# Bass
# Strategies

MINNETONKA, MINNESOTA

# Bass Strategies

Printed in 2008.

**Tom Carpenter**
Creative Director

**Jen Weaverling**
Production Editor

**Teresa Marrone**
Book Production

**Contributing Writers:** Paul Canada, Bill Dance, Ryan Gilligan, Mark Hicks, Steve Huskey, Dan Johnson, Scott Liles, Al Lindner, Don Lindner, Clark Montgomery, Spence Petros, Zell Rowland, Jeff Samsel, Jon Storm, Tim Tucker, Don Wirth.

**Photo Credits: George Barnett:** 49. **Shawn Bjonfald:** 14, 15, 16, 17, 18, 70, 74, 98, 139. **Ryan Gilligan:** 147, 148, 149. **Mark Hicks:** 43, 107. **Merlyn Hilmoe:** 102. **Steve Huskey:** 11. **Dan Johnson:** 104, 105. **Mitch Kezar:** 142. **Mark Kingsbury:** 111. **Scott Liles:** 48. **Bill Lindner Photography:** 4-5, 6-7, 8, 19, 20, 21, 22, 23, 24, 38, 40, 42-43, 44, 45, 50, 53, 58-59, 60-61, 62, 63, 64, 69, 72, 75, 83, 87, 92-93, 94, 98, 100, 106, 109, 110, 112, 116, 120-121, 122, 125, 152, 154, 156. **Tommy Martin:** 99. **Steve Pennaz:** 5 (inset), 126, 127, 132, 136, 141. **Roger Peterson:** 132. **Spence Petros:** 89, 91, 103, 123, 124, 131, 133, 136. **Steve Price:** 107. **Jerry Robb:** 26, 27, 68, 139. **Jeff Samsel:** 151. **Bill Siemantel:** 26, 37, 76. **Cory Suski:** 90. **Tim Tucker:** 13, 38, 41, 57. **Don Wirth:** 25, 27, 28, 79, 82, 117, 118, 119, 137, 138.

**Illustration Credits: Chris Armstrong:** 10, 29, 30, 31, 33, 35, 36. 37, 56, 65, 66, 67, 70, 74, 78, 84, 85, 88, 89, 97, 101, 108, 113, 115, 150-151, 153. **Mark Atkinson:** 23. **Shawn Bjonfald:** 34. **Jim Haynes:** 39, 40, 140, 144, 145, 146. **David Rottinghaus:** 46, 47, 81, 117, 128, 129, 134, 135.

**Special thanks to:** Kurt Beckstrom, Mike Billstein, Shawn Bjonfald, Terry Casey, Janice Cauley, Julie Cisler, Mike Hehner, Jill Nachtman and Steve Pennaz.

4  5  6  7  8  9  10 / 10  09  08
© 2006 North American Fishing Club
ISBN 10: 1-58159-274-4
ISBN 13: 978-1-58159-274-0

North American Fishing Club
12301 Whitewater Drive
Minnetonka, MN 55343
**www.fishingclub.com**

# CONTENTS

Introduction 4

**Strategies** 6

How Bass Attack 8

Topwater Revolution 14

Zell Talks Topwaters 19

Deadsticking 24

Weightless Wormin' 29

Jig Hopping 34

Gettin' Down 38

Golden Retrieves 42

When Big Is Better 45

Small Wonders 50

**Situations** 58

Dockin' Bass 60

Crank It Up For Shallow Bass 64

Full-Circle Brush 69

Vegemat Bass 72

The Point Man 76

Over The Edge 79

Big Bass From Secondary Lakes 83

On Solid Ground 87

**Seasons** 92

Bass Before Bedtime 94

Bass Before The Spawn 100

Bass On Top 104

Deep Down Bass 106

Fall Creek Bassin' 112

Suspended Animation 116

**Smallmouths** 120

Smallmouths By The Numbers 122

Spring Smallmouths 127

Rock Solid Smallies 132

Lethal Weapons 137

Big River Smallmouths 142

Crawdaddy 147

Hot Dam: Four Tricks For
Tailwater Smallmouths 150

Up, Down, All Around 152

**Index** 157

# INTRODUCTION

Part of bass fishing's allure is the level of challenge involved with finding and catching fish on a relatively consistent basis.

What fun would it be to go bass fishing if you nailed them every time? Catching five-pounders would be old hat and you'd quickly move on to a new addiction. On the other hand—would you keep coming back for more if you never found success?

Most of us in fact operate in that middle water, where sometimes things go right and sometimes they don't. Of course, there's nothing wrong with the goal of catching more and bigger fish … doing things more "right," more often!

How to accomplish that? To start, you can fish more. The more experience you get, in the widest array of habitats and under the broadest range of conditions, the better bass angler you will become.

But do you have to figure it all out for yourself? No way. That's where this book, *Bass Strategies,* comes in. This elite collection of "best of the best" bass-fishing stories from the pages of North American Fisherman magazine will help you take your bassing to a higher level.

You'll start by gleaning top strategies from today's best bass pros. Then move on to essential secrets for solving the challenges of specific bass-fishing situations. Every season of the year presents new bass-fishing opportunities, and we show you how to fish through the calendar. A section devoted specifically to small-mouths—the other bass we all love to catch—completes the course.

If you're like me, bass are a part of your life, and you're always scheming for ways to find more time on the water in pursuit of these challenging, exciting fish. This book-full of strategies is going to help you find more success on the journey.

Steve Pennaz
Executive Director
North American Fishing Club

# STRATEGIES

*M*astering a variety of key strategies is essential to consistent bass fishing success.

# HOW BASS ATTACK

*by Steve Huskey*

When you fish top-waters for bass, you'll see fish strike in different ways. Sometimes they blow up on a bait—throwing water in all directions and leaving a boil or small whirlpool to mark the carnage. At times there's merely a slurp as a bass sucks the lure in; sometimes, the bait suddenly and silently disappears.

By understanding the mechanics of how largemouth bass feed, as well as the different ways they attack their prey, bass anglers can predict which lures and techniques will be the most productive depending on how the fish are feeding at any given time.

## HOW FISH FEED

Feeding mechanics in fish has become a hot topic among a group of researchers known as functional morphologists. What we attempt to do is find the link between the design of a fish or animal and the environment in which it lives. Fish, by far the most

---

## Florida Vs. Michigan: Battle Of The Big Mouths *by Steve Huskey*

There are about 27,000 different species of fish in the world. Although some large groups of closely related fish, like minnows, darters or sunfish, look quite similar, many are quite different in appearance. Body shape, coloration, fin size and position, and eye position are just a few of the ways they differ.

Another way fish differ is the mouth—size, shape, gape (dimensions of the mouth when open), types of teeth and function. These relate to what the fish eats, and are extremely important in maintaining a diverse fishery, since eating different foods is one mechanism that allows so many types of fish to co-exist in the same body of water.

Until recently, it was assumed that, though there is some variation in the jaws among individuals of a single species of fish, they would be similar no matter where that species lives. To test that assumption, I compared the jaws of largemouth bass from the northern and southern extremes of their natural range to see if the mouth dimensions of bass feeding on various prey species would be similar or different.

I found that Michigan bass had larger mouth openings (gape height and width) than Florida bass. Intuitively, that seems backward. A larger gape allows the

> **"Body shape, coloration, fin size and position, and eye position are just a few of the ways they differ."**

predator to eat larger prey, and Florida bass are known to grow faster and larger than their northern cousins. Since a bass gets more energy return from eating large prey rather than small food items, it seems like Florida bass would have the larger gape.

My research indicates that the benefits gained from a large or small mouth transcend the ability to eat bigger forage. Adult Michigan bass, fish over 14 inches long, eat fish almost exclusively. The lakes I studied had relatively little aquatic vegetation—and prey species, primarily sunfish, minnows and yellow perch, are captured in relatively open environments. Actively swimming prey in open water is a perfect target for ram-feeding. And a larger gape increases the success of such behavior.

On the other hand, many adult Florida bass consume large amounts of grass shrimp. As the name implies, grass shrimp live in dense vegetation. Capturing elusive prey in dense vegetation calls for suction feeding. The smaller gape increases the success, because suction is greater through a smaller opening than through a larger one. Thus, my theory is that a small gape translates into greater efficiency when foraging on and in dense vegetation.

## Modes Of Attack

**Ram-feeding**  **Suction feeding**  **Ram-suction feeding**

Ram-feeding (left) is an aggressive attack used in open water on schools of shad or other baitfish. Suction feeding (center) is used to pick prey from bottom or thick vegetation. A hybrid of the two, ram-suction feeding (right), occurs when bass feed on baitfish or other prey items suspended off bottom. Note the weightless worm, a great bait for such a feeding scenario.

diverse group of vertebrates on earth—numbering more than amphibians, reptiles, birds and mammals combined —provide the perfect model for these comparisons; and their feeding mechanisms provide the perfect examples for study because of the vast diversity displayed between various groups of fish.

Some species, like barracuda, have extremely long jaws lined with razor-sharp teeth, allowing for a large gape and superior prey-holding efficiency. Others, like the sheepshead, have small, robust mouths housing teeth similar to human molars, capable of reducing an oyster shell to bits of chalk.

The barracuda needs quick jaws to overtake and capture prey as it tries to escape. In contrast, the oyster isn't going anywhere, so the sheepshead can take its sweet time processing the shell to get at the meat inside. As functional morphologists, we examine these feeding systems relative to their prey, in order to understand how and why so many fish species exist today.

## FEEDING TYPES

Before we can characterize and quantify feeding behaviors of largemouth bass, we must first discuss the different modes of feeding in fish. In short, there are three recognized types.

The first, as in the barracuda example above, is called "ram-feeding." As the name indicates, the predator moves in a forward motion toward its prey and overtakes it with greater velocity and acceleration. The second is "suction feeding," where the predator exhibits very little forward velocity, opens and expands the mouth extremely fast, and sucks prey in along with the water that rushes in to fill the void.

The third is known as "biting," and is characterized by using the jaws to excavate and process prey such as urchins, corals and mussels by simply grabbing a piece and chewing away, as in the sheepshead example. Oftentimes, fish exhibit some characteristics of each behavior during a single feeding bout.

## BASS BEHAVIOR

Largemouths' propensity to "suck in" topwaters leads to misconceptions about how they attack prey. In reality, sucking prey into the mouth is but one way bass feed. They also ram-feed, overtaking prey with a surprise attack, their mouths open and with quick acceleration. Despite what the "tap-tap" of a bass picking up a plastic worm feels like, they technically do not "bite."

Feeding, a complex behavior that ends when the prey is in the predator's gullet, is really a progression of actions. To explore feeding behavior, I'll begin by describing the sequence used by bass where they do most of their feeding—below the surface.

I have analyzed hundreds of largemouth bass feeding events, filmed at up to 2,000 frames per second. An adult bass typically makes a relatively slow initial approach, rarely more than 2.25 mph, from any angle or direction. At close range the bass then accelerates so it is traveling about 4.5 mph when it reaches the prey. When it gets to within two to six inches from its target, it begins to open its mouth.

The mouth is fully open (what we call maximum gape) just before it reaches the prey. Once a bass reaches maximum gape, it will flex the muscles at the back of its head, causing the head to lift. At the same time, muscles in the floor of the mouth (known as the hyoid) expand downward and the gill covers flare outward. A lot of individual actions occur when a fish opens its jaws to take prey, but they all take place very quickly, in just 6 to 8 milliseconds, many times faster than a fisherman can blink, much less set a hook.

The coordinated head lift, hyoid depression, and gill cover flare create a negative pressure, or suction, into the mouth. At the point of contact with the prey, the bass has reached its maximum forward velocity. It swims directly "through" the prey, engulfing it with the mouth and, at the same time, drawing it in with some slight suction.

Another element further increases the odds of a successful attack. The jaws of most fish have an interesting mechanism known as a "protrusible premaxilla." The premaxilla is the bone on the tip of the upper jaw, and it is linked to the lower jaw via the maxilla bones (the other bones of the upper jaw). When the lower jaw of a bass is dropped, it transfers this movement through the maxillas to the premaxilla, causing it to jut forward toward the prey.

Next time you catch a bass, before you release it, hold the fish by the body and open and close its mouth. This protrusion of the upper jaw gives the bass a little extra forward movement, helping close the gap between predator and prey a few milliseconds faster.

## Largemouth Bass Anatomy

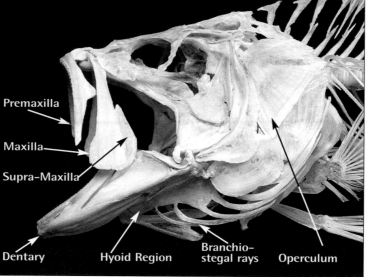

Premaxilla
Maxilla
Supra-Maxilla
Dentary
Hyoid Region
Branchio-stegal rays
Operculum

## BASS IN GRASS

When I analyzed and compared the feeding habits of bass in Michigan and Florida lakes, I found Florida bass tend to consume large amounts of small grass shrimp, which cling to submerged vegetation. Logic dictates that ram-feeding shrimp would lead to a mouthful of coontail or hydrilla. So, I devised experiments where I could film bass feeding on grass shrimp clinging to plastic plants in our laboratory.

Behold, a whole new feeding behavior. The bass approached and attacked the shrimp at one-third the speed of ram-feeding, open-water bass. They also appeared to decelerate as they attack, to avoid plunging headfirst into the vegetation with their mouths open.

Most importantly, the sequence of events from maximum gape, to maximum head lift, to maximum hyoid depression, to maximum gill flaring took only two-thirds as much time (4 to 5 milliseconds) as it did when the fish was ram-feeding.

Also interesting is that the bass I observed feeding in mock vegetation actually spread their jaws almost twice as fast as fish ram-feeding in open water. My explanation is that, by opening its mouth faster, a bass creates stronger suction, which compensates for its slower approach.

My observations indicate that grass shrimp are elusive and hard to catch; small fish use the weeds as obstacles. Feeding bass must move stealthily and strike quickly, with increased suction. Ram-feeding is not as effective here as it might be in open water. The bass not only efficiently captures prey, it does so without a mouthful of veggies.

This feeding behavior may explain why bass hit a soft plastic bait or jig dragged slowly through the weeds or along the bottom differently than they do a crankbait in open water. When you chunk and wind a crank over a hump or ledge, the bass sees an actively swimming prey and no obstructions. To maximize the chances of success, the bass shifts into ram-feeding mode and bam, you feel the strike all the way to your elbows.

Conversely, a jig or plastic lure moves slowly—apparently not a strong swimmer—and is tight against the bottom or working through vegetation. The bass approaches with less speed and turns on the suction. You feel a "tap," a "tick," or maybe your line just barely twitches as your bait jumps into the bass' mouth. The bass got what he went after and may or may not swim off. Set the hook.

## Mats, Shrimp And Bass *by Dr. Hal Schramm*

Aquatic vegetation holds bass food. Lots of it. A cubic yard of densely vegetated water may hold dozens of baitfish. Some of these fish are fingerlings that will grow larger, like bluegills or redear sunfish; others will attain only a couple inches as adults. That same cubic yard of water may also hold hundreds of invertebrates. Many of these are small and provide important food for sunfish and young-of-the-year bass.

In southern waters, one of the more abundant invertebrates is the grass shrimp. While generally abundant in many stands of dense weedbeds, they are especially abundant in surface matted vegetation. Unlike most native aquatic plants, hydrilla (and to some extent Eurasian watermilfoil) keeps growing after it reaches the surface. This continued growth often results in dense surface mats several inches thick. After several weeks, a filamentous algae begins growing in and on the hydrilla mat. This is a haven for grass shrimp—I have collected more than 100 shrimp from only a few square feet of matted hydrilla.

Grass shrimp are small; a large adult is only about 1 1/2 inches long. But bass love them. I have seen bass up to 5 pounds with their stomachs packed full of grass shrimp. Interestingly, while small bass tend to have a few, large grass shrimp in their gut, the big girls tend to be stuffed with dozens of small and intermediate-size shrimp.

Learning about grass shrimp and other small forage that lives in the vegetation, as well as the food habits of bass in densely vegetated habitats, gave me two hints about how to catch largemouths in lakes with surface-matted hydrilla: where to fish and what to fish. The "where" part of the equation is simple. Fish in the dense mats of hydrilla, particularly areas with patches of bright-green filamentous algae. Knowing "where" is good, but knowing "exactly where" is better, and exactly where is right beneath the surface mat.

Yes, I'm talking six inches under the surface, in water commonly four feet to eight feet deep. The deeper the better, but feeding bass, and probably less active bass, too, will hover right below the mat. It offers the only substrate and cover to both forage and bass, shading out everything beneath.

What to fish: A slender plastic worm with a straight, transparent green (watermelon) or chartreuse tail. The straight tail is needed to

*Tiny grass shrimp are a major prey item for adult largemouth bass in many southern waters.*

make the worm fall through tiny gaps in the mat. A jig won't go through, and a curly- or paddletail worm will hang up. Even a straight-tail worm needs at least a 1/2-ounce bullet sinker in front of it. The green or chartreuse tail mimics grass shrimp, which are almost transparent in the water (some folks call them glass shrimp), but their hydrilla mat background is green.

Use a flipping approach. Find a gap in the mat; look for algae since the hydrilla beneath it tends to be thinner. Flip the worm through the opening and let it drop. Reel it back so it's just under the mat. Deadstick it, give it a little shake, then deadstick again. No bite? Move on and repeat it. One final tip, hold on to the rod, this is not a small bass pattern.

# TOPWATER TIME

Bass have two different topwater feeding modes, which they appear to change to suit the environment, prey or maybe even their mood. A "blow-up" is the result of ram-feeding at the surface. The bass swims rapidly toward its prey and engulfs it. To avoid launching itself into the air, which of course does occur sometimes, a bass quickly changes direction, throwing water or creating a boil.

Suction feeding, as is used to snap up a grass shrimp from a submerged leaf or stem, allows the bass to "suck in" your topwater, sometimes without a sound. Whether the bait quietly disappears or the strike is signaled by a slurp or a pop is related to how much water the bass pulls into its mouth to capture the prey.

Blow-ups are more likely when fishing a fast-moving topwater, like a buzzbait or Zara Spook, in open water. Quiet strikes are likely when fishing a stickbait, popper or other slower-moving lure in lily pads or surface-matted vegetation—a place where the predator can conceal itself.

Bass will modulate feeding behavior based on their prey's location and speed, and the amount of vegetation around the prey. Anglers should check out their surroundings to get an idea about the habitat they plan to fish.

Keep in mind that the act of feeding is a complicated process, but by understanding feeding behavior and recognizing how it changes from one environment to another, you may just put more fish in your boat.

*Editor's Note: This story is based on the author's extensive laboratory research on largemouth bass feeding behavior. We present these ideas for you to compare with your own observations, and consider as you select your own bass fishing presentations.*

---

## Nine Reasons Why Bass Strike by Roland Martin and Bill Dance

1. Hunger is the number one reason why bass strike a lure. Hunger-based strikes account for about a third of all our strikes in a year's time, and about 35 percent of those come when fishing during the early morning or late afternoon hours.

2. Twenty-five to 30 percent of the bass we catch are the result of a reflex strike. The reflex action of a bass is no different from the behavior of any predator, such as a cat pouncing on a mouse.

3. The third most important reason why bass strike is anger. Sheer anger. Often, the first cast you make to a spot produces a reflex strike or a hunger strike. But if you don't get an immediate strike at a spot where you think a bass should be holding, you can sometimes aggravate the fish into striking by casting over and over again.

4. You can't leave out the protective instinct during the spawning season. For the short amount of time that bass guard their beds, they nail anything that comes near their nests.

5. Some bass strike out of curiosity. It may only account for two or three percent of my strikes each year, but that small percentage is important in clear-water situations.

6. A strong motivation for strikes, particularly in deep-structure situations, is competition among bass that are schooled together. When they are congregated, the strike from one bass can ignite interest in other members of the school, creating a feeding frenzy.

7. A year-round reason why bass strike is their strong territorial instinct. This is usually a trophy-fish situation where a big bass is guarding its territory.

8. Killer instinct is another reason. Have you ever wondered why a tiny bass will attack and try to kill a giant lure like a Musky Jitterbug? The bass can't possibly eat it. All it's attempting to do is kill it.

9. There is one last reason why bass strike—sheer ignorance. In this day and age it's hard to find bass that have never seen a lure, but when you do, take advantage of it.

# TOPWATER REVOLUTION

*by Ryan Gilligan*

Aside from a few relatively rare exceptions, soft plastics are denizens of the subsurface. We Texas-, Carolina- and wacky-rig them, or fish them as add-ons to jigs or specially weighted hooks.

We get down. And it works wonders.

When the bite's on the fishes' ceiling, however, most of us abandon our plastics and throw only buzzbaits and the usual hardbait fare.

That is, aside from today's most savvy bass anglers—members of this select group have learned to use soft plastics as boisterous topwater lures and are increasingly using them in place of traditional surface baits. And the trend is catching on as manufacturers produce plastics specifically geared for the top, while retaining the sexy subsurface qualities anglers have learned to lean on.

Although these baits range widely and include more traditional "creature" lures with modified flipper arms, the newest and most exciting are frog-style creations with legs that function like miniature buzzbait blades.

Rigged weedless and weightless on a wide-gap hook, they produce a subtle sound and undulating surface action bass simply haven't seen. Even better, the baits open up vast expanses of thick cover because they can be fished in the nastiest slop without hanging up, yet still produce their signature topwater action.

## TOP TRICKSTER

Cleveland, Ohio, bass pro Frank Scalish is one of the select anglers who has begun to see the potential of these plastics and has developed a precise system for fishing them. His favorite is a bait he fished on Arkansas' Lake Ouachita, the Yum Buzz Frog.

Like other members of this breed of plastic, the bait sports a frog shape and a heavy, horizontally flattened body with flipper legs.

Scalish says the feature that sets it apart is the shape of its feet. "Its legs have wedge-shaped feet—like the tail of a Yum Samurai Shad. They produce the look and sound of a plastic-blade buzzbait on a straight, steady retrieve," he says.

"The really unique thing is that when it's at rest, the legs spread apart. This lets you kill the bait during the retrieve in a promising pocket, let it sink for a moment, then pop the rodtip. The legs slap together like a real frog

---

### Ring My Bell

Surface soft plastics are no doubt versatile right out of the package—they can be rigged almost any way and because they're softbaits, you can easily modify them. Adding sound is a prime example.

Uncle Josh staffer Matt Bichanich likes to add rattles to increase the surface commotion of the Sizmic Toad. "Push a worm rattle into the soft plastic body, and it really adds to the presentation," he says. "It's important to insert the rattle in the head of the bait."

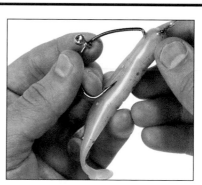

*A craft-store jingle bell slid into the hook gap with a split ring adds another triggering stimulus to topwater plastics.*

**Uncle Josh Sizmic Toad**

According to Bichanich, that's another way in which these lures beat hollow-bodied floating frog baits. When anglers add rattles to those lures, they tend to roll to the back of the body cavity on the retrieve. "When a fish hits, the rattle gets in the way and prevents good hooksets. But with these solid-body baits, you can position the rattle in front, and it stays there," he says.

Bichanich also adds bells. "I like to thread a small bell, like you find at craft stores, onto the hook shank—those with with a single BB inside." Adding a split ring makes it easier to slide them onto the shank.

---

## Lead-The-Way Lead

Bass pro Randy Howell loves topwater plastics. For good reason—he pulled off a sixth-place finish in the recent Bassmaster Southern Open while fishing a prototype of Berkley's new Gulp! BatWing.

Howell says the bait excels because it creates an unparalleled scent trail—an added trigger when bass miss the bait on their first attempt. Stall the bait and let it drop into the cover after a miss, and bass often inhale it.

*Randy Howell pegs a ¹/₁₆-ounce bullet weight in front of the Gulp! BatWing. The added heft lets him burn the bait across the surface.*

Although the bait's dense Gulp! body makes it heavy for its size, Howell finds it's better to add some weight when conditions call for burning the lure across matted grass and other subsurface cover. "If you really crank it in, the head can lift up and the lure will start skipping across the surface," he says. "It's like trying to fish a spinnerbait with a big blade and a light head—you're not going to be able to retrieve it too fast and maintain the right action."

**Gulp! BatWing**

To adjust, Howell pegs a ¹/₁₆-ounce bullet weight immediately in front of the hook eye. It's simple, but effective. "That head stays down so you can hit the speed you need to trigger fish."

and any following bass pounds it."

Although new frog-style plastics lend themselves best to topwater presentations, other softbaits traditionally fished on jigs, Carolina rigs or as subsurface jerkbaits work on top, too. Rigged weightless, the Gary Yamamoto Kreature, for example, can slide across the surface while its rear appendages whip the water. The Yum Houdini Shad is another good crossover, with one minor tweak—cut a diagonal slit halfway through the paddle part of its tail. The altered bait gurgles and splashes across the surface on a steady retrieve.

This begs the question: Why not use floating rats and frogs for these same situations? Aside from increased action, the reason lies in the hooksets. "Soft plastics, especially the new frog-style baits, are far more effective than floating frogs, because you

## Tweaking The Toad

Palestine, Texas, bass pro David Gregg is among the growing cadre of innovators using today's topwater plastics, and his favorite is the Zoom Horny Toad. "Whenever the water's 60 degrees or above, you can fish this lure like a buzzbait," Gregg says. "Bass love it."

To get the most from the bait, he pushes a wide-gap, 5/0 Mustad hook into the bait's nose and out the bottom, just as you'd begin a typical Texas rig, then alters the bait before completing the rigging. "I cut it lengthwise between the legs about ¼ inch, then skin-hook the point along the cut surface of either leg. This accomplishes two important things: First, the legs become longer and more flexible, so they produce a better surface action. Second, it allows for better hooksets because the point doesn't have to penetrate as much plastic before sticking a bass."

*To enhance action and hooksets, David Gregg cuts about ¼ inch between the Zoom Horny Toad's legs and skin-hooks the 5/0 on the inside surface.*

**Zoom Horny Toad and Horny Toad Hook**

Gregg adds a dab of Super Glue behind the hook eye before sliding the Toad's head in place, as it has a tendency to slide back in heavy vegetation. Zoom also offers a new hook designed to increase hooksets and keep it on the hook. The aptly-named Horny Toad Hook features an extra-wide gap and screw-in attachment.

have that one single hook. Your ratio of bites to landed fish goes way up," he says.

Hook size and shape is crucial for maintaining this edge, however. Scalish relies on 4/0 and 5/0 wide-gap hooks to ensure hooksets on the meaty plastics. "The key is using a hook with a gap that's twice the bait's width (belly to back)," he says. "The Excalibur Tx3 Wide Gap is great because of the relatively short distance between the eye and gap. This lets the plastic get out of the way when a bass strikes."

Soft plastics also excel over floating frogs because you can let them sink and fish them as jerkbaits on a whim, triggering reluctant bass. Try that with your conventional topwater lures.

## TOP SPOTS

Scalish fishes surface plastics whenever bass come shallow and relate to heavy cover like matted vegetation, but also timber, brush and gravel piles.

"You can throw them almost anywhere—they come through unbelievable stuff without hanging up," he says. "Actually, I've learned they're effective just about anywhere I'd fish a typical topwater bait."

Some of his favorite places are matted weedbeds, and he has a unique mindset when fishing these gardens that lends itself perfectly to plastic.

"I look at mats as if they are actually underwater humps: the mat itself is the top of the 'hump' and the fringes and scattered clumps off the main mat are 'breaks'," he says. "Those breaks are the place to throw first—most

strikes come in pockets and fringes, where you can pause the lure, let it sink momentarily and pop it before resuming your retrieve."

Scalish also makes hay fishing wood, which he breaks down into two types: "hard" wood like fallen timber, and "soft" wood like willows, pines and other brushy cover. He's dialed in a specific approach for each.

"When fishing hardwood blowdowns, I position the boat and cast parallel to the trunk. Most strikes occur where the root system or thickest part of the trunk meets the bank," he says. "Another usual spot is the first major fork in the tree, where branches begin to spread from the main trunk. The third spot is the outside edge of the limb tips."

To hit all of these spots without spooking fish, he begins by positioning his boat a cast length from the limb tips and buzzing the bait through. He then moves to the tree's first major fork and then on to the root ball,

*"Hard" wood like fallen timber is excellent cover for buzzing plastics. Cast to sunken limb tips before moving into the main branches and trunk.*

## Bead It

Reaction Lures designer and owner John Dean has developed a simple yet highly effective trick for fishing topwater plastics like the company's Ribbit: simply adding a bead, like one used in a Carolina rig, to the line in front of the hook eye. "The bead breaks the flow of water hitting the front of the lure, keeping the bait upright and running true," Dean says.

Add a Carolina-style bead to the line in front of the bait. The lure will run better and won't pick up as much slop.

"The bead also helps guide it through cover and keeps off grass and other weeds." Although subtle, little tricks like this make the topwater plastic presentation even more effective.

**Reaction Lures Ribbit**

---

although he makes sure to watch for patterns and follow them.

"A lot of times, for example, I'll get all the strikes on that first big fork, but not on the branches or root ball," he says. "When that happens, I move right in and cast the frog to the forks."

When fishing soft wood, he runs the bait right through the brush, hitting every inch, but especially any variations within the cover itself. In the rare scenario where the brush is too thick to allow pulling the bait through, Scalish positions his boat to the side of the cover, which lets him make angled casts to the brush edges. This forces the bait to make contact with the cover during much of the retrieve.

"It's absolutely critical that the plastic bumps the emergent twigs and branches," he says. "Bass are often holding tight within these piles and need that contact to trigger them to strike."

Scalish lets the bass dictate retrieve style, but starts with a straight, steady retrieve, letting the bait buzz across the top. "If that doesn't trip their trigger, I'll go to a pull-pause-pull-pause retrieve, which looks like a bullfrog making its first few kicks as it tries to escape a predator," he says.

Setting hooks requires perfect timing and patience—something that isn't always easy given the nature of the strikes this presentation triggers.

"Remember to wait on your hook-set until you can feel the fish pull. Then set that hook—not before," he says. "It takes some getting used to because these are not subtle bites, even compared to the type of blow-ups you get when fishing other top-water baits."

## TACKLING UP

Scalish generally fishes surface plastics on 20-pound fluorocarbon in open water, but goes to braided line in slop because of its low stretch. Cast length factors in, too. "If I know I'm going to be making long casts, I'll definitely use mono or braid—even in open water—because these lines float and keep the bait churning water on top," he says. "Fluoro sinks and makes it more difficult to keep the bait up on a long cast."

He predicts that topwater uses for such plastics are only the beginning. "Although it's something currently only being seen on the professional circuit, some guys are already Carolina rigging frog-style baits and flipping them in pockets like they normally would a craw or tube," he says. "We have only begun to see the applications."

As always, those who stay on top of these trends and use them to pioneer new bass fishing techniques will stay more than a few steps in front of the masses.

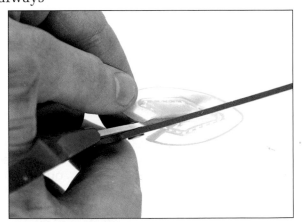

Frog-style creations aren't the only soft plastics that work on top. Frank Scalish turns the Yum Houdini Shad into a topwater bait by making a diagonal cut from the front side of the paddle tail ending at the center of the bait's perforated diamond.

# ZELL TALKS TOPWATERS

*by Zell Rowland with Jon Storm*

**W**ith any fishing technique, from tossing topwaters on down to crankbaits, it's hard to get that edge that keeps you ahead of the next guy. I'm well known for my topwater abilities, and have been for almost two decades now, but the thrill of seeing a big fish blow up on my bait still excites me.

In my tournament experience, I've fished against some tough competition—guys like Denny Brauer, Guido Hibdon, Kevin VanDam—so I'm always looking to gain that edge. Fishing topwaters can often separate me from the crowd. I'll go to topwater baits even when conditions turn tough.

Most bass anglers think topwaters only work when the weather and water are warm. But the truth is, you can catch bass on topwaters nearly all year long. No matter how cold it gets, some bass in every lake are going to stay shallow,

especially if they have access to cover and forage. The added benefit is that most anglers will be targeting those fish in 15 to 25 feet of water. By staying shallow, I'm avoiding the crowds and competing against far fewer fishermen.

During March and April, you're most likely faced with prespawn bass—fish that are heading toward the bank. The first places I start to look for them are along shorelines where deep water is close to the bank, maybe a creek channel, or it could just be a drop-off.

Believe me, prespawn fish will hit topwaters, and not just at dusk and dawn. Bait choice, of course, is highly dependent on water temperature. There are basically five styles of topwater hardbaits: buzzbaits, jerkbaits, prop baits, chuggers and walking stickbaits.

We'll cover them all, but during the prespawn, jerkbaits and buzzbaits are the top choices, so I'll start with them.

## JERKBAITS: SIZE MATTERS

Whatever the season, I always have one rod rigged with a jerkbait. They're productive because you can vary the action from a subtle twitch to an explosive jumpout-of-the-water snap. Let the fish guide your presentation.

In seminars, I tell anglers to keep their color selection to a minimum. I'm a professional angler, as well as a member of the pro staffs for Bomber, Rebel, Cordell, Heddon, Smithwick and a number of other brands of lures. I have every lure color under the moon, but that's because I fish from coast to coast and from Texas to Canada. But most anglers who fish a few bodies of water, or one specific region, would do better to expand their selection of lure sizes and styles rather than stuffing their tackle boxes with baits featuring every color of the rainbow. A good base of colors

*Give jerkbaits added appeal by adding a prop (top), or even removing the diving lip (bottom).*

would include some gray, silver, black, blue and white pearl (shad colors), as well as purple, blue and green (bluegill colors).

For example, the Smithwick Rogue comes in several sizes. You cannot use just one and expect to catch all the bass you would with various sizes. Plus, you need some jerkbaits with different actions and profiles, like a Bomber Long "A," Rebel Minnow and Excalibur Ghost Minnow, to name a few that I use.

They all resemble baitfish, but some have a tighter action while others wobble more. Consider these factors over stocking eight colors of each bait.

Size is important because, let's say you and I go fishing on Toledo Bend. We know the lake has a lot of fish between 3 and 10 pounds, so we'd throw an 8½-inch lure instead of a 3 incher. We won't get 50 bites, maybe just seven or eight. But those fish will have eyes six inches apart. We effectively took the smaller fish out of the game. Favoring style and size over color gives you more options.

Variety doesn't end with size and color. Take the Rogue as an example. I fish a Rogue that I'd say 99.9 percent of anglers throw away. If a jerkbait's bill snaps off, don't toss the lure! Quite often, I'll fish a Rogue with no bill because of its wild, erratic action—like a real wounded baitfish. If you want

to remove the bill yourself, use a pair of pliers and wiggle it back and forth until it breaks free.

Other times, I fish a Rogue with a prop. With a small propane torch, it's easy to add a prop to almost any bait. I hook a thin piece of wire into the rear eyelet, then heat the wire. It transfers heat to the eyelet and loosens the glue. Now, with pliers, I can easily unscrew the eyelet, add a prop, and screw it back in. Do this, and you'll have a bait almost nobody else has got, and I catch a million fish on it.

Over the years I've added props to a variety of baits—Spooks, Excalibur Spit'n Images, and so on. It allows me to fish them effectively during different times of the year because I can slow them down and keep them near the cover longer.

Jerkbaits are productive because they're versatile.

## BUILD A BETTER BUZZBAIT

As I said, it's important to work topwaters slowly during this time of year, and in order to get a buzzbait to fish at a leisurely pace, I bend the blades a little more than they already are. Closing the angle makes slow retrieves possible.

When it comes to choosing a buzzbait, it must have a very good hook, but equally important is that it has a flat head, which makes the bait come to the surface quicker. A round head takes longer to reach the surface, and you won't be fishing as efficiently.

Some anglers prefer buzzbaits with a built-in clacker, but I prefer to make my own. Simply open up the wire and remove the buzzbait blade, slide on a Colorado blade, then replace the buzz

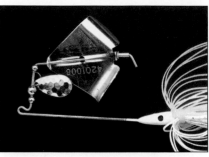

*When bass literally need to hear the dinner bell before they eat, try Zell's easy-to-assemble clacker buzzbait. Straighten the wire behind the blade and remove the rivet and blade. Slide on the Colorado spinner blade with or without a clevis (between metal beads). Replace the buzzbait blade and rivet and re-bend the wire.*

*By the way, notice this bait features a flat head. A flat head planes to the surface upon splashdown, and stays there better than a round or pointed head.*

blade. When retrieved, the buzzbait blade hits the Colorado blade and makes more noise than any clacker-style buzzbait on the market.

## WALK THE WALK

Of all the topwaters, walking stickbaits like the Zara Spook are the toughest to fish. You have to snap the rodtip and crank the reel at the same time, which requires very good hand-to-eye coordination. When you jerk a walking bait, it turns at about a 45- to 50-degree angle from your line. The quicker you snatch it back, the better you avoid fouling the hooks in the line.

If you want to get good at creating the walk-the-dog motion you have to practice coordinating the snapping motion with one hand and taking in line with the other. Get one of your old or broken rods and a reel that doesn't turn easily, then saw the rod off at the fore grip. Start with the fore grip pointing to the two o'clock position and begin the jerking motion. With each jerk, lower the fore grip a bit, as if the bait were moving toward the boat. Don't physically crank the reel handle. Instead, keep your hand relatively motionless and let each jerk turn the reel handle.

As the rod gets near to being parallel with the water, it may help to turn your wrists so the back of your palming hand faces upward. Continue lowering the fore grip with each jerk until it's pointed toward the ground. On the water, your rodtip should be at the surface as the bait nears the boat.

Another critical consideration with walking baits is line weight. With 10-pound line, the bait may turn almost 90 degrees. It's a good choice when bass are active and want a lure with a lot of action. With 25-pound, it might turn about 30. Of course, cover dictates what weight line you use, but getting comfortable with

your mechanics often means understanding the role that line plays in how a bait walks.

Lastly, and perhaps most importantly, is to add an additional treble hook to your walking baits. I don't use a Zara Spook that doesn't have a third hook in the belly. I even add a hook to the Spook Jr. It's real easy to do. Just screw an eyelet into the bottom of the bait, apply 5-minute epoxy, and it's there. You will be amazed at how many fish you catch that have that middle hook in their mouths.

## CHUGGERS

I tend to use chuggers more after the spawn, and everybody in the world knows my favorite bait is the Rebel Pop-R, especially when fishing clear or semi-clear water. In stained or dirty water, I start moving toward baits like an old Lucky 13 because they tend to dive more forward, and down into the water.

As much as I love the Pop-R, I don't believe it's built

exactly right, so I customize each one. I sand the bait down to give it a narrower body, and thin out the edges around the cupped face. It makes the bait float higher. Instead of the low-pitched gurgle you get with a Pop-R right out if the box, I can skitter a modified bait easier, which sounds like a shad flicking the surface.

The modifications also allow me to retrieve the bait in a walk-the-dog fashion, which you can't do with a stock lure. Remember, this is a bait that's as small as 1½ inches, so that's pretty remarkable.

Also, I use a feathered treble hook on all my Pop-Rs. Feathers are the only thing that has action when you barely move the bait. I call it blink-of-the-eye action. When you pull the bait forward, the feathers close extremely fast, then return to their original shape. In other words, the bait is reacting, even while sitting still.

If a fish blows up on a Pop-R, but misses, nine times out of ten I can catch him because the feathers make him come

### *Paint and Create*

If an angler wants to paint his own baits, there are several methods that are easy, quick and not too messy. I use a professional airbrush kit, but you can use Tester's model spray paint. I paint all my baits solid white, then add other colors. For example, I'll often spray the bottom of the bait with pearl, then paint the back green, black or another color.

Next, put some metal flake, which you can buy at any craft store, in one hand and apply spray glue to the part of the bait where you want the appearance of scales with the other. Hold the bait in front of your face and blow the flake from your hand onto the bait. This will give the appearance of fish scales.

If you want a not-so-messy scale job, build a small, square frame out of Popsicle sticks, then stretch a piece of pantyhose over the frame and staple it all the way around. Hold the side of the bait against the pantyhose and run the spray paint once across the side, through the pantyhose. The fancier the pantyhose, the fancier the scale effect.

*When custom painting topwaters, stick to the basic light belly/dark back pattern, but choose shades that closely match the predominant forage in the waters you fish.*

back. It's also because of my hooksetting technique. Let me explain. As soon as a big bass blows up on a bait, too many anglers jerk the rod instantly, yanking the bait toward the boat at about 60 mph. Compounding the mistake, they then reel in the slack and throw the bait right back to where the hit occurred.

That bass didn't grow to 6 or 7 pounds because it was a dummy. When it tried to get that "shad," the baitfish jumped about 65 yards in the air. Never in its lifetime has that fish seen a shad jump that far. Plus, when the angler recasts, that shad lands right back where he was a minute ago. You'll rarely get a bass to strike again with this method.

Instead, when a fish blows up on a bait, I don't jerk the rodtip. If it misses, I either stop the bait right where the bass struck, or I continue the action, trying to make the fish think its prey is trying to get away.

If I stop the bait, I know exactly where that fish is. He's sitting underneath it, making up his mind whether he should try again. I turn the reel handle not even a quarter-turn, which moves the bait about one-half inch. Just that little movement makes the feathers close so fast it looks like lightning hitting the ground.

The bass eases a little closer, and as he does, the feathers open slowly. Nine times out of ten, the fish cannot stand

*A feather trailer has a subtle action that pulls a bass' strike trigger better than any other type of trailer, says Zell.*

that. He has to get it. And that's the reason for the feathers on the back.

I put feathers on every top-water I've got, from jerkbaits to Pop-Rs, and it's amazing how many times a bass will have just the rear treble in its mouth. I tie them myself, starting with an Excalibur hook, then adding hackle feathers, which you can get at any fly fishing shop.

I use white for a base because I believe there are three colors a fish sees all the time—dark, light and red. Every fish that swims has a light-colored belly, a dark back and red gills. So I always start with white, then sometimes tie on red or dark colors.

## TOP PROPS

Prop baits are very "tolerant" because there are lots of things I can do with them I can't do with other baits. When bass are spawning and tucked in a bush, for example, it's logical that you increase your chances for success by keeping your bait near cover. Of all the baits in my tackle box, I can keep a prop bait around cover the longest.

I bend the prop (or props) toward the front of the bait so it won't move as far when I snap the rodtip. If I bend them all the way forward, I bet I can jerk that bait 15 times and not have it move more than a foot and a half. So now my bait is around that piece of cover, and my odds of getting a strike are much better.

On the other hand, if I'm fishing in the dead of summer and want the bait to move faster, I bend the blades rearward. The farther back I bend them, the farther the bait moves when I jerk the rodtip.

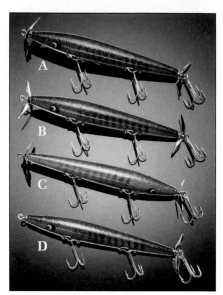

*Prop baits fish well as they are right out of the box (A), but you can easily modify them to meet specific needs. If bass are tight to cover, or want a slow-moving bait, bend the prop blades forward (B) so the bait travels a shorter distance with each rod twitch. Bend them backward so the bait glides farther when the bite is hot. Swapping the line tie and rear treble end-for-end (C) makes the Devil's Horse prop bait more aerodynamic so you can cast it into the wind more easily. Finally, remove the front prop altogether (D) to allow the bait to zigzag with each rod twitch.*

Though prop baits can sometimes be difficult to cast, I seldom let the weather or wind keep me from casting a bait I want to fish. Whenever possible, I generally have one style of bait for calm days and a different style of the same bait for fishing in the wind.

Smithwick's Devil's Horse, for example, is one of the toughest baits to throw on a windy day. Because the head of the bait is much fatter than the rear, it's easy to tangle the lure in the line because you're trying to throw the lightest end of the bait into the wind.

To overcome this, I reverse the front and rear by putting

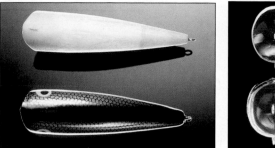

*Zell uses sandpaper to give his Pop-Rs a more streamlined profile (above) than a stock production model, and to sharpen the edges of the cupped face (above right, top). The modified bait, he says, skitters more like a shad. He repaints the bait with an airbrush.*

the line tie on the tail end and the rear treble on the front. When I cast the bait, the heaviest end goes into the wind first, and it will cast forever.

One final tip I can offer is to remove the front prop entirely if you want the bait to walk-the-dog.

## ROD CHOICE

Be choosy about the topwater rod you use. Mine is an All-Star TWS, which stands for Topwater Special. I designed this particular rod, and it's markedly different than any others I've seen.

An excellent topwater rod, in my opinion, is one that goes from an extremely light-action tip to a heavy butt section. The light tip gives a bass another second to pull the bait into its mouth. As that happens, the rod loads up, and as long as the hooks are sharp, you don't need to set the hook. Just reel and the fish will hook itself.

Reels are important, too, and I use a high-speed (5:1 to 6:1) reel after the spawn and during summer, and a low-speed (4:1 or less) reel during the late fall, winter and early spring. This way, it's harder

to fish a bait too fast.

As for line, I prefer monofilament for all topwater fishing. Line size is also important, because with any topwater bait, the lighter the line, the more action you can give the bait, and the more strikes you will get. However, it's also true that the lighter the line, the harder it becomes to work the bait. It's not that often that I meet an angler who fishes a Zara Spook on 10-pound line. Most prefer 14 to 17, and some even throw it on 20 or 30. But I fish it on 10-pound line when conditions dictate.

Fish a variety of baits and line sizes until you find something that works, or that targets the size fish you want. If I tie on the smallest bait in my box with the lightest line possible, for example, I might get 30 strikes, but the bass will only be anywhere from 10 inches to 5 pounds.

## PUT IN YOUR TIME

Improving your topwater game means examining all of its aspects. You need to focus on bait style, the speed you fish the baits, the extras you add (like feathered trailers and props), as well as the equipment you use.

Just as important, you need to realize that bass, especially big bass, are opportunistic feeders, and they will hit topwaters under almost any circumstance, provided you make the correct presentation. It takes practice and the willingness to fish hard, but believe me, the results are worth it. When it comes down to it, topwater fishing is the most exciting way to catch bass, and your heart will never grow tired of seeing big bass bust your finely-tuned topwater.

### *The Progressive Retrieve*

As a rule of thumb, Zell tries to get as much action out of a bait as the law allows, and the lighter the line, the more action a bait will have. But light line sinks extremely fast. By holding the rodtip high at the beginning of the retrieve, then progressively lowering it as the bait moves toward the boat, he can negate the problem. Snap the rodtip upward until the rod is about parallel with the water, then start snapping it downward.

You can also keep the line from sinking by applying wax or fly line dressing to the first six feet of monofilament.

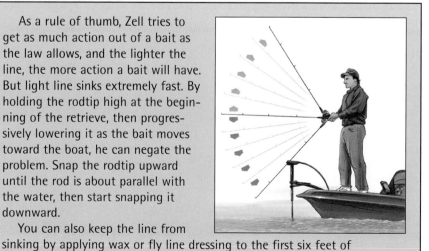

# DEADSTICKING

*by Don Wirth*

Here's an incredibly effective early-spring tactic for putting more big bass in the boat—deadsticking minnow-type jerkbaits. It's the very antithesis of the run-and-gun approach used by so many top anglers, and may be best described as live bait fishing with artificials.

It's so effective, most fishermen who use the technique are extremely reluctant to talk about it. But as Woodward and Bernstein discovered when reporting on the Watergate break-in, persistence can pay off.

Here are three deadsticking variations, each with potential to put giant bass in your boat

from late winter into the spawning season.

First, a word of warning: If you're the typical hyperactive tournament angler who loves the high-speed approach, deadsticking is definitely not for you. It requires more patience than many competitive fishermen can muster, but when properly performed, it'll put you in the winner's circle. It's true, the best retrieve is often no retrieve at all.

## COLDWATER "TREATMENT"

Bass expert Lou Treat is a master at deadsticking in

cold-water conditions. The Flippin, Arkansas, angler is a supervisor in the fender department at Ranger Boat Company's trailer plant, and a veteran of the regional tournament scene. He's won a total of 10 tournaments, including two events each on the Central Pro-Am and Red Man circuits. All four victories came on jerkbaits.

Treat's deadstick method works best during the initial warm-up phase typical of his region, which occurs sometime between late February and mid-March. The exact timing, of course, depends on warming trends and water temperatures, so time your fishing trips to fit conditions in your area.

"Usually our deep reservoirs get down to around 41 degrees in winter," Treat explains. "Prime time for deadsticking occurs when the water first warms up 3 or 4 degrees. That's when bass will absolutely eat it up!"

The key factor in Treat's deadsticking strategy is structure, and he searches out two distinct situations in early spring—rock transitions and isolated standing timber.

Rock transition areas, where one size or type of shoreline rock changes into another, might be a sheer limestone bluff that changes to chunk rock, or where chunk rock changes to gravel. The second area involves timber, more specifically "pole timber," which occurs in many highland reservoirs and resembles spindly telephone poles jutting out of deep water.

Once Treat locates a likely area, he evaluates water clarity. "Most anglers think of jerkbaits as clear-water lures, but if you deadstick 'em,

they'll work in water with only a foot of visibility," he says.

If the water is murky, Treat often finds bass suspending closer to the surface and tighter to the bank; if it's clear, they'll hold farther out and deeper. "Bass at 15 to 20 feet aren't uncommon in cold, clear water," he notes, quickly adding, "It really doesn't matter how deep the water is if it's clear, because a reflective jerkbait is highly visible, and will draw bass from long distances."

To execute his deadstick method, Treat uses a Suspending Super Rogue or Suspending Pro Rogue, approaching the target area cautiously and

*Arkansas angler Lou Treat targets steep rocks and transitions. Confidence pattern: Clown.*

keeping his boat well off the bank, or away from the timber, for the initial casts.

"Sometimes the fish will suspend a cast and a half off the bank, so you don't want to roar right up on 'em and spook 'em," he warns.

After splashdown, he cranks the lure to its maximum running depth (10 to 15 medium-speed handle cranks), then pauses, allowing the lure to suspend. As it sits, he makes sure there is sufficient slack in the line to compensate for boat drift, especially when it's windy, and keeps his eyes glued to the slack line. If it suddenly jumps or peels off, he knows a bass has taken the bait. He reels up the slack and makes a side-sweep hookset.

---

## Jig Connection *by Roland Martin and Bill Dance*

*The best winter bass bait? It's still tough to beat the rubber-skirted jig.*

On the question of what's the best wintertime lure of all, we are in complete agreement—the rubber-skirted jig. The jig is absolutely our favorite lure for cold water. Under these conditions, you'll catch more bass on jigs than on any other bait. During the coldest months, it often boils down to either a jig, or jigging spoon, with the jig the better choice.

There is something about a jig with a plastic or pork trailer that is unmatched when it comes to triggering strikes from sluggish bass.

### Winter Weight
Here are some tips. Use the lightest jig you can get away with. And remember that concentration is more important than ever. You will get only a limited number of strikes, so you need to be thinking "strike" the second the lure hits the water. Sometimes the strike is so light, all you feel is a heavy sensation on your line. When that happens, set the hook immediately.

### Other Approach
Target the back ends of creeks and other protected areas where you can find the warmest water. In the backs of those creeks, look for little depression areas, stumps, logs and deeper spots.

Always try to find cover. Stumps are key cover elements in cold water. If you can find stumps, it's usually a good deal.

## California Monsters

Deadsticking is a good technique for enticing strikes from reluctant largemouths. But there's more than one way to get it done. Bill Siemantel, renowned big-bass specialist from Castaic, California, has his own deadsticking technique that regularly produces 12- to 18-pound Florida-strain bass in the waters he fishes.

Siemantel drifts a Castaic Trout Bait behind the boat

*Bill Siemantel deadsticks monster bass with giant plastic trout.*

as he works a point with another lure ("Trophy Hunter," April 1999). The deadstick rod sits unattended in a rod holder, yet regularly produces his biggest catch of the day. However, since that article was published, Siemantel has developed another deadly tactic using a soft plastic trout from Castaic.

"Western anglers regularly deadstick worms for as long as 10 to 30 seconds," he says, "and I commonly deadstick magnum floating baits at the surface, but now, I've started deadsticking magnum sinking baits right on the bottom.

"The new Castaic soft plastic trout is perfect for this method. My typical approach is to slow-roll the bait up a ridge, then after the bait comes over the top, I let it sit on bottom, dead still. Sometimes the bass strike as it's sitting, other times it comes just as I begin to move the bait. Sometimes I shake the lure in place. It depends on what's working that particular day.

"Another great tactic is to work the edge of a grassline. I cast past the edge and slow-roll the trout bait up until it just ticks the grass. Then, I kill the retrieve, so the head is stuck in the grass with the tail sticking out. Bass cruising the edges will annihilate this deadstick presentation."

---

If you simply can't stand it any longer and have to move the bait, he says, move it with the rodtip, not the reel. Treat p-u-l-l-s the line three to four inches at a time, then pauses. "Don't jerk, just pull smoothly," he insists. "Move the lure just enough so it barely rocks back and forth."

Don't be surprised if you happen upon bunches of bass while using this method. "I once deadsticked 10 fish on 10 consecutive casts," he says. "I've caught five largemouths weighing 26 pounds without even moving my boat."

Remember, this method is intended to snare lethargic bass in icy water, fish that are too sluggish to chase down a moving lure. Later, as the water warms into the upper 40s and low 50s, Treat gradually switches to a more aggressive retrieve to meet the changing mood of the bass.

## SITTING DUCK

Lebanon, Tennessee, bass guide Jim Duckworth is on the water at least 325 days a year. Spring in Tennessee often means volatile weather, and most anglers head for calmer water when the wind whips up. But Duckworth uses it to his advantage, employing a deadstick surface tactic that's nothing short of amazing.

"One March day, I was guiding a novice bass angler on Dale Hollow Lake," he recalls. "The wind was blowing 35 mph and waves were crashing onto a main-lake point. I threw a crankbait against the bank a couple of times, without a strike. Then, my client cast a floating jerkbait, and his reel backlashed. As he picked at the line, his bait sloshed back and forth in the waves."

Duckworth was helping his client straighten out the mess, when the rod nearly flew out of the boat. "I quickly grabbed it and discovered a bass had hit the floating jerkbait." He quickly handed the rod back, and his client boated a 6-pound, 2-ounce smallmouth.

The pair spent the afternoon seeking out the roughest banks and points, deadsticking floating jerkbaits in the waves. "We caught two more big smallies, a 4-pound spotted bass and a 6-pound largemouth—all by letting the waves wash the lures back and forth."

Since then, Duckworth has spent considerable time playing with this do-nothing jerkbait method on windy spring days. "It works best in water ranging from 49 to 58 degrees, on shorelines with a 45-degree slope," he says. "Bass use these relatively steep banks as migration routes from deep to shallow water in spring, and pick off crayfish and baitfish as they travel. I believe they use the wave action to their advantage, and will grab an injured minnow that's bobbing in the breakers."

Although Duckworth's deadsticking method seems straightforward, there are a few key points to remember. First, he recommends fishing an unweighted lure; flashy colors on sunny days, flat colors under the clouds. Especially productive is a Floating Super Rogue or Rattlin' Rogue in laser craw pattern—red with an orange belly.

Cast the lure about three feet from the bank into the heaviest waves. Lower the rodtip and peel off some slack. "The line shouldn't go tight until a fish takes the lure," he says. Let the lure slosh back and forth in the

*Tennessee guide Jim Duckworth plays the wind to his advantage. Confidence pattern: Laser craw.*

waves for at least 30 seconds. If you're not getting bit, wait longer.

Always keep the lure in sight. If it disappears, or if you see a bass strike, reel up the slack quickly, but don't set the hook. "Strikes are usually very light," says Duckworth. "Sometimes a bass swims up, closes its mouth around the lure and moves away slowly. The fish may just flash on the Rogue and get hooked on the outside of its jaw, and a hard hookset will rip the bait away. If your hooks are sharp enough, you'll stick the fish by just tightening down."

High-percentage areas for this unusual method include stump-covered points, rock transitions and Duckworth's favorite—deep, chunk-rock points at the mouths of tributaries. It's less effective on flats and slow-tapering points where wave action is not as intense.

## BEDTIME BASS

Bass pro Mark Davis helped pioneer the use of suspending jerkbaits on the professional tournament trail. The Mount Ida, Arkansas, bass legend has won two BASS Angler of the Year titles and a BASS Masters Classic, and credits suspending jerkbaits for much of his success. Like the others, he primarily fishes Rogues, although other jerkbaits will work just as well. Davis even throws a Rogue when bass are on their beds, a time when most other pro anglers reach for a tube or lizard.

"Sight-fishing a Suspending Rogue is the most exciting fishing imaginable," he says. "Seeing a big fish actually take the bait is something you never get used to—it makes my heart pound just talking about it!"

Bass spawn in waves, not all at once. When the water warms to about 55 degrees, some fish—often the biggest—begin moving into sheltered coves and quiet tributaries to spawn. Bedding continues until the water reaches about 70 degrees.

For his deadsticking, Davis prefers the Suspending Super Rogue when the weather is

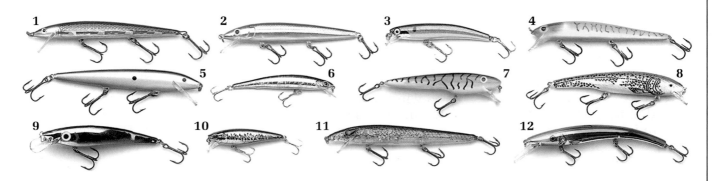

1. *Bugley Prizm Image Bang-O-Lure; 2. Rapala Husky Jerk; 3. Yo-Zuri Twitch'n Minnow; 4. Storm ThunderStick; 5. Rapala Husky (floating); 6. Mega Bite Twitchn-L; 7. Berkley Frenzy Floating Minnow; 8. Mann's Loudmouth Jerkbait; 9. Luhr-Jensen Suspending "Power" Minnow; 10. Owner Rip'n Minnow 65; 11. Smithwick Dead Stick Rogue; 12. Reef Runner RipStick.*

## The Baitfish Connection

Bass don't feed in the winter nearly as much as they do when it's warm, but they do feed. As evidence, ice fishermen regularly catch bass.

So why do cold-water bass strike a motionless jerkbait? Many predators have a search image—a prevalent forage that becomes a preferred target. The search image concept is usually applied to the predator seeking some conspicuous aspect of the prey's appearance. But might it also include the prey's behavior?

Unfortunately, studies of bass forage behavior, especially shad, have largely been restricted to estimating populations. However, there is indirect evidence that shad may be less active in cold weather. For example, the number of shad that pass through reservoir water control structures (called entrainment), or are caught in the water-intake filters at power plants (called impingement), is generally higher in winter months. Although several explanations can account for this, it could result from inactive shad being pulled to a water discharge or intake structure.

Furthermore, shad die-offs are common when the water begins to warm in the spring. And just before a die-off, they appear sluggish, swimming slowly and

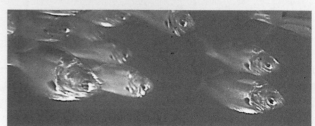

*Baitfish, especially shad, are sluggish when the water is cold. Deadsticking mimics well their movements at this time, triggering a natural feeding response.*

erratically, and are often unresponsive to things that would normally cause an escape response.

It seems like a suspended jerkbait would mimic this behavior better than a rapidly vibrating shad imitation. Since the dying shad are likely to rise to the surface, a bait rocking back and forth in the waves may be an especially good imitation.

While we wait for bass psychologists to explore the bass ego, you might try thinking like the prey. Deadsticking a jerkbait would be a very good start.
—Dr. Hal Schramm

---

stable, and the smaller Suspending Pro Rogue under frontal conditions or when the water is exceptionally clear. He also fishes a new lure he and lure designer Jim Gowing developed, the suspending Dead Stick Rogue.

This one doesn't have the exaggerated wiggle that's typical of minnow-type baits with a long diving lip. Rather it produces a straight, tight swimming action, much like a real fish, that's perfect for Davis' pattern.

Wearing polarized sunglasses, Davis scans the water for signs of bedding fish, maintaining a safe distance from

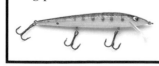

*Mark Davis sight-fishes early-season bass. Confidence pattern: Log perch.*

potential target areas. When he spots a fish, he makes a long cast past the bass, jerks the lure sharply two or three times until it's over the fish, then kills the retrieve.

While the Rogue suspends over the bed, Davis barely twitches the rodtip while keeping his eyes on the lure. "You don't want the bait to move forward, just rock in place," he says. Alternate between twitching and deadsticking to trigger strikes, and when the bass mouths the bait, use a side-sweep hookset. If the fish appears uninterested, come back to it later, or try another color.

Davis also uses a variation of this method when bass are bedding in deeper water, out of sight. This is a common scenario early in the season and in gin-clear lakes. He casts to likely spawning areas—open pockets in grass and shallow tributary inlets.

"Jerk the lure down once or twice so it suspends two to three feet down," he says. "Often you'll see the bass rise up and eat it, even if the bass isn't visible at first."

## MORE FROM LESS

Good information never comes easy, but now you have the inside score on patterns that will produce this spring. Cold-water bass, or bedding fish, need a little coaxing and in these cases, the best retrieve is often no retrieve at all.

# WEIGHTLESS WORMIN'

*by Don Wirth*

The reservoir was high, and as I idled my boat toward the back of a tributary, hundreds of willow bushes inundated by rising water gave proof to the fact. I picked up a spinning rod rigged with a floating worm, a straight-tail plastic 'crawler impaled on an offset hook.

Talk about a plain-Jane rig—no sinker, no rattle; not even a wiggling twister tail to entice Mr. Big. But there was something off-the-wall about its color—shocking pink! The color of one of those gaudy Cadillacs driven by women who sell Mary Kay cosmetics for a living.

Any bass angler schooled in the art of finesse would no doubt have viewed the neon-colored worm with amusement. It looked like a cheap novelty that some prepubescent boy might drop down the back of his sister's blouse.

I cast the worm to a flooded bush and let the weight of the hook pull it slowly down. A twitch of the rodtip sent the worm darting, and the biggest bass I've ever seen shot out, opened its bucket-size mouth and sucked it in.

Even at casting distance, the take was easy to spot. One second I saw bright pink and the huge, dark shape of the fish. The next second, no pink, and the shape was on the move. I set the hook.

The bass boiled angrily beneath the surface, then bulldozed for the bush. Suddenly, the line cut upward as the fish tried to jump, but it was simply too big to clear the surface. When it shook its head, I saw pink at the corner of its mouth, the hook point buried solidly.

Two more bulldog runs followed, then I lipped the bass with both hands. It weighed 9 pounds, 15 ounces on a digital scale.

I caught 14 more bass that day from 1 to 6 pounds on that goofy pink worm. And unlike bass caught on a crankbait or Carolina rig, every fish hit in plain sight. Bass fishing, my friends, just doesn't get more exciting than this.

There are many ways to catch bass using floating worms. A great presentation I stumbled on years ago was to turn a worm into an erratic surface lure. To get extra casting distance, crimp on a large split shot about 18 inches above the hook. Then, during the retrieve with a 7-foot spinning rod, wave the rodtip from side-to-side, holding the sinker above the surface. This certainly offers a different look, one the bass aren't conditioned to. Plus, it covers a lot of territory.

I use 10- to 14-pound superline tied to a small swivel, along with an 18-inch mono leader. Rig the worm with an exposed hook, or weedless, depending on the cover. When a bass strikes, drop the tip and delay the hookset a second or two. A long spinning rod allows you to make longer casts, and lets you more easily swing

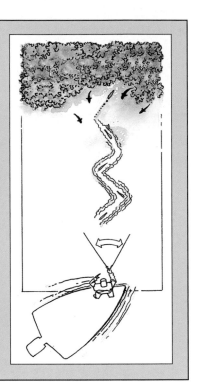

the weight back and forth above the surface to create the side-to-side dart that triggers strikes.
—*Spence Petros*

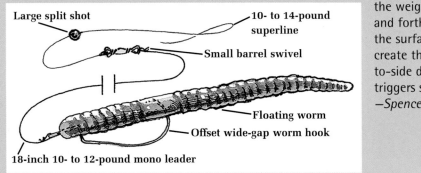

Large split shot

10- to 14-pound superline

Small barrel swivel

Floating worm

Offset wide-gap worm hook

18-inch 10- to 12-pound mono leader

# RETURN OF FLOATERS

"Bass anglers have been fishing the so-called floating worm for 50 years, but lately the method has skyrocketed in popularity," says Wayne Kent of Creme Lures. "Ever since Nick Creme invented the plastic worm in 1949, bass anglers have learned to rig them in endless ways, including on a plain hook.

"Of course, bass fishing is a game of trends, many of which are driven by pro anglers on the national tournament circuits. For years, the Texas rig with a sliding sinker was the gold standard in wormin'. Then came the Carolina rig, with a heavy sinker, swivel and leader. Now the big buzz on the pro tour is the floating worm."

One reason the floating worm is enjoying a high-visibility status among the elite bass anglers is because major

tournament circuits, including B.A.S.S. and FLW, have revamped their schedules. Fewer events are held during the summer these days, more in the spring, and spring is when floating worms are especially effective because so many bass hold in shallow water at this time.

This spring-heavy schedule also tilts the playing field in favor of pros who are adept at targeting bedding bass. Keen-eyed competitors know the floating worm is one of the deadliest of all sight-fishing lures.

Although there are variations on the theme, the basic floating worm rig is a 6- to 8-inch straight-tail plastic worm rigged with only a hook to make it sink. Virtually every soft plastic manufacturer makes a worm specific to this technique. The best floaters, including Creme's Scoundrel, are made with high-grade plastics cooked at exactly the right

temperature to achieve the desired buoyancy. Unrigged, they ride the surface. When rigged on a hook, they sink very slowly and respond with sinuous action to the slightest twitch of the rodtip.

# OUTRAGEOUS VS. NATURAL

Color is always a hot topic among bass fishermen, including floating worm aficionados. And the biggest question is whether you should use a bright-colored worm, or one that's more subdued and realistic. Many anglers (myself included) prefer hot colors such as pink, school-bus yellow or white when fishing a floater. Not only do bass often react aggressively to these high-vis shades, they're easy for the fisherman to see. Alabama pro angler Randy Howell, one of the youngest stars on the tournament circuit, feels the ability

## Skip Casting

Skip casting is a mandatory skill when fishing docks or overhanging trees. Use a strong sidearm cast, aiming the worm at a patch of water in front of your target area. With enough practice, you'll soon be able to skip the bait four or five times to fish hanging back under cover.

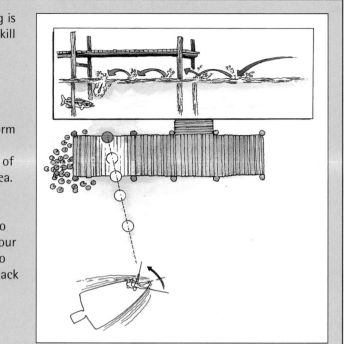

to see the worm provides a tremendous advantage.

"Erratic movement is one of the most important factors in triggering a strike," he says. "If you're fishing a brightly colored worm near the top of the water column, you can easily see it a cast length away. When you spot a bass moving in, you can 'kill' the worm (stop the retrieve so it sinks slowly), twitch it slightly, or swim it rapidly, all the while watching how the bass reacts.

"This is harder to do with a realistic looking worm that blends into its surroundings, and impossible to accomplish with a Texas or Carolina rig in deep water. I usually fish a white worm; it glows like a neon tube in the water."

Sometimes, he admits, bass will either follow a bright-colored worm without striking, or fail to respond at all. In either case, it's time for a more natural hue. "Try to match the predominant forage," he says. "For example, when you're fishing around overhanging trees or bushes, green is good because it mimics a live caterpillar. Water snakes hatch in spring and are easy targets for bass along the margins of the lake; a black-and-yellow floating worm is a convincing imitation of a baby snake."

## PROS FISH FLOATERS

There's more to fishing a floating worm than flipping it out and twitching it back. Randy Howell, along with Jay Yelas of Texas and Rickie Harp of Alabama, are three of the best when it comes to flinging floaters. Each of these competitors has earned thousands of dollars using these buoyant baits. And they all have specific ideas about the most productive ways to fish them.

## Howell: Arrow Straight

"My biggest bass on a floating worm weighed 10 pounds even. I typically use a 6½-inch Hawg Caller rigged on a 4/0 hook with an offset shank. This gives me enough weight to get the lure down to that 'twilight zone' where you can barely see it, and plenty of bite for hooking big bass.

"A 6½-foot, medium-action spinning outfit, strung with 10- to 12-pound mono, provides the flex to cast a light lure, and enough muscle to fight the fish.

"I'm a real stickler for a straight worm. It should hang dead straight when you hold it by its head. If it's got a kink, its action will be unnatural and will twist the line as it comes through the water.

"Often when you take a worm out of the package or your tackle tray, it's got a bend in it from sitting in storage for a long time. I lay several worms on the deck of my boat at the start of the fishing day so the sun will soften them and make the kinks disappear. Finally, the worm must be hooked absolutely straight, not off to one side even slightly, or it'll twist your line.

"A floating worm is most effective from pre-spawn to post-spawn, in water from 55 to 75 degrees. I fish it around laydown logs, isolated weed patches and other shallow cover. It's also a dynamite bait around boat docks, brush piles, weedlines, you name it.

"Anybody, even a kid who's just learning to cast, can catch a big bass on a floating worm, but for anglers who can skip cast, the chances of hanging a trophy escalate dramatically. When fishing the back of a cove or the banks of a creek arm, both classic situations for floating worms, an overhand cast will either get hung up or won't reach many of the fish. When bass are pressured, as they often are during a tournament, they tend to retreat back into flooded bushes and other shallow cover, and skipping is the way to reach them.

"Skipping a worm is like skipping a stone. You want the lure to hit the water with enough speed so it skitters into the fish zone. The idea is to make a sharp, sidearm snap-cast so the lure hits the water in front of your target. If you make a whip-cracking stroke with the rod, you can skip the worm four or five times so it scoots under overhanging branches and into spots overhand casters only dream of reaching. Here's where the medium-action rod comes into play: you can't get the whip-crack effect with a rod that's too light or one that's too stiff.

"I fish a floating worm pretty fast, alternately turning the reel handle, twitching the rodtip and letting the bait sink a little, always keeping it high enough so I can see it when standing up. Many anglers fish this lure way too slow. Use it to trigger a reaction strike from bass, to shake 'em up a bit and elicit an immediate response."

## Yelas: Ready Backup

"The floating worm is a great lure for clear to moderately-stained water. I fish a 6-inch Berkley Power Floatworm, pink mostly, on a wide-gap 4/0 hook with a 6½-foot, medium-action spinning outfit and 10-pound mono.

"Skipping is definitely the key to catching quality bass on a floating worm. Any guy or gal who can skip a worm under overhanging trees and boat docks will outfish an overhand caster 10-to-1. Like riding a bicycle, the skipping technique is hard to describe in words, but with practice you'll get it right.

"I've caught some huge bass on floating worms in tournaments. It's even more fun than fishing topwaters, because you can see everything—the lure, the fish's approach, and the take. In fact, the floating worm is so exciting to fish, the greatest danger is that it'll entice you into staying with it too long.

"Bass will turn off this lure as quickly as they turn on to it, so you must be prepared to leave it in favor of another lure when the bite subsides. Fortunately, it's easy to tell when the floating worm begins to lose its magic—just watch the way bass react to it. If they rushed out of cover to eat it an hour ago, and now only nip its tail or follow it half-heartedly, it's time to switch to a backup. Good choices include tubebaits, finesse worms, lizards and centipedes on a pegged worm sinker, or jig head, and fished on bottom.

"During bedding season, it's critical to view these backup lures as part-and-parcel of your floating worm program, not as separate lures and presentations. I seldom present the same lure to a bedding bass two casts in a row. Instead, I keep several rods rigged with all the baits mentioned and, to keep the fish agitated, I rotate among them.

"I fish each of the backup baits the same way, by holding the rod at 10 o'clock and gently shaking the tip. The idea is to keep the weighted head on the bottom while the lure pulsates."

## Harp: Extreme Wormin'

"I won a berth at the Bassmasters Classic one year by winning a Federation tournament on Tennessee's Fort Loudon Lake on a yellow Creme Scoundrel floating worm. It was the only lure I used during three days of competition, and caught more than 27 pounds of bass. Once, when pre-fishing another tournament, I caught seven bass weighing 41 pounds on this worm. It's an awesome lure for big fish.

"I take the floating worm to extremes. I rely on it in clear or muddy water, shallow or deep, nearly year-round. I'll fish it from early spring through late fall, whenever the water temp is above 55 degrees.

"My favorite worm is an 8-inch Scoundrel on a 6/0 offset worm hook. The hook is much heavier than what most anglers use because my line is 6/30 Spiderwire, which has zero stretch, and my rod is a 6-foot, medium-action baitcaster. The super-tough line, heavy rod and big hook let me put maximum pressure on big fish in thick cover.

"I use an underhand cast, keeping the worm close to the surface, to get it as far back into cover as possible. A lot of strikes occur as soon as it hits the water. Superline helps me stick fish that would probably come unbuttoned on stretchy mono.

"Let the bass tell you how to retrieve a floating worm. I vary retrieves from active to very slow, depending on the fish's mood. When bass are surface-feeding, fish the worm on top like you'd walk-the-dog with a stick-bait. If that doesn't work, twitch it out from the cover quickly, then gradually slow it down as it moves toward the boat, letting it sink to around six feet.

"After bedding season, bass that were hanging around shallow wood and grass move out in front of the cover and suspend in deeper water. Slow-twitching the lure at their level can pay off big.

"Changing colors is critical with this lure. I'll often make a half-dozen loops around an area, using a different color worm on each pass. On sunny days, dark colors like purple and black seem to work best, while brighter colors produce better on overcast days.

"When a bass takes the worm, wait a second or two before setting the hook. I've watched big bass swim up and chomp down on the middle, carry it off a few feet, spit it out, then take it again from the head. If you set the hook immediately, you'll miss a lot of fish."

# FISH IT

The biggest mistake you can make with a floating worm? Not fishing it. This lure is a deadly tool, and it puts the fun back into bass fishing. And every serious angler could stand to have a little more fun.

## Alternate Worm Rigs

Floating worms are as versatile as they are productive. You can rig them a number of ways to fit any specific need. Here are a few examples, but no doubt you'll discover others as you become more experienced with the lure:

Swivel rig—*Rig the floating worm as you normally would, but add an 18-inch leader of abrasion-resistant mono and a small barrel swivel. The leader should be at least the same strength as your main line, heavier if you're fishing snaggy wood cover. This rigging method substantially reduces line twist.*

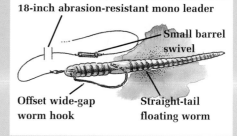

18-inch abrasion-resistant mono leader
Small barrel swivel
Offset wide-gap worm hook
Straight-tail floating worm

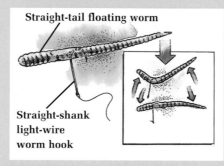

Straight-tail floating worm
Straight-shank light-wire worm hook

Wacky Worm—*Pierce the middle of a straight-tail worm with a straight-shank, light-wire hook. Cast, and allow the worm to settle a bit, then twitch the rodtip. Both ends of the worm will alternately flare backward, then straighten out. The wacky worm is a great presentation when bass are holding in weedbeds topping out to a foot or so below the surface.*

Swimming Worm—*Legendary big-bass angler Doug Hannon showed me this rigging method. "The Bass Professor" has caught largemouths up to 16 pounds on it. Run an offset worm hook through the head of a straight-tail worm as you normally would when Texas rigging, but before reinserting the point into the body, twist the body slightly with your fingers.* Hannon fishes his swimming rig on a 12-inch leader of 30-pound mono behind a billfish swivel, casting it to grassy points and retrieving it steadily so it swims across the surface like a water snake.

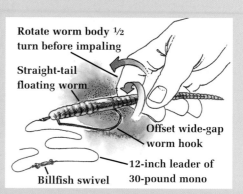

Rotate worm body ½ turn before impaling
Straight-tail floating worm
Offset wide-gap worm hook
Billfish swivel
12-inch leader of 30-pound mono

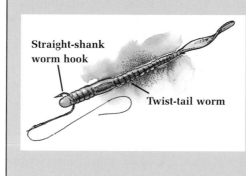

Straight-shank worm hook
Twist-tail worm

Open Hook—*For maximum action, run a straight-shank hook above the thick ring of a twist-tail worm, letting the point protrude. Twitch the rodtip repeatedly so the body arches and tail wiggles. This is a great presentation when bass are holding around boat docks and weedlines.*

# JIG HOPPING

*by Jon Storm*

Unless you fish the Tennessee River Valley or follow the professional bass tours closely, odds are you've never heard of "jig hopping." Known also as "stroking" and "jig-jerking," it's a relatively obscure technique practiced by top pros like Mark Menendez and Mickey Bruce that has never truly caught on in other parts of North America.

But, as these two gentlemen have proven time and again, jig hopping is at home anywhere bass inhabit clean to clear waters. And if you think spinnerbaits, or other "moving" baits, are the only way to provoke reaction strikes, you're about to discover a brave new world of jig fishing.

Mickey Bruce employs jig hopping frequently on the BASS Masters Classic trail, from Lake Lanier to the Louisiana Delta. It's practiced most on Kentucky Lake, but works anywhere you're faced with deeper water and inactive fish. The whole jig-hopping philosophy is, as red-hot pro Mark Menendez describes it, "a system within a system that includes tackle, line, jig and trailer, in various combinations."

But the most amazing thing about the system is the actual technique itself. "I rip that jig so hard, you'd think I was setting the hook on a 10-pound fish," says Bruce. "Each and every rip is that violent."

## HOPPING: WHERE, WHY

For most bass anglers, the jig is the perfect weapon for fish holding tight to cover—pitch and twitch, hook a fish. The jig excels along the bottom, too, and draggin' jigs has dredged up countless big bass. But when bass are relating to cover, but not covered up—when they're suspended above and around structure or cover—most anglers go to a spinnerbait, crank or other fast-moving lure to provoke reaction strikes. Sometimes it works, other times it doesn't, and then it's time to hop a jig.

This technique is really at its best in the postspawn through early summer period, when water temperatures reach 70 to 72 degrees and fish move out of creek arms en route to summer residences. But it's good right now, too, as the bass follow shad migrations back into creek arms.

According to Menendez, "During October, you can get on any major creek channel and follow the shad. Somewhere along that creek channel, from the mouth to the back end of the creek arm, you will encounter a population of fish, and that's the place you want to hop a jig. The top of the drop may be only four feet, and the bottom of the channel may only be eight, but this is a deadly technique in that situation."

Deadly in other situations, too, like summertime when fish set up on deep ledges or rocky points, or when they relate to rock humps and sunken islands, but suspend far enough above or away that bottom-fishing won't provoke their ire. And it's a three-punch combo, effective on largemouths, smallmouths and spots.

## RIP IT GOOD

To prepare for jig hopping, mark the structure you plan to fish either mentally or with a marker buoy, and position the boat in deep water, perpendicular to the area you wish to fish.

Once you've marked a ledge, flat or other area, and

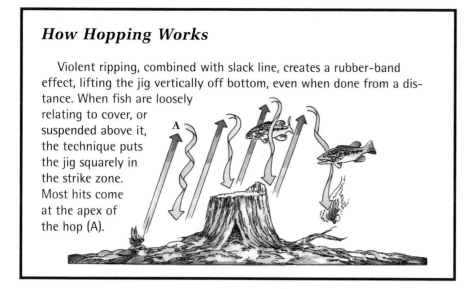

### How Hopping Works

Violent ripping, combined with slack line, creates a rubber-band effect, lifting the jig vertically off bottom, even when done from a distance. When fish are loosely relating to cover, or suspended above it, the technique puts the jig squarely in the strike zone. Most hits come at the apex of the hop (A).

can mentally picture what's below the water, cast the jig and let it settle to bottom. Next, align the rod with the jig and hold it at the 10 o'clock position. There should be some slack in the line. Now, get ready to rip.

"See how hard you can jerk that rod a minimum of three feet," is how Mickey Bruce describes it. Menendez adds, "When you stroke that rod up, and you do it right, your line should sound like a bow and arrow. If you hear a 'wheeoush' you'll know you're on the right track."

You really can't rip the jig too hard, but you can rip it too far. Be sure to end the stroke above your head, in about the 1 o'clock position, then pause and let the jig fall on a semi-slack line. By ripping the jig so violently, it shoots vertically off the bottom, then descends back down. It's a way of getting a jig straight up off the bottom, and right on the nose of a fish, even when the jig is far away from the boat.

Both pros agree 95 percent of the bites occur just as the jig reaches its apex and begins to sink back down. The other 5 percent of the time, a fish will pick the jig off bottom, and when you go to rip again, it will darn near break your wrist. Setting the hook, however, is not easy. With the rod behind you at 1 o'clock, if you feel a tick or thump, the best you can do is reel back down to about 11 o'clock and try to take up slack. It's a chance game, and you might get him, you might not.

Menendez discusses the payout. "You're going to lose more fish than you're going to catch with this technique, but the trade-off is you'll get more bites. So your ratios may be different, but your catching is going to be the same or better."

## TACKLE BALANCE

The combination of violent ripping and hit-or-miss hooksets directly affects which setups work best. Foremost, use a high-speed reel; a minimum of 6:1. This lets you take up line as quickly as possible and get a handle on a lightly-hooked fish.

For rods, Menendez and Bruce differ in their approach. "I use a 6½ footer," says Menendez, "which is the best go-between for moving the bait vertically in the water column, and moving it horizontally toward the boat. Anything longer, and the stroke moves the bait out of the strike zone. It also needs to have a heavy to medium-heavy action, with a short handle—either straight or pistol grip. I'm working with Shakespeare right now and we're releasing a rod made specifically for jig hopping."

Mickey Bruce largely agrees, but his jig-hopping rods run a little longer. "I use a minimum of 7 feet, most often a 7½ footer, so when I rip the jig and the rodtip is at a high angle, I can follow that jig down with a limp, but not totally slack, line and detect a strike. The length gets the slack out quicker."

When building your own system, try a 6½- to 7½-foot rod, coupled with a high-speed reel. But here's where things get tricky. Yes, the rod and reel are integral pieces, but the real key is balancing the jig, trailer and line to achieve the rate of fall that works on a particular day.

Basically, each component affects the manner in which the bait hops and falls. Changing one affects the entire system, so you must consider the whole package.

We'll start with line. Menendez prefers lighter monofilament. "I use 10-pound Triple Fish Camoescent for two reasons. First, its hard coating makes it very stiff and sensitive. Second, it's highly abrasion resistant. When you stroke that jig, if you're hitting brush or rocks, you need a tough line. Also, the 10-pound diameter allows the jig to fall at the correct speed. You get bites on 12-pound, but not as many, and even fewer with 15-pound."

### *How to Hop*

1. Cast the jig, then let it settle to bottom. Raise your rodtip to about 10 o'clock, making sure there's some slack in the line.
2. Rip the rod as hard as you can, stopping at about the 1 o'clock position.
3. Pause, and let the jig fall on semi-slack line. A strike will register as either a "tick" or solid thump. Most hits come as the jig reaches the high point of its hop.
4. If you feel a strike, reel down quickly and set the hook. Understand, you will lose some fish.

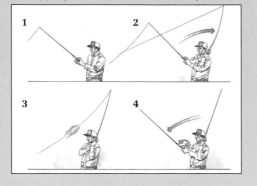

Bruce goes heavier. "I use 16-pound Momoi saltwater mono. When casting, it combines the smoothness of monofilament with the low stretch of superline, and it's the best go-between I've found."

Selecting the jig and trailer gets a little more complicated, and again, each pro differs somewhat, but agrees that experimentation is mandatory. They provide their systems as a starting point only.

"My most productive combination is 16-pound mono with a 9/16-ounce Stanley jig and Zoom Big Chunk trailer," says Bruce. "I also keep rods rigged with 7/16- and 3/4-ounce Stanley Jigs, with smaller and bulkier trailers close at hand. If a jig doesn't come with rattles, I try to add as many as I can on the jig, trailer or both."

Menendez fishes Riverside jigs, and claims, "The key size is 1/2 ounce. I rarely use a 3/4-ounce jig. Since this technique really started with a No. 11 pork frog, I use the Riverside Beavertail Chunk, which is of a similar size, but won't dry out when I set it down. If I want the bait to fall

faster, I go to a craw worm, like the 3-inch Big Claw."

"Generally, in the spring you want a faster-falling jig. During the summer, I slow down and that's when I use the Beavertail Chunk. In colder water, I'll go even bigger, using a 3/4-ounce jig paired with either a 5-inch Riverside Big Claw craw worm, or something else equivalent to a No. 11 pork frog. Plus, the fall turnover milks up the water and I want a bulkier jig with a bigger profile. Use a hook with a thin point and small barb, to help get the hook started."

Of course, line diameter plays into each change in jig weight and trailer, but there's no universal rule. Having a few rods rigged with different combinations will start you down the path, and by adjusting to water temperature, clarity and mood of the fish, you'll eventually dial in a pattern that produces.

Color is the least important factor in jig and trailer selection. Black-and-blue typically scores best, but if the water is clear, try a translucent color like pumpkin with green glitter, or other crawdad imitator.

Menendez adds a few Kentucky Lake combinations to the mix by suggesting black/blue/brown, which he starts using in July when the water starts to clear, plus black-and-brown for very clear water.

## BRANCHING OUT

Once you have the system down, there are a few more refinements that deal largely with the structure or cover you're fishing. It's a great ledge technique, and works on flats, too, plus points and humps, as mentioned. But it's important to decipher where, exactly, the bite is occurring and fish that depth precisely.

For example, if fishing a ledge, Menendez starts with his boat perpendicular to the ledge, then casts from deep to shallow. However, if he discovers the fish are biting just as the ledge drops off, he'll reposition the boat at a 30- to 45-degree angle, which maximizes the time his jig hops along, rather than down, the drop-off.

"This technique targets three specific groups of fish," explains Menendez. "It's perfect for catching fish suspended above and around cover, as well as fish suspended just off a drop-off, or those using the drop-off itself for cover."

Bruce often targets specific cover elements atop a ledge, or attempts to understand exact fish positioning in relation to the ledge. "If there's a stump or brush pile atop the ledge, I'll usually cast beyond it and start ripping. If the fish are relating to the ledge itself, you need to envision exactly what's happening underwater. Sometimes you may only rip it three feet but it falls 10 feet, according to the steepness of the drop, yet ripping it up that three feet puts the bait right on the nose of the fish."

Menendez also expands the technique to other baits. "This whole technique, from my understanding, basically came from Toledo Bend. Larry Nixon was a guide there in his younger days, and he used the lift-and-drop technique to win the Classic one year, but with a worm. There are many times when, if they won't bite a jig, I'll try hopping a Texas-rigged Big Claw craw worm or Riverside Ribbon Tail worm. "It also works on the Great Lakes, but with a tube bait. I've found that many times, when you get into high-pressure areas on Lake St. Clair, Erie or Ontario, most guys are dragging tubes. Now that's a very effective technique, but if I can find a flat with a little drop, even three or four feet, and I know there's fish there, I'll try hopping a tube. Most often, it's a ⅜- or ½-ounce insider weight on a 4-inch tube."

There's really no limit to what jig-hopping can accomplish, given the right conditions. Whenever bumpin' cover fails to produce, whenever you mark fish relating to cover but not buried inside, prepare for a good workout and start hopping jigs. It's a "secret" technique that's a secret no more.

## Bill And The Boomerang Rig

The Boomerang concept is simple: improve a dropshot rig by incorporating a length of elastic spectra fiber. It's quite similar to the theory behind hopping a bass jig, because it keeps a bait off bottom, and in the strike zone, for a longer period of time.

The Boomerang has undergone significant modification, thanks in large part to big-bass specialist Bill Siemantel.

"Joe Renosky sent me a prototype of the rig and asked for some feedback," recalls Siemantel. "Immediately, I knew the setup was ingenious, but it needed some simplification. I started tying the hook directly to the line with a palomar knot, as I would in normal dropshotting. I then attached the line to the 'boomerang' section of spectra elastic, and affixed a Bakudan-style weight below. But I later modified it by flattening the bottom, and angling it slightly, to resemble a walleye walking sinker.

"The system still amazes me. I've already caught bass up to 14 pounds on it. Really, the sky is the limit because the action is so unbelievable. You can do things with the Boomerang that you simply can't do without it. For example, one of my favorite ways to fish a crawdad uses a new glider jig head, instead of a standard hook, tied above the elastic Boomerang cord and weight. With this setup, I raise my rodtip to lift the crawdad off the bottom and stretch the Boomerang cord, then drop the rodtip quickly. As the line goes slack, the Boomerang snaps back, turning the craw backwards and sending it scurrying back toward the weight. You have to see it in person to believe it. It's the most natural action for a crawdad I've ever seen."

*Testing the new Boomerang, Bill Siemantel stuck this 26-inch, 14-pound largemouth on California's Lake Castaic.*

Use this rig below docks, near shore and especially along the deep weed edge. Bass have never seen a bait that sticks its nose out, then backs up and disappears into the weeds.

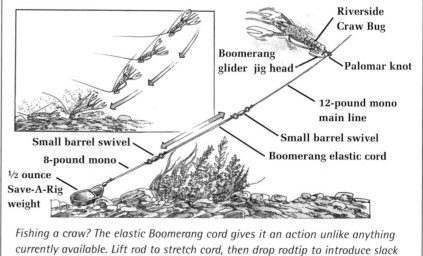

Riverside Craw Bug

Boomerang glider jig head

Palomar knot

12-pound mono main line

Small barrel swivel

Boomerang elastic cord

Small barrel swivel

8-pound mono

½ ounce Save-A-Rig weight

*Fishing a craw? The elastic Boomerang cord gives it an action unlike anything currently available. Lift rod to stretch cord, then drop rodtip to introduce slack line. The elastic cord will snap back, turning the craw tail-first and scurrying backwards. No other presentation gives artificial crawfish such realism.*

# Gettin' Down

*by Bill Dance*

*Whether you fish 'em shallow or deep, spinnerbaits take largemouth bass.*

There's no telling how many bass are caught on spinnerbaits each year, but the number is huge. And I'd be willing to bet my favorite casting rod that the majority of them are caught in less than 5 feet of water. There's a good reason for this. That's where the majority of anglers fish these versatile baits. But I'm here to tell you that bass that live down deep will take spinnerbaits just as well. In fact, one of my most productive techniques throughout the year involves the art of probing deep structure.

## Why They Work

Fishing spinnerbaits in deep water allows you to search for bass more quickly than with a plastic worm, jig or another lure that requires a slow presentation. And it allows you to feel for isolated cover along, or near, the structure you're fishing. Plus, it's especially effective in older lakes where shallow, woody cover has eroded and bass have moved deeper to key structural features.

But beyond these considerations, you should understand why, exactly, spinnerbaits are so deadly in deep water.

- Spinnerbaits have a wide zone of attraction. Their action, flash and vibration draw bass from great distances.
- A spinnerbait can trigger aggressive reaction strikes from bass that might otherwise ignore slow-moving lures.
- Spinnerbaits represent baitfish better than most other lures.
- They can be fished in a wide range of water clarities and temperatures.
- They can be fished effectively on the bottom, or several feet above it.
- Spinnerbaits are effective throughout the year.
- Spinnerbaits produce within a wide range of presentations, including slow-rolling, free-falling and bottom-bouncing.

## Deep Probe

When fishing depths of 15 feet or more, I throw a ¾-ounce lure, unless faced with current or windy conditions. Then, I'll go to a 1-ounce model for better control.

Selecting the right blade or blade combination for deep-water spinnerbaiting depends a lot on the time of year. During the warm months when bass are most aggressive, I select a spinnerbait with medium-size, willow-leaf

## Turn Around

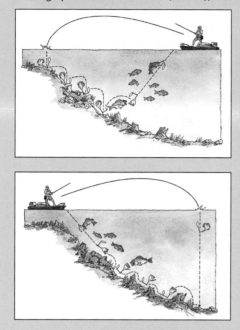

Conventional strategy calls for positioning your boat in deep water and casting spinnerbaits shallow (above), but Dance says you can take more bass by turning things around.

When pulling a spinnerbait down a break, you'll find it's more difficult to maintain bottom contact. Plus, when you do hook up, bass that are trailing your fish are drawn into open water where they become disoriented. It often takes them several minutes to find their way back to their holding area.

By holding your boat in the shallows and casting deep, however, you can easily keep your spinnerbait close to the bottom. Plus, bass that trail a hooked fish quickly return to their holding cover, making it easier for you to stay in contact with them.

blades, simply because they create less lift and the lure stays deep on a fast retrieve.

This allows me to search for bass between hotspots, such as along a deep shoreline flat, rather than move directly from one piece of structure or cover to the next. This not only helps me connect with cruising bass, it allows me to locate subtle, isolated bottom features that may hold fish.

When fishing a willow-leaf spinnerbait through open water, I make long casts. When the lure hits the surface, I pull back slightly, keeping a semi-tight line so I can feel strikes during the fall. Once the bait reaches bottom, I give it a quick jerk to start the blades turning, then begin a slow retrieve.

I occasionally stop the lure to allow it to stay in contact with the bottom. It's very important that the blade or blades spin, and the lure follows the bottom contour.

During the cold periods of the year, I've had much better success with a round-style single blade like a Colorado or Terminator's new "Oklahoma." These blades produce a stronger thump, and can be fished more slowly for cold, sluggish bass.

When fishing a round blade through open water, I cast and closely watch the line as the lure falls to bottom. Once it hits, I give it a slight twitch to get the blade turning and begin the retrieve. Every few feet I pause and lift the rodtip to pull the spinnerbait upward, then allow it to fall back to bottom and start over again. I work the bait in this yo-yo fashion all the way to the boat.

It's important to keep a semi-tight line to stay in contact with the lure at all times. As you'd expect, most strikes come as the lure falls to bottom. Another benefit is that this technique covers a lot of water, so you'll often detect

subtle structure that would otherwise go unnoticed.

Although I work spinnerbaits through secondary areas, I usually attack known structure first. For example, I've caught a world of bass by bouncing a big spinnerbait off stumps and rocks along a deep-water ledge. Chunk rock, boulders and riprap are also perfect cover for this type of spinnerbaiting.

In the summer, you can often fill the live well by targeting deep grass patches with a heavy spinnerbait. If vegetation is growing in 10 to 12 feet of water, for example, I count the lure down to the top of the grass, then bring it back so it ticks the weedtops on the retrieve. Over the years, I've refined my countdown techniques to know exactly how fast my baits fall, and you should as well. Start by assuming the lure falls at one foot per second, and fine-tune it from there. If I know I'm coming to the edge of a grass patch, I'll slow the bait down and try to shake it off the edge right to where bass are most likely hiding.

When fishing submerged grass, the key is to either skirt the tops of the plants, or parallel the edges and any irregular features like cuts, pockets or points.

Standing timber is another situation where deep spinnerbaiting can outproduce other techniques. With standing timber, I cast to the trunk of a tree, let the bait sink to bottom, then pump it a foot or so before letting it settle again. I fish it similarly to the way I work a worm in deep water.

If the line crosses a limb, I'll pull the bait up until it bumps the limb, then work it over and let it fall back to bottom. This method often produces difficult-to-catch bass that suspend in deep brush or trees.

Regardless of the situation, it's critical to vary the retrieve. Instead of reeling straight back to the boat, speed up, slow down, or impart other erratic movements to the lure.

# STAYIN' DOWN

Spinnerbaits, by design, have a tendency to rise on the retrieve, but there are a few tricks to keep them down. If you're having trouble keeping the spinnerbait near the bottom, try downsizing the blade.

Also, if the deep structure you're targeting will permit it, it's much easier to keep your spinnerbait close to the bottom by casting from shallow to deep, instead of from deep to shallow. Working up a breakline is much easier than working down it. But I should point out that you run the risk of hanging up more often if cover is present.

Another advantage in positioning your boat shallow and casting to deep water occurs once you hook up. Other bass tend to follow a hooked fish, and when you pull a bass from deep to shallow, the trailing fish move a certain distance, then quickly return to their original location.

When you battle a bass into deep water, however, the trailing fish become disoriented, and it takes them much longer

*To shorten a spinnerbait's arm, cut it so the blade will run ahead of the hook point (left). Use a needle-nosed pliers to bend a new loop and re-attach the ball-bearing swivel and blade (right).*

to regroup. I'm convinced that you will catch more fish from a deep-water area by casting from shallow to deep.

# SLOW GOES IT

When spinnerbaiting deep structure or cover, perhaps the most important element is your level of concentration. You've got to stay tuned-in to what your lure is doing at all times. Your presentation should be slow and steady, with an occasional drop to maintain bottom contact.

Patience is the key. It takes time for the lure to drop 20 feet, and it takes patience to slow-roll the spinnerbait along the bottom. But if you are willing to work at it, your effort will be consistently rewarded.

Avoid overpowering your retrieve by reeling too quickly. Many anglers have better success with a reel that has a low gear ratio like Quantum's Energy or EX model baitcasters with 4.4:1 ratios. This forces a slower pace and provides more power once a fish is hooked.

For deep spinnerbaiting, my rod choice is a 6½- to 7-foot, medium-heavy IM6 graphite Quantum Dance Class baitcaster. The action and length provide more sensitivity and power for controlling heavier spinnerbaits, as well as the backbone needed for a solid

## Blade Retrieves

**Round Blade Retrieve:** When the weather is cold and fish sluggish, Dance fishes secondary areas between pieces of structure or cover with a round-blade spinnerbait. He makes long casts and allows the bait to drop to bottom. Then, he snaps the rodtip up to start the blade turning (A) and begins reeling. After a few feet, he lifts the rodtip, then lets the bait drop again (B). Most strikes come as the bait falls (C).

**Round Blade Retrieve**

**Willow-Leaf Blade Retrieve:** Aggressive fish call for a spinnerbait with willow-leaf blades retrieved a bit faster. After making a long cast and letting the bait drop to the bottom, snap the rodtip up to kick-start the blade(s) (A). Then, begin the retrieve close to the bottom. Instead of lifting the lure, however, simply pause to maintain bottom contact (B). Aggressive bass usually hit the lure as it's moving (C).

**Willow-Leaf Blade Retrieve**

hookset. The extra length also allows you to move a lot of line on the hookset, and helps you get a big bass out of the thick stuff.

When deep-water spinner-baiting, it's also important to use a low-stretch, thin-diameter monofilament line. Personally, I don't fish anything heavier than 16-pound test. Anything above 16-pound test has too large a diameter and creates additional drag, which can hurt the maximum depth of the bait and cut distance off each cast.

## CONSIDER COLOR

When it comes to color selection for blades and skirts, I keep it simple. Silver is my favorite for blades because it reflects more sunlight in the water than other colors. But I place more importance on the skirt color since this is where the hook is, and it's what I want the fish to home in on. I highly advise experimenting with skirt color; different shades have better visibility in certain types of water clarity and light conditions.

It might surprise some of you to learn that black is my favorite skirt color for deep spinnerbaiting. Although I also use chartreuse-and-white and solid white on occasion, black is best for this technique because it holds its identity underwater better than any other color, regardless of the light or water conditions.

Deep spinnerbaiting places a premium on concentration and patience. If you have what it takes to slow down and probe the depths, you just might catch more bass than you ever did spinner-baiting the shallows.

## Kevin VanDam On Deep Structure

Kevin VanDam has earned a reputation as bass fishing's top spinnerbait technician. Here is what he says about taking them deep.

*Kevin VanDam is among bass fishing's top spinnerbait technicians. He may use other baits to locate deep fish, but once they're found, a spinnerbait is his lure of choice.*

"Deep spinner-baiting is a deadly technique in depths from 10 to 25 feet, especially during the heat of summer. If I catch a fish on a piece of deep structure with any bait, I never, ever, leave that spot without thoroughly working the area with a spinnerbait. I may use other baits to locate fish, but once they're found, my No. 1 catch lure is a spinnerbait.

"The reason they work so well in deep water is because at least a few fish will suspend over deep structure. With a spinnerbait, I can maintain a controlled fall through the entire strike zone and catch fish that would otherwise ignore a jig, worm or deep-diving crankbait. In these situations, 99 percent of my spinnerbait strikes come on the fall.

"Head weight, along with the shape and size of the blade, determine a spinnerbait's running depth, retrieve speed and rate of fall. It's critical that anglers understand the interrelation of these factors.

"Let's start in 10 feet of water. Here, if I want a fast fall, I use a 1 1/4- to 1 1/2-ounce lure. This triggers active bass when the bite is on. Sometimes, though, I want a slow-falling bait, so I go to a 1/2-ounce lure with a Colorado blade. This bait falls considerably slower, making it a good alternative in cold or murky conditions when the bass are tentative.

"Moving out to depths of 15 to 20 feet, I prefer a small willow-leaf combination or single willow-leaf blade to achieve a fast fall. Basically, the deeper I go, the smaller my blades become, regardless of head weight. Sometimes, it may seem like a gross mismatch, but small blades are extremely effective.

"My best all-around, deep-water combination is a 3/4-ounce or heavier spinnerbait with a single size 4 1/2 to 5 willow-leaf blade. I throw this combination all through the summer months. I flutter it down through the deep-structure strike zone and it consistently loads the boat with bass.

"However, willow-leaf blades don't vibrate or lift as much as Colorado or Indiana blades so it's tougher to stay in contact with them. I've found that size 4 1/2 is the smallest I can go on a willow-leaf blade and still maintain contact with the bait. I stick with sizes 4 1/2 and 5.

"The problem with out-of-the-box baits is most large spinnerbaits come with tandem blades. I cut the clevis and the front blade off a tandem spinnerbait to create a deep-water, single-blade spinnerbait. If you're going to fish a spinnerbait as a drop bait in deep water, you've got to have a very short arm to achieve a tight vertical fall and spin. So I'll further doctor my spinnerbaits by shortening the arms.

"Strike King's Pro Ledge series, for instance, comes with tandem blades and a three-inch arm. I cut that arm down to 1 1/2 inches, remove the front blade, then bend a new loop in the end. This gives me a small, single blade on a very short arm that gives me the tight fall and spin I need. Of course, this can't be done with titanium spinnerbaits, which is one of their drawbacks."

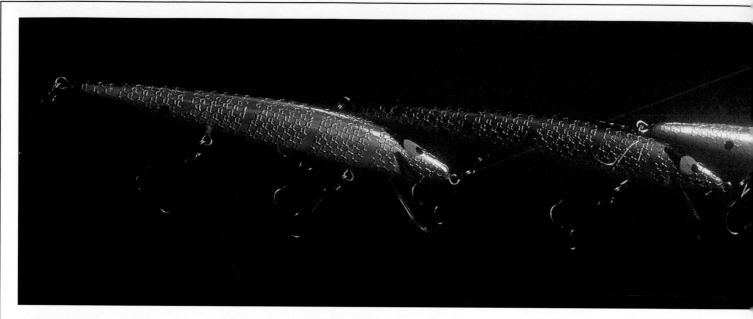

# GOLDEN RETRIEVES

*by Ryan Gilligan*

Jerkbaits catch bruiser bass, especially in spring. Countless tournament victories and firsthand experiences of bass hunters nationwide confirm it. Yet, few anglers understand how to wring the full potential from these lures.

Bass pro Mark Menendez of Paducah, Kentucky, is one who does. He has tremendous success on the tournament trails, and says jerkbaits deserve much of the credit. In fact, he once set a record three-day total of 60 pounds, 3 ounces on Smithwick Rattling Rogues during a B.A.S.S. Top 100 tourney on Pickwick and Wilson lakes.

The reason, he says, is simple. "In cold, clear-water periods, there's no better bait for big bass—I'm talking 5-, 6-, 7-pound fish, and better. The minnow shape is something bass, particularly larger fish, really key on.

They let me cover a lot of water, and make my job a whole lot easier."

Of course, like any lure, a jerkbait isn't magic—catching fish consistently depends on knowing where, when and how to use them. If you're missing any of these puzzle pieces, you might as well be fishing in a bathtub.

Through his extensive experience fishing jerks from early spring through summer in waters across the country, Menendez has developed a formula for success. He breaks down spring water temperatures into four distinct ranges, and uses specific jerkbait styles, retrieve speeds and cadences for each, to match predominant bass behavior.

Armed with his secrets, you too can unlock jerkbaits' true potential for duping largemouths this spring. Let's examine his proven formula.

## Water Temp: 38 To 42 Degrees

These temps are downright chilly, but such conditions, combined with clear water, are hot for jerkbaits.

"When you've got clear water in the 38- to 42-degree range, it's prime time."

Under these conditions, Menendez chooses a deep-diving rattling jerkbait. Although a shallow-diving rattler is his go-to lure for much of the spring, he gives the deep diver the nod early on because of its 12- to 13-foot running depth.

"This time of year, deep divers outshine all others. They get down to where bass are holding, which is critical when water's cold—bass won't chase lures far."

He targets main-lake points and ends of bluffs adjacent to river channels, positioning his boat in as deep as 40 feet of water and casting into 20 to 25. There, he says, bass often

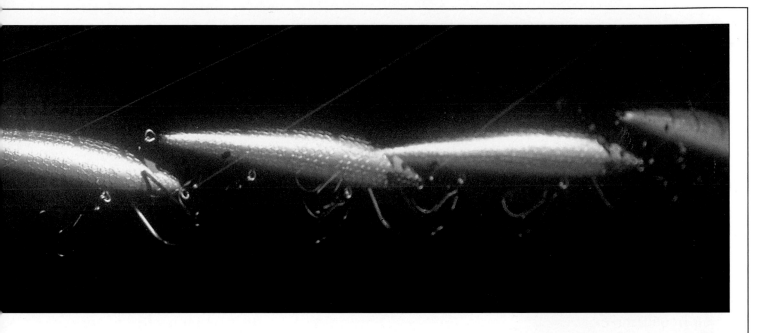

suspend 12 to 15 feet down—perfect for deep divers.

Rather than jerk or twitch the lure, Menendez reels it down to maximum depth, then uses a slow, sweeping-style retrieve—as if he's fishing a Carolina rig. He sweeps the bait forward, pauses two to three seconds, and repeats.

Add up all those pauses and pulls, and it may take up to two minutes to retrieve a bait. "That can feel excruciatingly slow," he says, "but it's absolutely deadly on big, cold-water bass."

To fight the temptation to speed up, he sits down while casting. "I find I'm much more patient and trigger a lot more strikes when I just take a deep breath and force myself to settle down in that front boat seat," he says.

## Water Temp: 43 To 48 Degrees

When the temperature rises above 42, Menendez will switch gears slightly. He finds bass in about the same areas, but now they'll chase the bait. For these fish, he ties on

a 4½- or 5½-inch suspending rattler, usually a Rogue because he likes the way it sits in the water column.

"I like the 45-degree head-down posture this bait produces. The angle lets it quickly dive to that 7- or 8-foot range, and you can cast farther. More importantly, though, 45 degrees is a non-natural angle for healthy baitfish. In early spring, gizzard shad are dying all over the place and they have that same head-down posture. When bass see that, it often triggers a strike."

If your lure doesn't produce quite the right posture, apply lead tape to the front half of the bait or add weight to the lead treble. Use the lightest line possible; Menendez prefers 8-pound Excalibur. Thinner line lets the bait dive faster and produces a better action.

At these temperatures, he uses a jerk-jerk-pause retrieve, but Menendez says there's no set-in-stone formula for overall speed or pause duration.

"I generally start with a three-second pause, softer

*Jerkbaits are bass pro Mark Menendez's favorite presentation for duping big bass in spring.*

jerks and a moderate speed when water temps are in the low to mid-40s," he says. "But I've been known to pause as long as 12 seconds. Every day I go out, it's my job to find the speed and cadence bass respond to."

If, for example, you're getting strikes, but fish are hooked on the back trebles, lengthen the pause and slow down the overall retrieve speed.

## Cool Jerks

**38 To 42 Degrees**
5½-inch deep-diving jerkbait
Ultra-slow, sweeping retrieve,
long pauses.

**43 To 48 Degrees**
4½-inch to 5½-inch suspending jerkbait
Jerk-jerk-pause retrieve; three-second
pauses, soft jerks and a moderate speed.

**48 To 55 Degrees**
4½-inch to 5½-inch suspending jerkbaits;
floating jerkbaits as temperatures rise
Twitch-twitch-twitch retrieve; moderate to fast speed.

**55 To 65 Degrees**
4½-inch floating jerkbait
Twitch the bait in place over bedded bass.
Keep the lure in the strike zone for extended periods.

## Water Temp: 49 To 55 Degrees

When water temps climb into this range, it's crossover time. Using bass behavior as a guide, Menendez begins to abandon suspending jerkbaits in favor of straight floaters.

"Bass are more active and will move farther to capture a baitfish. That means you don't have to get the lure as close to their depth—and that means you can cover more water."

He also whittles down his pauses to one or two seconds. "I also start jerking the bait harder, depending on the bass' mood. You have to let the fish dictate your retrieve style."

Toward the upper end of this transitional period, Menendez begins exclusively using a 4½-inch floater and a significantly faster twitch-twitch-twitch retrieve.

"At this time I'm moving fast, and this presentation lets me do just that. If I'm fishing a tournament, this pattern is my go-to way to fill a limit," he says.

## Water Temp: 55 To 65 Degrees

At 55 to 65 degrees, bass move into the shallow spawning areas and floating jerkbaits displace suspenders and divers. The floaters stay in the strike zone, letting Menendez goad strikes from temperamental fish.

"Bass in spawning areas hate having a jerkbait over their heads. I cast over the fish and twitch the lure in place. Eventually, they take a swipe at it," he says.

Menendez warns that it's critical to keep your hooks razor sharp in these situations. "A lot of bites you'll get from bedding bass will be slashing strikes. If your hooks aren't sharp, they'll slide away from the fish's mouth."

## SEE THE BIGGER PICTURE

Aside from water temperature, a host of other factors further dictate presentation.

Menendez says clear water is a must for jerkbaits. "You need a minimum of 18 to 24 inches of clarity," he says. "Murkier waters call for different presentations.

"If you can't see your bait a couple feet through the water, jerkbaits aren't going to work, regardless of temperature," he says.

It's also imperative to use highly visible colors. For Menendez, that usually means lures with a white belly; orange in questionable water clarity.

"Wind is another big factor," he says. "I really speed things up when the wind is blowing, because I've found fish are more active and willing to strike."

A warm, calm day calls for the contrary. "When you've got no wind and high, blue skies, use patience, even if the water's a little warmer. You need a slower retrieve and longer pauses between jerks."

So keep your eyes on your surface thermometer and attention on detail when you hit your favorite bass spot this spring. Use 'em right, and jerkbaits will be your ticket to success.

# WHEN BIG IS BETTER

*by Scott Liles*

Locating bass on a lake with thousands of fishable acres can be intimidating, especially when fish are concentrated in small schools and tucked into heavy cover. Rather than getting caught up in trying to pinpoint these isolated hotspots, it's often better to focus on massive structure that's easier to see—and fish.

"I certainly haven't learned where all the good places to fish are, but I do know that big structure almost always produces a few fish," says noted angler Bill Dance. "If the lake has a large riprap bank, a massive bridge over the water, or steep bluff walls, these huge, visible structures can be phenomenal hotspots for big bass."

Dance recalls encountering a perfect example of this situation years ago while motoring to a fishing spot on a reservoir in northern Mississippi. He was passing under a large metal bridge, which was supported by colossal concrete pillars, when his trademark "T" baseball cap blew off his head. When he circled back to pick it up …

"I noticed the propeller wash was sloshing against a concrete bridge pillar," he explains. "The turbulence threw shad against the pillar and I saw a 4-pound largemouth bust a baitfish."

Dance quickly pulled a rod from the locker and began casting. It wasn't long before he'd caught and released several largemouths weighing from 2 to 7 pounds each.

"I was lucky enough to catch a few in that one area," he says. "Since then, I've learned that big structures such as bridge pillars are among the finest bass-holding real estate available."

# BRIDGES OVER BASS

Anglers who study bridges and their structural details will see that these massive spans offer a variety of prime fishing areas. The hottest features are concrete support pillars, deep-water channels, adjacent shallow feeding flats, and riprap on the bank.

To keep bridges as short as possible, they're usually built where the expanse between the shorelines is narrowest. Naturally, this bottleneck accelerates the current flow and concentrates baitfish as they pass through the area—making them easy pickings for hungry bass.

But it also means largemouths must continually fight the current, so they use the giant pillars as protection from the flow.

When targeting these "resting" fish, position your boat with the bow facing into the current. Cast upstream and reel with the flow. This allows increased lure control and a more natural-looking presentation.

Dance makes his first few casts along the edge of a pillar, working the lure parallel to each side. Fish often hold close to the structure, where the water moves more slowly.

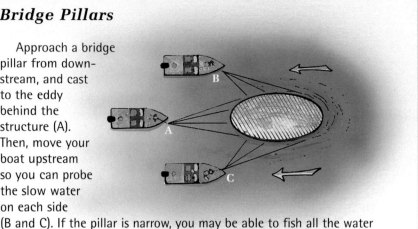

## Bridge Pillars

Approach a bridge pillar from downstream, and cast to the eddy behind the structure (A). Then, move your boat upstream so you can probe the slow water on each side (B and C). If the pillar is narrow, you may be able to fish all the water from the same position.

"But you also want to fish each pillar from different angles," he adds. "If there's a noticeable current, I often catch the most bass from behind the pillar, on the down-current side."

Big structure acts as a current break, and fish burn less energy holding in the calm, stable water directly behind a pillar. It's also an ideal spot from which to ambush unsuspecting baitfish caught in the current.

When Dance packs his tackle box for fishing bridges, he's partial to crankbaits, grubs and jigging spoons. This arsenal enables him to cover the entire water column.

Naturally, it is difficult to predict the presentation or lure size and color that will produce.

"You don't know from one day to the next what lure will work best," Dance explains. "That's why I take several sizes and colors. With a big selection of lures, I can experiment with different combinations until I figure out what the fish want."

Typically, Dance begins with a shallow-running Bomber Fat Free Shad, then switches to a medium diver followed by a deep diver. At some point he'll figure out the bass' preferred depth range that day, as well as the presentation that triggers strikes.

If bass don't respond to a fast-moving lure, Dance slows things down with a grub or jigging spoon. The vertical presentation keeps his lure in front of the fish longer, allowing them more time to react. Again, it's important to stay flexible, he says.

"If I'm vertical fishing near a bridge pillar with a 3-inch grub rigged on a ¼-ounce jig head, and I don't have any luck, I'll go to a larger grub," he says. "Another option is to use the same lure size but try other color combinations. It's a matter of trial and error until you figure out what the bass want at that particular time and place."

One final word on current is especially important during the winter months: "When the water temperature dips below the mid 50s, it requires too much effort to fight the chilly current," Dance says. "At these cool temperatures, water becomes more dense and it's not what bass prefer."

# RIPPING RIPRAP

The bank at the bridge abutment normally features some sort of erosion control structure, either riprap or a seawall. Both structures hold bass.

"Riprap banks and concrete seawalls provide an ideal spot for algae growth," Dance explains. "Since algae is a food source of baitfish, they are naturally attracted to these areas, drawing bass, too."

While either type of structure will hold bass, riprap is the better of the two because it offers more cracks and crevices in which small plants and animals live. Normally, there's a superb shallow feeding area somewhere along this rock-covered bank, but you may have to probe the bottom with your sonar to locate it.

"The bottom contour under each bridge is different and it's important to become familiar with the available structure," says Dance. "Once you get a feel for the area, you can pick out the shallow hotspots, as well as irregular features along a riprap bank. If you do this, you'll have every base covered."

When fishing a shallow feeding area, give it at least 10 to 20 minutes. If you do not find active fish, move on. But make sure you return to the flat from time to time throughout the day because when inactive bass get the urge to feed, they'll move into the shallows.

Another advantage riprap and bridge pillars offer is that constant boat traffic often sparks fishing action. Boat wakes slapping against the rock and concrete dislodge algae and plankton, attracting baitfish—and bass. This is

**Bluff Banks**

With your boat parallel to the wall, run a worm or jig along short ledges extending from a bluff bank (A). If the ledges jut out from the bank, hold away from the wall and hop the lure from one ledge to the next (B).

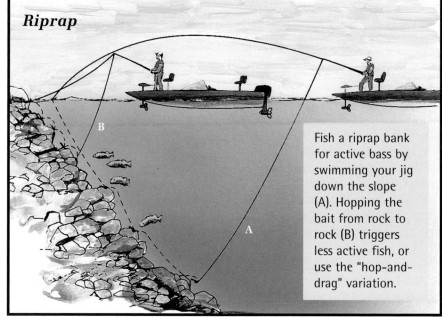

**Riprap**

Fish a riprap bank for active bass by swimming your jig down the slope (A). Hopping the bait from rock to rock (B) triggers less active fish, or use the "hop-and-drag" variation.

one time you won't mind company on the lake.

Along with bridge abutments, riprap is also a common sight along dam embankments and other erosion-prone shorelines. That's where Missouri state trooper and avid bass angler Scott Pauley spends many of his fishing hours.

Pauley, who lives in Columbia, fishes riprap whenever possible, and says

the best time to be there is when the dam operators open the huge gates, creating a current on the lake. Soon after the water begins to flow, bass turn into feeding machines, he says.

Pauley surmises that the current pulls baitfish toward the dam and crayfish come out of their hiding spots to snatch passing forage. All this activity provokes bass into a feeding binge.

During a typical early-morning fishing trip, Pauley begins by focusing on extremely shallow fish. He positions his boat close to the rocks and casts a Rebel Pop-R topwater, Zara Spook or buzzbait parallel to the shoreline.

If nothing bites, he moves the boat away from the bank 5 to 10 feet and tests the slightly deeper water. Another option is to keep the boat about 20 feet from the bank and fancast toward the shoreline. This allows you to cover various depths quickly, he says.

The topwater bite rarely goes beyond 10 a.m., depending on sunlight levels. That's when Pauley switches to a tandem Jewel spinnerbait fitted with a white skirt and silver blades. He first tries a steady retrieve, switching to slow-rolling just above the bottom if that doesn't work.

Another excellent lure for ripping a few riprap bass is a jig-and-pig combo, as long as the jig is fairly light.

Even though a heavy jig is easier to fish, Pauley recommends going with an ⅛-ounce head because it won't hang in the rocks as easily. While pork trailers are the tried-and-true choice for this technique, he prefers a synthetic Jig Tail trailer.

"The synthetic material is thin and has much more action," he says. "Any slight movement of the jig, and the trailer wiggles and flutters. Bass just can't stand it."

Pauley casts the jig to the shoreline and allows it to sink to the bottom, then steadily swims the bait along

## Dancin' With Duck Blind Bass

While bass anglers love to fish visual cover, there are prime pieces of real estate that often go overlooked—duck blinds. These fish-holding structures are normally located on shallow flats, and when bass are up in the skinny water, fishing can be unbelievable.

*Duck blinds give up more than ducks. Dance never passes up a chance to fish them.*

"Every time I come across a duck blind, I just have to stop and give it a try," says Bill Dance. "If you use a common sense approach, there's no doubt you'll fool duck blind bass."

Boat position is important. As you approach the blind, maneuver the boat into a position where you can make accurate casts to all the potential strike zones around and under the blind.

Other factors to consider are the direction of the sun and current. Both help determine where bass will hold around the duck blind.

"When I'm fishing a duck blind where there's current, I catch more fish on the up-current side," says Dance. "I position the boat parallel to, but not too close to, the blind, then cast into the current and retrieve with the flow."

Bass face into the current, waiting for baitfish to wash past. Any spinnerbait or shallow-diving crank that comes into the strike zone usually draws a strike.

Shade is also a key factor, especially if there's no current to keep the water cool. Cast to the shady spots, but do it from an angle that keeps your shadow off the water near the blind.

The final ingredient is confidence that fish are in the area. "You've got to believe bass are present, or you'll simply go through the motions. Without that confidence, you lose concentration, and maintaining a clear focus on your technique is very important." —*Scott Liles*

the slope. Occasionally, he stops the retrieve and allows the jig to sink, just to make sure it's following the bottom contour.

"This simulates a crawfish or baitfish swimming from the bank toward deeper water," he says. "If the bait swims about four to eight inches above the rocks, and it passes anywhere near a bass, he just can't keep from smashing it."

If swimming the bait doesn't trigger strikes, Pauley recommends switching to a slow-hop. Cast to the shoreline, lift the rodtip while

cranking the reel handle a few times, then drop the tip and allow the jig to sink to bottom. You can jiggle the rodtip to create action in the tail, or simply allow it to remain motionless for three to eight seconds before beginning another "hop-and-stop" retrieve.

When bass refuse to hit either of these presentations, Pauley falls back on his "hop-and-drag" presentation, which accurately simulates a feeding crawfish. It's a perfect solution when bass are inactive and will not take anything moving too fast.

Crankbaits also have their place among the rocky riprap. Like the swimming jig, try to bump the lure off the rocks. The racket will call bass to the lure, and even if they're not hungry, you should draw some reaction strikes.

## BLUFFING BASS

A rocky bluff is another oversize structure that provides excellent bassin' opportunities. But these massive bass magnets are also among the most intimidating structures bass fishermen ever encounter.

Bass on a deep-water bluff can be hard to locate and even harder to catch, but the rewards can be great.

"I've found that the best bluffs have ledges that extend outward under the water," says Bill Dance. "One way to tell if a bluff has this feature is to examine the wall above the waterline. If you can see ledges in the wall above the waterline, it often indicates there are also ledges under the surface."

Bluffs can be composed of rock, mud or clay, and are found mainly in midland and highland type lakes. Often, bluff banks are a result of a creek or river channel washing into the bank. Along with ledges, cuts, pockets, slides and points are also key substructures.

While a bluff usually indicates deep water, it doesn't necessarily mean bass are holding deep. Water clarity has a big influence on bluff bass. If the water is clear, bass tend to move deep under bright skies. Start fishing at 6 to 10 feet and work deeper if you come up empty. But if it's dingy, the best action may be fairly shallow.

Position your boat parallel to the bluff and fan-cast a jig-and-pig or plastic worm along the walls. This way, you can fish the bluff quickly, but more importantly, you keep the lure in front of the fish.

"If you fan-cast, the lure remains in the strike zone 80 to 100 percent of the time," notes Dance. "The only time this approach is not as useful is when bluff ledges extend way out into the lake. Then, it's best to cast directly into the bluff and work the lure from ledge to ledge."

Hopping a jig or worm from ledge to ledge takes practice. If you lift the rodtip too high, it will probably miss the target. The trick is to move the lure only a few inches, then lower the rodtip so it drops straight down to the next ledge. Ledge-hopping isn't the fastest fishing method, but it's effective.

Massive bridge pillars, long stretches of riprap and sky-high bluff banks seem intimidating, but don't overlook them. They may be big, but so are the bass that call these special places "home."

---

## Science Of Stumps *by Roland Martin and Bill Dance*

One of our favorite types of bass cover—stumps—are created when trees are clear-cut by loggers prior to initial flooding. The flat-top remnants remain on the lake bottom, a perfect haven for bass.

*When it comes to bass cover, stumps can't be beat. Throw weeds into the mix and big bass are bound to be nearby.*

### Studying Stumps

You can catch bass around any stump, but to save time and quickly cover more water, you should concentrate on fishing stumps that are positioned on or near a drop-off. Likewise, you should always fish a stump situated on a point. Often, a point stump will be your best bet for a big bass. You can fish an entire cluster of stumps and not get a single strike until you fish the outer one.

Also, keep in mind that where there are fewer stumps, the bass will be more concentrated, and you can often catch a number of fish from the same spot.

### Angle Of Attack

With visible stumps, the shady side is usually better than the sunny side, so cast first to the shady side. And it's very important to cast a few feet beyond the stump. The bass might not be right on the stump, but close by. By casting past the stump, you can cover the back, one side and the front with a single retrieve. If the lure plops down directly on top of the bass, though, the fish will likely spook.

Find stumps and fish them. You won't be disappointed.

# SMALL WONDERS

*by Dan Johnson*

When it comes to bass baits, bigger is better, right? After all, everyone knows the old adage, "Big bait, big fish." Yes, big can be good—but not always. There are plenty of times when just the opposite is the case; situations when downright tiny lures are absolutely lethal for behemoth bass.

Witness the phenomenal success of dropshotting, which hinges in many waters on dangling downsized plastics above active and tight-mouthed bass alike. In a similar vein, another of the hottest trends in bass fishing is the growing popularity of downsized crankbait presentations.

True, small cranks aren't new. If you're like most anglers, your tackle boxes include at least a handful of baits like the size 5 Shad Rap, Bandit 1100 series, Bomber Model "A", or something in Norman's venerable "N" family, to name just a few. But are you making the most of these small wonders?

The same holds true for jerkbaits. Anglers and manufacturers are pushing the envelope with micro jerkbaits —lures small enough to be eaten by traditional minnow-baits—further expanding lure choices and tactics for taking bass almost year-round.

As a result, never in the history of bass fishing have we enjoyed more options in downsized cranks and jerks, and the techniques with which to fish them. Best of all, downsizing works from the Canadian Shield and Great Lakes to the Carolinas, impoundments like Dale Hollow and Cumberland, as well as in clear-water western reservoirs.

## WHEN SMALL RULES

Pint-size jerks and cranks are the best option in several situations, particularly in clear, cool water when the bass are in water 10 feet deep or less. Sounds like early sea-

son, right? To be sure, but these little lures also take bass in clear, warm shallows, as they roam feeding flats and inside weed edges early and late in the day.

Downsizing also works well in shallow, stained water or other low-visibility situations, river and lake, throughout the summer, when bass are keying on small forage like young-of-the-year shad. Did I forget to mention clear-water river spots and smallies? The list goes on, limited only by your imagination and willingness to experiment.

Small baits offer many benefits. In tough fishing conditions, such as the wake of a brutal cold front, downsizing allows you to cover water quickly and trigger reaction strikes from neutral fish, thus locating bass faster than standard finesse baits like jigs and plastics. When you're fishing active summertime bass—whether along a riprap bank or early-morning weed tops—small baits offer biological advantages. These

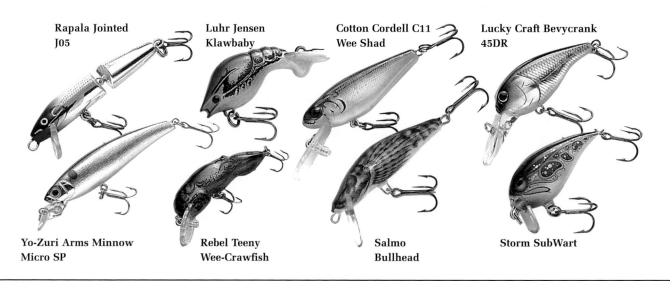

Rapala Jointed J05

Luhr Jensen Klawbaby

Cotton Cordell C11 Wee Shad

Lucky Craft Bevycrank 45DR

Yo-Zuri Arms Minnow Micro SP

Rebel Teeny Wee-Crawfish

Salmo Bullhead

Storm SubWart

include matching forage size, as well as triggering a strike response from fish conditioned to expend as little energy as possible to fill their bellies. Research has consistently shown that, while bass may strike the occasional big, wounded baitfish, day in and day out, their prey of choice is actually much smaller than the largest meal they can fit in their mouths.

## DEFINE SMALL

Size is a relative thing. If you're fishing a 5½-inch, 1-ounce Rebel Minnow, then switching to the 4½-inch version will seem like downsizing. For this discussion, let's set the top of the jerkbait spectrum at 3½ inches and ¼ ounce.

This seemingly narrow window is actually quite broad, and includes a variety of baits new and old, like the 2¾-inch Rapala F07 Original Floater (old) and 3½-inch Bass Pro Shops Lazer Eye Extreme Floating Minnow (new).

With crankbaits, which are typically shorter but fatter, 2½ inches and ⅜ ounce is an appropriate max. As with jerks, such tight parameters

actually include a wide array of baits, including the 2½-inch, slow-floating SPRO Prime Crankbait 25, Rebel Teeny Wee-Crawfish, Lucky Craft Bevy-shad 60 and Bevycrank 45DR, Matzuo's ¼-ounce Depth Charge and the Yo-Zuri Aile Killifish, which measures just 1⅜ inches and nudges a delicate scale ¹⁄₁₆ of an ounce.

## MATCHING TACKLE

It almost goes without saying that small baits demand light tackle. Rods must be long enough, with enough tip flexibility, to achieve casting distance. When fishing jerkbaits, try a 6½- to 7-foot, medium-light graphite rod with a fast tip, which is key to getting the most action from the lure on the "jerk" part of the retrieve.

Crankbaits call for 6½-foot, medium-action glass or glass composite, which is better for the steady retrieve so common when cranking. They're also more forgiving should you try to set the hook a bit too early.

Line choices typically hinge on monofilament, fluorocarbon and mono-fluoro

hybrids in the 6- to 12-pound range. Light line with fairly low stretch produces the most action, especially with jerkbaits, while a stretchy line will absorb the snapping action of the rodtip. On the flip side, the extreme low stretch of braids is not an option because tiny trebles are too apt to rip free during the fight.

While there's no debating the need to lighten up, the debate on casting vs. spinning gear goes on. Many fishermen switch from casting gear to spinning when downsizing, for good reason. A medium-light spinning outfit is perfect for casting baits that weigh half an ounce or less, especially into the wind. Still, many diehard baitcasting fans refuse to give up the power and control of 'casters. In the end, gear choice depends on the type of tackle you're most comfortable, and effective, fishing.

## THINK SMALL

Small cranks and jerks work spring through fall, in a variety of common bass fishing scenarios. Let's start with a few hot-weather patterns you can use now.

**Cabela's RealImage Livin' Minnow Shallow Diver**

**Cultiva Rip'N Minnow 65**

**Matzuo Fantastic Jointed Minnow**

**Matzuo Depth Charge**

**Bass Pro Shops XPS Lazer Eye Extreme Minnow**

**Lucky Craft Pointer 65SP**

**Lucky Craft Bevyshad 60**

**Ugly Duckling 7JF**

## Going Lipless *by Roland Martin and Bill Dance*

Although they've been around for years, lipless crankbaits are hot as ever for largemouths and smallies under a wide variety of conditions.

Lipless cranks' biggest advantage is how much water they cover in a short time. Plus, they're effective in a variety of depths, are high-percentage strike attractors and, thanks to built-in rattles, they're great all-around fish attractors, especially in low-visibility conditions.

### Fish Callers

Lipless cranks also shine under tough conditions—such as when bass hunker in the shade of thick hydrilla beds and deep bulrushes to escape summer's heat.

Lipless crankbaits are also deadly on bass around wood—docks, logs, standing timber and stumps. Plus, because they don't have a lip, they're less prone to snag than traditional cranks. Whenever you feel the crankbait bounce off woody cover, pause a few seconds to let the bait fall; bass often strike on the drop.

Lipless baits are also good fish locators when bass stage on the flats in spring, or run shad in fall. In my book, no other lure is better suited for finding scattered fish. The compact, heavy body casts a country mile and can be retrieved fast enough to cover a tremendous amount of water.

Color options abound, but chrome variations—such as a chrome body with a black or blue back—are among the best. For many applications, a 1/2-ounce bait on a 6 1/2- to 7-foot baitcasting rod spooled with 10- to 17-pound mono is perfect.

***Weed flat finesse—***
Tournament pro Joe Thomas is a big fan of micro jerkbaits like Lucky Craft's Pointer 78SP. "Among my favorite situations to downsize jerkbait size are large weed flats and smaller, scattered weedbeds, where there is about five feet of open water above three feet of standing vegetation.

"With my boat positioned a 50- to 70-foot cast length away over deep water, or off to the side of the area I want to fish, I cast onto the weedbed. When the bait lands, I engage the reel, drop the rodtip about six inches off the surface and, with the rod at about a 45-degree angle to the bait, begin a snap-pause-snap presentation. I'm right-handed, so I palm the reel with my left hand and snap my right wrist to move the rodtip about three feet. Given line stretch and rod bend, this typically moves the lure six to eight inches."

Thomas varies the intensity of the snap, and pause length, until he finds the presentation the fish want. "It's a semi-slack line presentation,"

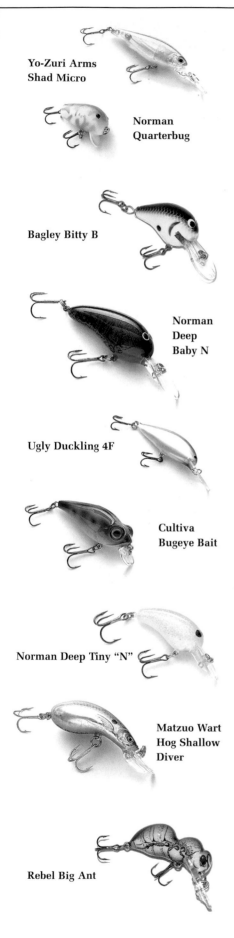

**Yo-Zuri Arms Shad Micro**

**Norman Quarterbug**

**Bagley Bitty B**

**Norman Deep Baby N**

**Ugly Duckling 4F**

**Cultiva Bugeye Bait**

**Norman Deep Tiny "N"**

**Matzuo Wart Hog Shallow Diver**

**Rebel Big Ant**

he notes. "Snap the rodtip, let the bait hang there on slack line while you take up some line, and snap again. Often, fish strike on the pause, so you don't know you're hooked up until the rod loads at the beginning of the snap phase."

When the rod loads, avoid the temptation to set hard. Often, bass slash at the bait and get stuck by only one hook point. A hard set can rip the hook loose.

"This technique is most effective early and late in the day during summer, as well as throughout the day in spring," he says. "With small jerkbaits like the Pointer, you've got realistic patterns in reaction baits that, on average, tend to catch bigger bass than plastics and jigs, and allow you to cover water faster in search of fish."

**Post-front largemouths—** As a successful tournament pro and the head of Rapala's field staff program, Mark Fisher is in a unique position to stay on top of bass fishing trends. He views the current move toward downsized baits as a reawakening of sorts. "One of the classic, yet largely overlooked times to downsize is following a severe summertime cold front," he says. "Before the front, let's say you were catching bass on the deep weed edge on large crankbaits like the size 9 Shad Rap, which is 3½ inches long. Then a front moves in, and the bite turns off for a day or more. Now what?

"Many fishermen tie on jigs or plastics and focus on the same deep cover, trying to nurse negative fish into biting. Downsizing your crankbait presentation is another option, which allows you to cover more water in

search of fish less affected by the front."

In such a scenario, Fisher turns his attention inward, to shallow water, where he fishes the inside weed edge and pockets in shallow weeds looking for cruising fish that are just a tad more likely to hit a moving bait than bass that remain in deep water.

"I fish a small crank like a size 4 Storm SubWart," he explains. "The 1½-inch, ⅜-ounce bait runs four to five feet deep, perfect for the shallow edge. I make long casts and use a slow, steady retrieve. Key spots to fish include anything that might attract bass, like a pile of rocks or patch of gravel on an otherwise soft, weedy bottom."

**River bassin'—**Stacy King is no stranger to small crankbaits. For decades, the longtime touring pro has fished them for early-season bass in the clear-water Ozark lakes near his Missouri home. "That's probably been my number one bass catching technique over the past 20 years," he says.

But he also thinks small in a number of other situations later in the season, including rivers. "Small, short-lipped crankbaits like the SubWart (as well as a number of the Bagleys, Bandits and other brands) are extremely effective for summer largemouths in off-color water like you find in the Arkansas River," he explains. "The small profile matches the size of young-of-the-year shad the bass are feeding on, and the bait bangs into the rocks with relatively few snags."

King targets rock jetties or wing dams. "Fish position on the jetty depends on the current and mood of the bass.

When the dams are letting water through and the current is strong, active bass will be on the tip of the jetty. In slack water, the up- and downstream sides can be better. You have to cover it all to determine a pattern for the day.

"Start from downstream," he says. "Fire a couple of casts into the corner where the jetty meets the shore. Then, move the boat up into the corner and make parallel casts down the jetty, slowly moving the boat out until you reach the tip. Let the boat drift away from the tip and cover it well, from several angles, before moving upstream of the jetty and casting parallel to the upstream edge."

In turbid water, nothing draws strikes like a loud, fast retrieve. "When the bait lands, crank it down until you hit the rocks and bang 'em all the way out to deeper water," he explains. "Keep the lure moving, too. I use a 6.3:1 gear ratio casting reel just for that reason."

King's summer river strategies also include targeting flowing water when brutal heat makes lake fishing tough. "A lot of times when the lake bite dies, you can run up small rivers and catch big large-mouths, smallmouths and spotted bass on these tiny crankbaits," he says.

While largemouths typically favor slower water behind rock walls and in timber-laden backwater sloughs, King seeks smallies and spots in fast water such as shoals, focusing on current-breaking boulders and logs.

It's hardly a southern phenomenon. Milwaukee-area bronzeback addict Bill Schultz targets small-mouths with Rebel Teeny Wee-Crawfish throughout northern streams and Great Lakes tributaries.

"In fast water, I make cross-current or slightly downstream casts and stick with a steady retrieve," says Schultz. "In slower current, I mix it up, twitching the bait on the surface like a topwater; cranking it down, then letting it slowly float back up; and making a few turns of the reel, then snapping the rodtip."

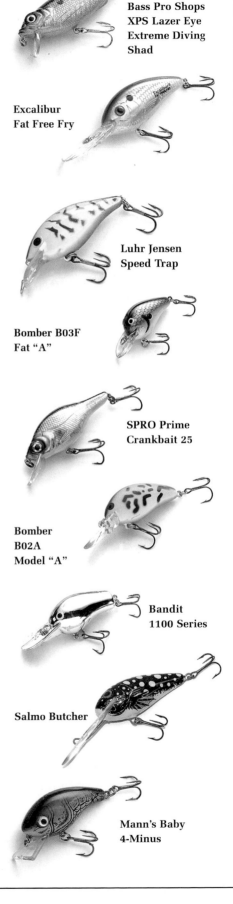

Bass Pro Shops XPS Lazer Eye Extreme Diving Shad

Excalibur Fat Free Fry

Luhr Jensen Speed Trap

Bomber B03F Fat "A"

SPRO Prime Crankbait 25

Bomber B02A Model "A"

Bandit 1100 Series

Salmo Butcher

Mann's Baby 4-Minus

## AUTUMN AND MORE

Small presentations hold their charm as the water cools. Like many anglers, Raleigh, North Carolina, pro Dustin Wilkes follows the fall migration of reservoir shad and hungry largemouths into shallow creek arms. There, however, the similarity ends.

"A lot of people throw big cranks in stained water," he says. "I prefer a smaller bait, like the Yo-Zuri Arms Crank Micro. In heavy cover, I bump it through the wood with a steady retrieve, pausing when the bait hits the timber. In open water, a stop-and-go cadence is better."

Wilkes fishes stained water, using bright, chartreuse patterns. To escape the crowds, he also fishes shal-low creek arms with clearer water. "Here's where a micro crank with a natural finish can really catch a lot of bass," he says.

After bass move deep during winter, small cranks and jerks typically can't reach the fish. Once the fish begin to move shallow in prespawn, however, downsizing can again pay big benefits.

"When the water temperature is in the mid- to upper 40s and the bass are moving onto major points, I fish a small, diving crank, the Yo-Zuri 3D Shad," says Wilkes. "Position the boat over 15 feet of water, cast to the bank, and bump it on bottom with a steady retrieve until you lose contact, then switch to a stop-and-go."

As the water reaches the low 50s, Wilkes dissects points with a suspending jerkbait, the Yo-Zuri 3D Fingerling, using cross-point casts and a sweep-pause retrieve. "When the bait lands, sweep the rodtip about three feet, then immediately throw slack in the line," he explains. "This is key with a suspending bait. Mix up the length of sweeps and pauses until the fish tell you what they want."

Another great small-bait spring pattern occurs during the early postspawn, when bass set up shop in ambush positions along grasslines, points and similar locations. In such situations, Columbus, Georgia, pro Bob Padgett favors Bandit Series 1100 cranks with a steady retrieve. "Another great opportunity is when you find postspawn bass on shallow stump flats," he notes. "Then, I beef up my line test and pop the baits off the wood."

## THINK SMALL

While small baits are no secret, the majority of fishermen have yet to realize their full potential. And, given all the new options in tiny cranks and jerkbaits (with more on the way), that potential keeps expanding every season. We suggest you consider making these diminutive but deadly weapons a major part of your bassin' strategies.

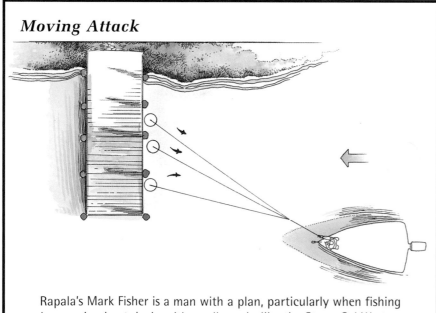

### *Moving Attack*

Rapala's Mark Fisher is a man with a plan, particularly when fishing early-morning boat docks with small cranks like the Storm SubWart. "Approach with the sun off your right shoulder, so long shadows don't spook bass," he says. "Fire casts behind roaming fish, which typically face the sun, so they turn to check out the splash and strike when the bait runs past. As you near the structure, cast parallel to the dock to pick up bass holding tight."

# Success With Finesse  *by Roland Martin and Bill Dance*

**Roland Martin:**

You will never hear me categorized as a light-tackle specialist. Give me a choice and I'll arm myself with a big flipping stick and heavy line. But there are times when all anglers—including myself—must downsize their attack and fish with finesse tackle.

At times, it is the only way to effectively catch bass. Other times, finesse tactics save the day when more heavy-handed techniques don't work.

Finesse tackle consists of spinning rods and reels with 6- to 10-pound line and tiny 1/32- to 1/4-ounce lures. Such gear has a place in the clear lakes of the North and some man-made impoundments of the South. When I fish places like Arkansas' White River chain of Lakes—Bull Shoals, Norfolk, Beaver and Table Rock—I'll usually rig up a couple of finesse outfits just in case I need them.

After a few years of watching finesse fishermen win some major tournaments, I have forced myself to learn to fish the smaller tackle. For example, 4- and 6-pound line tied to small grubs, jigs and plastic worms have paid big dividends for me in tournaments on Table Rock and Bull Shoals for all three species of bass—largemouths, smallmouths and spotted bass.

**Bill Dance:**

I have learned the same lesson over the years. During some of the toughest fishing conditions, from cold fronts to heavily pressured bass, I have resorted to finesse tactics to coax stubborn bass into biting.

Today's bass angler has a wide choice of lure sizes appropriate for

*Although Bill and Roland are fans of heavy tackle, they know that switching to spinning gear and light line often makes a huge difference in bass fishing success.*

use with smaller reels and light lines. Many are simply miniaturized versions of larger lures already familiar to most fishermen. Many measure well under 2 inches and weigh from 1/4- to 1/64-ounce.

**Roland Martin:**

Bill knows that one of my favorite finesse lures is a small jig combined with a 2- to 3-inch piece of pork rind. I prefer marabou jigs, which seem to breathe more, and a small Uncle Josh split-tail pork eel, which I often trim. I prefer jigs with light-wire hooks, similar to those that crappie fishermen use, and I like to swim them down drop-offs and ledges.

I will also fish a small plastic worm on 6-pound line in some open, clear-water situations. In that

situation, I use a small crappie-sized hook.

I reserve my finesse fishing for lakes that have limited cover and an abundance of open, clear water. I realize that 4-pound line will attract more strikes than 20-pound, but it makes it almost impossible to land big fish in heavy cover. This is where the small-diameter braided lines like SpiderWire really shine.

**Bill Dance:**

Finesse fishing requires more attention than fishing with heavier baitcasting tackle. You need to concentrate and stay on your toes. It's much easier to watch 20-pound line when you're worm fishing than it is to watch 4-pound line with a jig or grub. And it's usually easier to detect a strike, since most finesse fishing takes place in deep water.

You have to readjust your feel for strikes, which isn't easy to do since, many times, the strike occurs while the small lure is falling. Often, all you will feel is a little pressure on your line.

Roland knows that all of this eye-catching tackle and lures, however, is useless until the angler develops the skill that finesse fishing demands.

The angler, not the equipment, is paramount when tangling with a big bass raising Cain on a small hook and light line.

You don't simply reel in a bass on light tackle. No, you learn the true definition of the phrase "playing the fish." The victory is gained by capitalizing on the reel's smooth drag and the rod's flexibility to wear the prey down.

# SITUATIONS

*Knowing how to deal with specific bass-fishing situations makes you a more versatile angler.*

# DOCKIN' BASS

*by Ron Lindner*

As my boat careened around the point and I glanced into the bay, I was confronted by what seemed like an endless row of docks. Momentarily discombobulated, I scrambled for the map. Was I even in the right area?

The map confirmed my bearings, but my how the landscape had changed. The lake's near-pristine shore, dotted here and there with a short, wooden dock, had been transformed. And not just by the sheer number of new docks, but with the proliferation of super-structures sporting boatlifts, diving platforms, trampolines, jet-ski dockage, water slides and more.

In retrospect, I shouldn't have been surprised. The scene is the same on lakes across the continent. In many cases, these new docks have changed the face of bass fishing. They provide overhead cover with an extensive structural element. Such complex, shallow habitat—often located a few tail flaps from deep water—is bass paradise, and the fish are taking full advantage.

As a result, dock fishing is now more than ever a must-do for serious anglers. Each season, innovations lead to better ways to fish these structures. Keeping up with tactical trends is important if you want to catch the most bass possible. Check out the following 43 dock spots, tactics and tricks to help you do just that.

**1.** Docks where most of the walkways and platforms are in three feet of water are better than docks in five feet or deeper.

**2.** Always fish a big dock on the edge of a shallow, weed-choked bay. The same goes with docks on or near a point.

**3.** Docks surrounded by open sand alleys are usually better than weed-choked structures.

**4.** Low docks are usually more productive than those high off the surface.

**5.** Docks with a large pontoon or deck boat are better than those without.

**6.** A pontoon boat floating alongside the dock, rather than hanging from a lift, is even better.

**7.** Docks anchored on posts are usually better than floating docks.

**8.** Bass use certain docks (depending on their location) at different times of day. To pattern these activity swings, check back periodically.

**9.** Docks adjacent to lily pad and bulrush patches are usually more consistent fish holders than docks that are not.

**10.** The more docks in a row, the more likely bass are to use them. Conversely, lakes with only an isolated dock here or there rarely produce a consistent pattern.

**11.** In a row of docks, those on the ends usually hold more bass than those in the middle.

**12.** Docks located on gradually sloping flats consistently hold more bass than those along steep drop-offs.

**13.** Large, long, community docks (such as association or condominium docks) are usually not as good as those with open spaces between them.

**14.** A bright, sunny day is better for dock fishing than overcast weather.

**15.** Towels, chairs and water toys are signs of intense human activity. Such docks usually don't hold many bass—the activity pushes fish to quieter docks.

**16.** Some docks consistently attract and hold bigger bass than others—usually because of their location in relation to deep water, fertile flats or weedlines.

**17.** Docks that harbor hordes of small panfish are better bass producers than those that don't.

**18.** Docks in areas where schools of fish live on deep weedlines, or near a flat with heavy fish traffic, are better producers than docks isolated from that kind of activity.

**19.** Stuctures on sand hold more bass than docks on rocks. Note: smallmouths are a big exception!

**20.** Docks produce more bass during periods of high water than they do during dry years.

**21.** Docks that provide a lot of shade in the form of canopies, roof overhangs and large walkways are usually more fruitful than those with less shade.

**22.** Rickety, broken-down docks that have been in the water for years are always worth a look.

**23.** Covered boats that look like they haven't been used for some time indicate undisturbed bass. Fish the dock!

**24.** Complex docks are better than simple ones. However, they demand considerably more time to fish effectively.

**25.** Docks in clear to moderately clear lakes are better than those in stained or algae-laden waters.

**26.** Those with constant foot traffic are less

productive than those used less frequently. For example, resort docks and gas docks are usually poor prospects.

**27.** Windswept docks are never as good as those in calmer water.

**28.** Docks with dogs (especially the really annoying, barking types) are usually not worth the bother.

**29.** Conversely, docks with crabby owners are often very productive.

## FISHING TIPS

**30.** Some anglers fish the front posts, then work under the dock. Unless I'm picking a dock apart, I skip cast to the dark, shaded areas and ignore the peripheral spots.

**31.** When I'm fishing tubes, I prefer Berkley saltwater tubes with Lindy's E-Z tube inserts. Weightless, I tie on a Mustad UltraLock wide-bend hook and Berkley Gulp! 5-inch Sinking Minnow or 5-inch Senko. I also fish unweighted baits "wacky" style.

**32.** A variety of plastic and pork critters are effective baits. Most dock bass are active biters; fish 'em with a "bottom faller" such as a jig-and-pig, weighted tube, Texas-rigged craw and the like. For less active bass, use a "slight suspender" like an unweighted Berkley Gulp! Sinking Minnow, Senko or Slug-Go.

**33.** There are times "soaking" your bait is best. Use an unweighted lure that can be lightly jiggled and left to slightly suspend. If I know a big bass is under a dock, I might wait 30 seconds before moving the lure.

**34.** Topwaters, buzzbaits and spinnerbaits take bass in front of or alongside docks. But day-in and day-out, a jig or soft plastic is the most efficient and consistently effective lure.

**35.** Skip casting is the way to reach bass under docks, but it isn't easy. If your aim is off an inch, or your bait hits a small wave at the wrong angle, you're in trouble. Three words of advice: Practice, practice, practice.

**36.** How much time should you spend on a single dock? If I'm in a tournament, I give most docks a few casts, max. Unless I get a bump, I move on. If I'm out for kicks, I may fish a dock hard, just to see. If I suspect it holds fish, but it doesn't produce, I backtrack later and try the dock again.

**37.** Since most people are right-handed, casting to docks is mostly a right-to-left proposition—at least from the bow. It's no fun being a righty in the back of the boat.

**38.** You can fish docks with any boat, but rigs with low, flat decks are best. Proper lure skipping demands you be low to the water; high gunnels or windshields make low-slung casting awkward.

## TIMING DOCK BITES

**39.** Summer is usually better than spring or fall.

**40.** However, for a variety of factors including location, some docks only produce bass at certain times of year—often only in spring.

**41.** Midday is usually better than morning or evening.

**42.** On docks with a lot of daytime use, morning might be the only time the fish will be there.

**43.** Three or more warm days in a row tend to draw more fish to docks than post-cold front conditions.

*Ron Lindner melds tactical trends with structural savvy to catch big-bellied boat dock bass.*

# CRANK IT UP FOR SHALLOW BASS

*by Don Wirth*

One of the best ideas in bass fishing is the shallow-running crankbait. Shallow cranks aren't new. For more than 60 years, old-time wooden plugs like the Creek Chub Wiggle-Fish, credited with catching the world-record largemouth back in 1932, were the gold standard among bass anglers. Short metal lips sent these plugs diving only two to three feet beneath the surface.

Of course, there was little need for a deep-diving bass plug in the old days. America's vast reservoir system was still on the drawing board and most anglers pursued bass by casting to the banks of weedy, natural lakes. Deep structure fishing for bass wouldn't be popularized until the late '60s with the advent of tournaments, specialized bass boats and depthfinders.

Now, it seems the depth craze has reached maturity and manufacturers are banking on shallow-running cranks. It's good news for anglers, because designers have created totally new crankbait models designed to work the shallow zone, even when these shallows are littered with snarly, intimidating structure.

Never before have anglers had access to such a deadly arsenal of skinny-water specialty baits. Expanding concepts, colors and designs

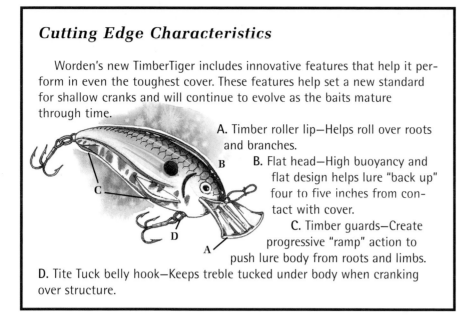

**Cutting Edge Characteristics**

Worden's new TimberTiger includes innovative features that help it perform in even the toughest cover. These features help set a new standard for shallow cranks and will continue to evolve as the baits mature through time.

A. Timber roller lip—Helps roll over roots and branches.

B. Flat head—High buoyancy and flat design helps lure "back up" four to five inches from contact with cover.

C. Timber guards—Create progressive "ramp" action to push lure body from roots and limbs.

D. Tite Tuck belly hook—Keeps treble tucked under body when cranking over structure.

ensure a blossoming portfolio of shallow tactics and techniques that let anglers fish where no crankbaits have dared to go before.

## SHALLOW GENERATION

"Shallow crankbaits have been largely neglected by lure manufacturers and bass fishermen alike," says Tom Seward, designer for Worden's Lures in Granger, Washington. "Until lately, mediocrity has reigned in the shallow crankbait category with very few good lures available. You see, it's much easier to design a deep diver than a shallow diver. Merely shortening the lip won't cut it. Attaining the correct body movement and vibration in a shallow runner is a real challenge."

Worden's new TimberTiger crankbait has several design elements that make it deadly in shallow water, says Seward. "Its special plastic mix, computer-modeled body, Timber Guard body fins and deflector lip have all

been specifically geared to maximize performance in shallow water. It features an advanced degree of snag protection so anglers can fish it with confidence through cover that would instantly snag other crankbaits."

Jim Gowing, lure designer for PRADCO in Fort Smith, Arkansas, feels changing habitat conditions have helped create an ideal environment for shallow crankin'. "Nationwide, many lakes have seen a proliferation of shallow weed growth. Vast beds of milfoil, hydrilla, coontail and other fast-growing varieties are literally choking the shallows, often where there was no aquatic vegetation a decade ago," Gowing says.

"These so-called 'junk weeds' provide sensational bass cover, and the latest shallow-running crankbaits, like the Excalibur Swim'n Image, are perfect for probing that narrow band of water between the surface and vegetation. These baits aren't weedless, but they're well suited to working water on

the top and outer edges of thick vegetation."

Bass pro Rick Clunn, well accustomed to bass conditioning, thinks you will catch more bass in highly-pressured waters by switching from their usual bank-probing artificials to shallow crankbaits. "Over time, bass become conditioned not to strike lures they see over and over again," he points out.

"For example, bass in certain lakes may be conditioned and unwilling to bite spinnerbaits, but they'll jump all over a shallow crank."

Anglers in northern, woodland lakes should exploit the shallow advantage as well. Many northern bass lakes are not only littered with downed trees, but growing beaver populations are creating some fantastic shallow cranking opportunities. Beaver lodges are well-known fish magnets and function much like a brush pile.

## SHALLOW BAIT BREAKDOWN

Shallow cranks come in two basic styles, either short-lipped or lipless.

### Short-lipped crankbaits

Unlike long-billed deep divers, shallow-running cranks have a remarkably short lip. Many are designed to dive only one to three feet on 10-pound line.

These baits vary widely in shape. Some, like Excalibur's Swim'n Image, are cylindrical and resemble a live baitfish. Others, like Mann's 1-Minus and Worden's TimberTiger, are short and plump, more toadlike than fishlike. Still others are thin with flat sides, like the Storm ThinFin and Poe's RC series.

Each style produces its own distinct movements, vibrations and sounds. Many bassers find slender, flat-sided baits work best on sluggish bass in cold water because they're quieter and emit tighter vibrations. The more rounded varieties, many of which are filled with rattles and swim with a wide wobble, tend to produce better in warm water.

## Lipless crankbaits

These popular lures, like the Bill Lewis Rat-L-Trap, Cotton Cordell Spot and Rattlin' Rapala, vary little from one brand to another. They all have flat sides, a hollow interior chamber loaded with shot or rattles, and no diving lip. Most sink at rest; a few models float or suspend.

Lipless cranks are designed to be "burned" quickly over submerged grassbeds, stumps and rocks, creating extreme noise and vibrations that trigger strikes from aggressive bass.

## TACKLE MATCHING

Shallow cranks demand the right tackle. Rods should deliver maximum casting distance and plenty of shock absorption. A long rod with a soft tip section will allow you to cast these often-compact lures to the nether-reaches of shallow structure. It will also make it harder for hooked bass to throw the bait. Good rod choices include either a casting or spinning rig, 6½ feet in length with a medium-light action.

High-speed reels are a popular choice for these lures, especially the lipless versions, but heed this warning: as speed increases, winching power decreases. While a fast-retrieve reel, like 6.3:1, might be fine for fishing shallow crankbaits across a slick river bar for 2-pound schoolies, it may be inadequate for pulling an 8-pound largemouth out of a glob of milfoil. A more powerfully geared reel with a standard retrieve ratio, like 5.3:1, is a better all-around choice.

Use abrasion-resistant lines testing at least 10 to 12 pounds with shallow runners,

and check your line for nicks constantly—gravel, brush and rocks will quickly chew it up.

Most weekend bassers are shocked to learn that tournament pros routinely fish shallow cranks on 20- and 25-pound mono. Yet, the reason is fairly obvious. Besides offering abrasion resistance and a combat advantage in tough cover, heavy lines make these baits run even shallower—nice to know when crankin' cover that almost kisses the surface.

## DARE TO GO SHALLOW

Shallow crankbaits can be fished in an amazing number of common bass fishing scenarios throughout the year. They can be used to intercept bass in their daily migrations. During the colder months, bass will take advantage of calm, sunny days and move into shallow areas adjacent to rocks. Heated by the sun, the rocks are bass magnets.

But they can also be used anytime bass occupy the shallows. Here are some top examples of where, and how, to fish shallow cranks.

---

### Crankin' Timber

Take today's shallow-running crankbaits right into the heart of timber, without fear of hanging up. Here's how it's done.

First, position the boat off the tip of the tree and cast along the trunk. After splashdown, keep the rodtip high and start cranking slowly (A). The bait will bump and run along the main trunk (B). Use the rodtip to control the lure's direction, moving from one side of the trunk to the other, pausing to clear the trunk if necessary (C). When the lure bumps a branch, pause, and allow it to rise above the obstruction (D). Once clear, continue the retrieve.

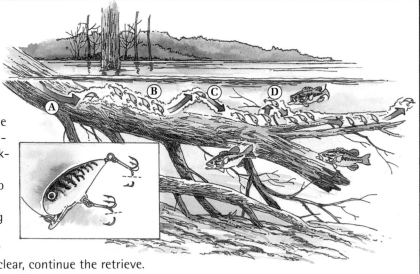

## Warm runoff

When warm, murky water enters a reservoir system in early spring, a shallow crankbait is your ticket to Lunkertown. Head up a tributary arm to the source of incoming water. A quick check of your boat's surface temperature gauge often reveals the muddy runoff to be 5 to 10 degrees warmer than the rest of the creek arm.

Cast a short-lipped or lipless crank around stumps, logs and rocks. Bass, having limited visibility in stained water, will hold tight to these objects and most strikes will occur the instant the bait bumps cover.

***Inside tip:*** *Runoff from warm spring rains can trigger a mass emergence of crayfish. Root a craw-patterned shallow diver slowly around bass-holding cover.*

## Brush piles

Many anglers would probably think, "Run a $6 crankbait through a brush pile? No way!" But a properly presented shallow diver is a deadly alternative to a jig or spinnerbait in this snarly cover. Working close to your target, use a short, underhand pitch to deliver the lure just past the brush pile, then reel slowly until you feel the bait contact cover. The instant it hits wood, pause, allowing the bait to float upward just enough to clear the obstruction, then resume the retrieve.

***Inside tip:*** *To reduce the likelihood of snags, cut the lead hook off each set of trebles.*

## Downed timber

Fallen trees offer some of the best bass habitat in any body of water. To make the

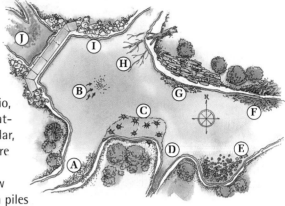

### Where To Fish Shallow Cranks

Shallow cranks can be fished effectively in a variety of situations. The diagram (right) illustrates a typical reservoir scenario, but anglers who fish natural lakes will find similar, if not identical, structure on their home waters.

Top spots for shallow crankin' include: Brush piles in creek arms (A); feeding school of bass in open water (B); stump flats (C); muddy runoff (D); weed-choked bays (E); banks being hit by wind (F); rock rubble at the base of a bluff (G); downed timber (H); riprap shorelines (I); and gravel bars in rivers or tailwaters (J).

most of the situation, align your boat with the tip of the tree and cast down the trunk. This not only puts your bait in the strike zone for 90 percent of the retrieve, it also increases the likelihood of bumping the cover. Each time your bait bumps the wood, it alerts nearby bass.

***Inside tip:*** *Keeping your rodtip at a high angle provides better lure control and reduces the likelihood of the bait wedging itself between the trunk and branches.*

## Submerged weedbeds

Milfoil, hydrilla and coontail beds attract droves of bass in warm weather, and a shallow crank is a great alternative to a jig, worm or spinnerbait. Gun for the most active bass first by burning a lipless crank over the top and along the edges. Then, swim a short-lipped bait just under the surface with a stop-and-go retrieve.

***Inside tip:*** *Bass commonly feed on small bluegills in thick weedbeds, so try an orange or firetiger crank.*

## River bars

Shallow crankbaits work much better in rivers than deep divers because they're less likely to be pulled past their mark by heavy current. Gravel and mud bars swept by moving water are perfect places for bass to intercept baitfish schools. Cast a short-lipped or lipless crank in a shad pattern upstream and retrieve it quickly along the bar.

***Inside tip:*** *Small bass will often chase a school of baitfish on top of a river bar, but for the big bite, bump a shallow diver against stumps or rocks on the downstream side of the bar, where it begins to taper into deeper water.*

## Flats

Good places for a quick limit in summer and fall. Grind short-lipped lures around scattered stumps in one to three feet of water. Burn a lipless crank through shallow baitfish schools at the edges.

***Inside tip:*** *A network of shallow ditches lined with stumps and brush often* *crisscross flats. Run a shallow crank through this cover for big bass.*

## Rock bluffs

Great bass hangouts in clear lakes. Target the rock rubble at the base of the bluff with a short-lipped crank. These rocks develop a coating of algae which serves as food for baitfish, and provides shallow concealment opportunities for bass. To cover the strike zone more efficiently, position your boat tight to the bluff and make long casts parallel to the structure, bumping the bait over shallow rubble.

**Inside tip:** *A short-lipped crank in a reflective silver or gold scale pattern works best on sunny days. Use a craw, perch or bone pattern when it's cloudy.*

## Mudlines

In clear lakes, a band of muddy water often forms against a bank buffeted by high winds. This creates an ideal concealment opportunity for bass that move in to feed on crayfish uprooted by wave action and baitfish forced into shallow water by wind currents. Cast a short-lipped crank in a craw or shad pattern right against the bank and retrieve it slowly into the clear water.

**Inside tip:** *This pattern is most reliable when the wind is from either the south or west.*

## Riprap

Large chunk rocks deposited along levees and erosion-prone banks provide a haven for crayfish and baitfish. Deep-diving crankbaits, Texas-rigged worms and jigs often get trapped, but shallow cranks ticked over the rock tops can work this cover effectively.

**Inside tip:** *Target riprap around dams during the initial minutes of current generation. A major forage movement usually takes place when current sweeps down the rocks.*

## Schooling bass

When bass are busting baitfish on the surface it's an ideal time to throw a shallow crank. While catching small schoolies on a topwater plug may be fun, running a short-lipped or lipless crank beneath the surface will often produce far bigger bass, maybe even a bonus striper or hybrid.

**Inside tip:** *When you spot small bass breaking the surface, cast a lipless crankbait past them and let it sink on a tight line. Often, the biggest bass in the school are hanging below the smaller predators feeding on injured baitfish, and will hit your bait on the drop.*

# KEEP CRANKIN'

It's no secret that the fastest bass action can occur along the bank, or deep inside intimidating structure. When faced with such a situation, most anglers immediately cast aside all thoughts of using a crankbait.

With all that's new in shallow cranks, start taking them where they haven't gone before. Instantly, you'll add a new hard-bait attack to your growing bass arsenal and catch big bass that other anglers miss.

*(1) Mann's Baby 1-Minus. (2) Poe's RC-1. (3) Bomber Model "A". (4) Worden's TimberTiger. (5) Mann's 1-Minus. (6) Rebel Wee Crawfish. (7) Excalibur Spit'n Image. (8) Rebel Crickhopper. (9) Storm Rattlin' ThinFin. (10) Possum Crappie. (11) Bagley Small Fry Bream. (12) Bagley Kill'r B2. (13) Bill Lewis Rat-L-Trap. (14) Rebel Humpback.*

# FULL-CIRCLE BRUSH

*by Jon Storm*

In bass fishing, brush piles are a bread-and-butter pattern. But many of us have become so conditioned to jump-fishing brush piles that we've forgotten how to fish them thoroughly.

Do you pull up on a brush pile, pitch a jig once or twice and then work the edges with a crank or jerkbait, only to motor away after a half-dozen "high percentage" casts? If

so, you can improve your success by learning to envision what these pieces of cover offer and using fine-tuned methods for triggering their occupants.

Few bass anglers have the know-how, let alone the patience, to effectively dissect a brush pile. Those who do are faces you recognize: They get one or two more big bites each day to consistently inch

out the competition and cash a first-place check.

They know that each brush pile has a heart that can be discovered only by exploring each potential boat position, casting angle and target area. This full-circle approach lets them form a mental picture of the pile and fish it strategically. Tim Klinger of Boulder City, Nevada, and Mark Kile of Payson, Arizona, earn their

# Tossin' Piles

## Mark Kile: Straight To The Heart

1. Kile casts beyond the brush pile to avoid spooking fish.
2. He retrieves his bait just under the surface until it is directly over the brush.
3. He then lets the bait freefall right into the heart of the brush pile.
4. If a fish doesn't hit the bait initially, Kile swims it along outlying branches.

## Tim Klinger: Beyond, Up And Over

A. Klinger casts past the brush pile and lets his bait sink to bottom.
B. He slowly pulls the bait along the bottom until it hits the far side of the brush.
C. When the bait hangs on a branch, he pops it free, then lets it fall.
D. Klinger continues to work the bait in this manner over the entire brush pile. Strikes come as the bait falls.

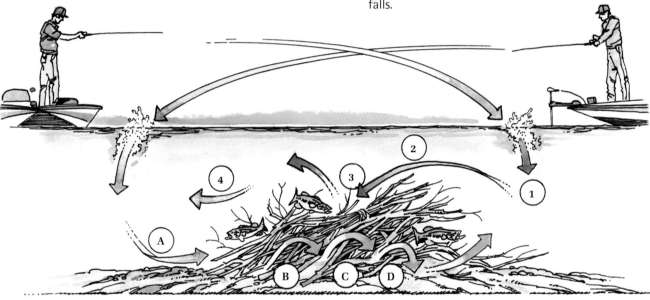

*Mark Kile says:* "My first choice for a brush pile is a 5-inch Tiki Stick with a 5/0 Gamakatsu heavy-wire hook pegged with a 1/32-ounce weight. I fish it on a flipping stick with 50-pound McCoy braid and a 25-pound fluorocarbon leader.

"If I can't get bit on the stickbait, I'll use the same approach with a 3/8-ounce green-pumpkin Lake Fork jig, unless the water's muddy, in which case black-and-blue is better.

"If I still can't get bit, I step up to a 1/2 ouncer in the same colors and swim the perimeter. Swim the jig down individual limbs.

"I remember each detail of how bites occur—boat position, angle and length of the cast, weather, time of day and more. When I return to that brush pile, I fish it the same way."

*Wave Tiki Stick with 5/0 Gamakatsu heavy-wire hook.*

*Tim Klinger says:* "When exploring a new brush pile, I start with a 3/8- to 1-ounce Yamamoto Flippin' Jig, which has an Arkie-style head, 4/0 Gamakatsu heavy-wire hook and modest weed guard. I use a pork trailer in cold water and a 2-inch Yamamoto Double Tail Grub when it gets a bit warmer.

*Yamamoto Flippin' Jig with Double Tail Grub*

"After I cast, I bring the jig forward until I contact wood. I keep total control of the jig—my finger is on the line so I can feel every little limb. Most strikes occur just after I've brought the jig up, felt a limb, popped it over and let it fall.

"Unless it's a high brush pile, you can usually just drop your rodtip to let the jig fall, but sometimes you need to freespool. Occasionally, I'll shake it on a limb for a bit."

livings fishing brush piles. Both pros continually reap big catches from brush piles that less experienced anglers might leave for dead.

## SETTING THE STAGE

Any time is a good time to fish brush piles, but prespawn is the best. Even so, brush piles remain exceptional throughout the spawn and into postspawn, as waves of fish continue moving in and out.

"As the water begins warming, start looking for brush bass," says Klinger. "I start looking during February in the Southwest, when water temperatures touch the upper 40s. Females begin staging on main-lake points and structure, but soon they'll move back toward spawning bays, stopping at brush piles."

Because the largest females tend to spawn first, they often use brush piles for weeks or even a month before an expected spawn.

"How deep they are usually depends on water clarity," he says. "In muddy water they might stage on brush in three feet on flats; in clearer water they might be as deep as 12 feet on a breakline. Brush piles near creek channel bends are usually the best. They offer shallow food and sanctuary next to deeper water, and these piles tend to 'recycle' better—that is, repopulate with new bass."

"Each lake is different, and you have to take everything into account," Kile says. "Search piles from the main lake all the way back into the spawning coves. I've seen instances, particularly on power-generation lakes in the South, where the coolest water is in the coves."

The anglers agree that finding brush is half the battle. Along with electronics, they use crankbaits to feel for that soft give that indicates a limb. "I mark each pile on my GPS. I have my bow and console units wired together, so I can mark the GPS from either place," says Kile. "With both units wired together, there's no need to run back and forth in the boat."

## ADVANCED PATTERNING

After locating and marking a good milk-run of brush, it's time to reset your focus. Throughout late winter and spring, bass are on the move. Large females travel from deep water to the bank and stage on nearby cover. They periodically leave to explore spawning sites and then return.

In short, keep checking piles throughout the day. Strong patterns are always a combination of location, conditions and time of day, so take each into account. Likewise, be aware that each brush pile will have its own distinct pattern. This is the true secret behind this fishing style.

## SWEET SPOT SEARCH

"I think bass in brush feed like fish on a point," says Kile. "They are used to getting their food from a certain direction. Maybe it's because of shade, current or a creek channel, but it seems bait comes from a certain direction each day. To get the big bite, you have to hit that sweet spot from the right angle.

"Advanced anglers often reverse position and fish from deep to shallow on a point, but you have to do the same thing on a brush pile," he says. "Learn the one cast, the one angle, that will get the big bite for each particular pile, then practice pulling up on them with a GPS."

Klinger agrees. "After I locate a brush pile, I circle the boat entirely around it, searching for the best angle," he says.

## BETTER BRUSH

Odds are, you've already achieved a certain comfort level with brush pile fishing—you've chosen your favorite baits and line, and probably have a few favorite piles. But if you fine-tune how you approach them, you'll maximize the potential of each bit of brush.

Just as you spend time developing a lake-wide pattern, you must put the same effort into dialing in that pattern for each brush pile. Fish full-circle to adjust your angles, find the exact approach that produces a big bite, and you'll have a go-to spot each time you hit the water.

# VEGEMAT BASS

*by Don Wirth*

There's something down-right scary about bass fishing in dense surface vegetation. Even approaching a big field of lily pads or a tangled hydrilla mat is enough to make the hair stand up on the back of your neck in anticipation of a strike from one of the giant bass that lurk in these seemingly impenetra-ble clots of cover.

A strike in a "vegemat" (my term for matted surface vege-tation) can take many forms.

If you're skittering a weedless spoon or a rubber frog over the surface, it might be a jolt guaranteed to rock your senses.

Or, let's say you reach into your live well and grab a fat 10-inch shiner,

Hook it up and pitch it to the edge of the vegetation, then freeline it, letting it swim under the mat. Eventually the hapless shiner swims one stroke too far, the mat humps up crazily and ka-boosh! Your shiner is toast,

and you have a 10-pound bass (and a bushel basket of grass) on the end of your line.

Or maybe you're fishing a tournament during a cold front. You ease your bass boat up to the mat, drop a jig or plastic worm down through it, and go on red alert as the lure falls into the danger zone. Suddenly there's the slightest twitch of the line (the kind your face involun-tarily makes when you're chatting with that friendly

IRS auditor), you rear back and hammer the hook home. Your flipping stick buckles, the bass shakes its head in protest, and your line snaps, echoing like a Saturday night special fired in a back alley. No check for you at the weigh-in today!

## WHY VEGEMATS?

"Despite the difficulties of fishing it, densely-matted overhead cover represents your best hope for a lunker largemouth in many waters nationwide," says Dan Thurmond, a legendary guide who has targeted big bass for three decades on prime Florida and Texas waters. Currently stationed in Conroe, Texas, Thurmond is an expert when it comes to fishing matted surface grass.

"A nationwide proliferation of so-called 'junk weeds' such as hydrilla and Eurasian milfoil has made vegemats today's primary big-bass attractors, converting many formerly mediocre lakes into lunker havens," he says. "There's no question that largemouths crave this thick cover. Vegemats represent the best possible sanctuary for big bass, particularly in heavily-pressured lakes."

Doug Hannon, the "Bass Professor," has studied bass in vegemats for years. "Bass use matted vegetation for many reasons," he explains. "Most anglers believe it's so they can shade their eyes from the sun, but this is non-sense—the largemouth is a member of the sunfish family, and the sun's rays don't hurt its eyes.

"A more likely reason they're attracted to this overhead cover is that it gives them a tremendous sense of security. Most threats to adult bass come from above, in the form of birds of prey or humans," Hannon says. "Hiding beneath a mat of lily pads or junk weeds undoubtedly provides ideal concealment from an aerial assault. They're awesome holding places during cold fronts, too, when bass will chill out and wait for weather conditions to improve."

Hannon says that upward visibility is dramatically restricted beneath vegemats, for bass and anglers. "This explains why you can go right up to the edge of a mat of hydrilla, drop a jig off the nose of the boat and haul up a big bass," he says.

So, if monster bass are hiding just below that matted surface slop, why the heck aren't we fishing it? "Vegemats are bass fishing's ultimate approach-avoidance conflict," explains Thurmond. "You realize the fish are there, but it doesn't take you long to grow weary of A. being constantly hung up, B. not being able to feel your lure, C. missing strikes, or D. hauling back a pound-and a-half of produce on every cast. No wonder so many bassers avoid these hassles by leaving vegemats—and the bass hiding beneath them—undisturbed in favor of easier-to-fish cover."

## FINDING SWEET SPOTS

Fishermen venturing out onto a weed-choked lake for the first time are often intimidated by those vast expanses of matted surface vegetation. It all looks so bassy, they wonder why a trophy isn't lurking under every lily pad and grass patch.

The biggest problem when fishing a lake with acres of surface vegetation is quickly editing out unproductive water, and focusing your precious fishing time on the most likely bass-holding spots. This might seem like an insurmountable task, but Thurmond and Hannon have some great pointers for pinpointing bass.

"I'll comb a big vegemat quickly when I first hit the water to locate concentrations of fish, then slow down once I've found them," says Thurmond. "Jigs, tubes and worms are not good search baits—they require way too methodical a presentation in this slop. Instead, I start by probing the open water at the edge of the mat with a spinnerbait or crankbait.

"On cloudy days, especially, bass will prowl the perimeter hunting bluegills and shiners. Then I'll move to the top of the mat with weedless spoons or topwater Scum Frogs, lures that cover a lot of territory," he says. "On my first couple of passes, I don't really care if I catch a fish. A missed strike, even a tell-tale movement in the vegetation, lets me know where the bass are holding. I can come back and fish a tube or worm for these fish later if they won't respond to a faster presentation."

"Bass are edge-oriented predators," adds Hannon. "Like a hawk circling above an area where dense forest meets open field, a bass using a vegemat will hold where thick weeds intersect a hole or open boat lane—or where one species of grass transitions into another. This maximizes their hunting

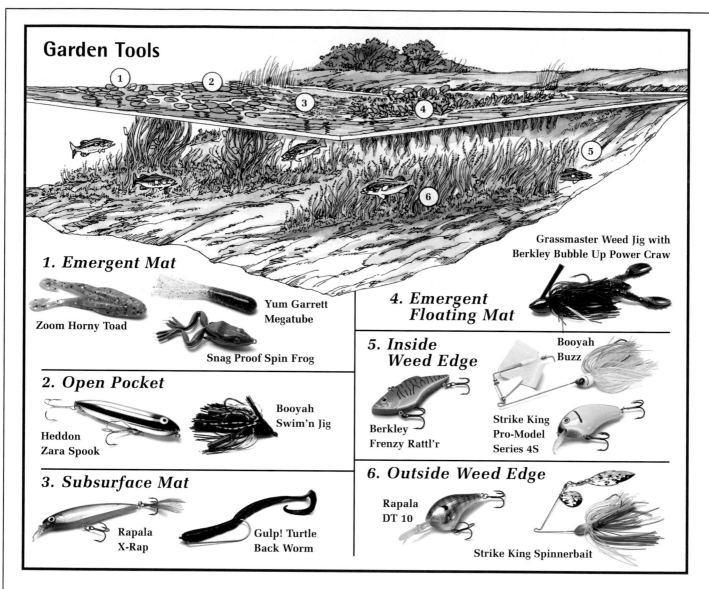

# Garden Tools

## 1. Emergent Mat

Zoom Horny Toad

Yum Garrett Megatube

Snag Proof Spin Frog

## 2. Open Pocket

Heddon Zara Spook

Booyah Swim'n Jig

## 3. Subsurface Mat

Rapala X-Rap

Gulp! Turtle Back Worm

Grassmaster Weed Jig with Berkley Bubble Up Power Craw

## 4. Emergent Floating Mat

## 5. Inside Weed Edge

Berkley Frenzy Rattl'r

Booyah Buzz

Strike King Pro-Model Series 4S

## 6. Outside Weed Edge

Rapala DT 10

Strike King Spinnerbait

---

opportunities by allowing them to take advantage of several prey species using different types of habitat."

Of the various species of vegetation that form surface mats, lily pads, which are rooted to the bottom, and water hyacinth, which drifts freely, are arguably the most predictable when it comes to determining bass location, Hannon says. "The outer edge of these weeds is the most obvious place to start. Be alert for subtle points or indentations, which bass use as ambush spots. Also watch for places where lily pads thin out or get thicker; this often indicates a change in

depth or bottom composition, another potential bass attractor.

"You'll often find the best lily pad fishing during midday," he says. "That's when the fragrant blossoms of these plants open wide, attracting droves of insects. The inevitable horde of bluegills follows, and bass move in to follow the forage."

# STEPS FOR FISHING MATS

**1. Work The Edges:** At first glance, super-dense hydrilla and milfoil beds can be daunting, but keying on bass-holding edges can put

you on fish quickly. Texas pro Larry Nixon likes to crank a Rattlin' Rapala around the edges of hydrilla mats in the early morning, before bass move too far under the weeds. "I cast parallel to the edge, running that bait hard and fast," he says. "When you contact cover, rip the bait free. If bass are hanging just under the mat, that'll get their attention."

Some types of vegemats, especially water hyacinth, can be fished effectively with live bait. "Hook a big wild shiner above the anal vent with a stout weedless hook, put your baitcasting reel in free-spool, drop the baitfish at the mat's edge, and it'll usually swim under the mat on its own," Hannon says. "When it does, it stands a good chance of getting eaten by a big bass. You can't believe the giants you'll catch using this approach."

**2. Over The Top:** When weeds grow to within a foot or so of the surface, burning a spinnerbait with two small Colorado blades, or a lipless vibrating crankbait like a Rat-L-Trap, over the top of the grass can provoke an arm-wrenching strike. A noisy surface popper works, too.

By midsummer, vegetation can grow at an amazing rate, and may form a mat all the way to the surface. "Weedless rats and frogs can crawl over this slop without getting mired down, and are a lot of fun to fish," Thurmond says. "Cut a small slit in the back and pack the hollow bait with ¼-inch pieces of plastic worm. This will permit longer casts on heavy tackle without compromising the lure's flotation. Dropping in a couple of glass worm rattles makes it easier for bass to hear the bait coming."

When vegemat bass want a smaller bait, try an alternative presentation. I recently fished a duckweed-clogged lake with South Carolina bass pro Davey Hite. He couldn't get a hit using a surface frog, so he switched to a 4-inch tube with a wide-gap hook and an ⅛-ounce sinker. Hite lubricated the tube with oily fish attractant, cast it onto the mat and slid it slowly across the top. He caught two dozen bass up to 6 pounds using this approach, the same presentation he used to win $225,000 in the 1998 FLW championship tournament.

Jordan Paullo also fishes tubes over dense lily pads near his home in Connecticut but he's begun to expand his arsenal with the introduction of the Booyah Swim'n Jig, which he says is the bait for fishing vegemats. "The key is to keep a steady retrieve so the bait makes a V-shaped wake across the top of the mat. Even if there's only an inch or two of water above the weeds, bass will hear the commotion from a distance."

**3. Punch The Mats:** Junk weeds such as hydrilla grow in towers with open water between them, but by summer these towers have exploded to the surface and folded over to form a nearly impenetrable vegemat. Instead of keying on the top of the mat, North Carolina bass pro Marty Stone prefers to pitch or flip a jig to bass holding in and around the weedy towers beneath it. He'll shake the jig until it wallows its way through the mat, or haul off and smack the jig through the surface layer with a sharp slap of his flipping stick. Then he lifts, drops and shakes the jig repeatedly until a bass grabs it.

Florida pro Bernie Schultz has plenty of experience punching mats as well. He prefers a Yamamoto Craw Worm, Kreature or Senko (junebug or green pumpkin color). Depending on the density of the mat, he'll use a ⁵⁄₁₆-ounce all the way up to a 1½-ounce weight to break through. He advises that once you bust through the mat, use your rodtip to keep the lure high in the water column. "Bass are most aggressive when they are hanging right below the canopy," he notes.

Several years ago, before underwater video cameras were widely available, Hannon got so hooked on fishing vegemats that he bought a cheap black-and-white surveillance camera, improvised a plastic housing for it and used it to scope out hyacinth mats for big bass on lakes near his Tampa, Florida, home.

"I'd move from one mat to the next, looking for bass. Sometimes I'd see fish hanging under the hyacinths that were so big, they were downright scary. It was almost as exciting watching them on the monitor as it was catching them—almost!"

Likewise, as exciting as it may be to watch pros haul lunkers from seemingly impenetrable cover, no thrill compares with catching them yourself. Don't let vegemats intimidate you; the right approach will get you off of the sidelines and into the trophy zone.

*Weedless rats and frogs can unlock vegemats. Be sure to eliminate unproductive water first, though.*

# THE POINT MAN

*by Ryan Gilligan*

If bass lived in aquariums, we'd all be tournament champs. We'd unfailingly cast right to big fish and drag our lures a hair's width from their prizefighter jaws. After all, we'd be able to see them—why would we cast anywhere else?

If a bass refused, we'd gauge its reaction and play trial-and-error with presentations until we found the magic combination. It wouldn't be a matter of *if* we caught big fish; it would merely be a question of when.

Of course, that's not how it works in the real world. Bass—even those in extremely clear lakes and rivers—wear a cloak of water that usually shields them from our prying eyes. Where they are and what exactly they're doing at any given moment remains unseen by the masses, even with the help of the latest, greatest electronics.

But this doesn't have to crimp our style. Bass magnet Bill Siemantel is proof. Unlike most of us, he's trained himself to break bass' underwater world into the same practical parts we do up on this side of the waves—something that's apparent in how he carves up one of bassin's most productive structures: points.

## MAKE A GOOD POINT

The Los Angeles fireman has a milk run of power points on his home waters' silicone-clear depths, and he has a deceivingly simple, minimalist method to fishing them. Best of all, the approach can be used to dissect bass-holding points from Fenway to the Golden Gate.

"The fish are there—they're not leaving the lake," Siemantel says plainly. "I just try to make it as simple as possible."

One of the keys to mastering his technique is understanding a concept he calls a "funnel attack," a situation where structure, baitfish and bass come together, forcing bass into attack mode.

"Bass like to pin prey against stuff when they eat, and points help them do this," he says. "Look at the room you're sitting in, where a wall meets the ceiling. If you were a bass, you'd push bait toward that intersection. That's a funnel attack situation.

"Now look at the corner of the room, where two walls intersect with the ceiling— that's another funnel attack, but it's better because more structural elements are funneling down to that one spot. In other words, funnel attacks pull fish into strike zones."

Our job when fishing points (and any structure for that matter), Siemantel says, is to present our baits in such a way that they roll through as many funnel attack situations as we can on every cast, then use that concept to make as few casts as possible, catch fish, and move on to the next point.

"Rather than put your boat in deep water right off the tip of a point, move 25 or 30 yards off to the side and launch a long cast as close to shore as possible, landing the bait along the opposite side of the point," Siemantel says. "Your bait is going to create a funnel attack when it butts up against shore, intersects the point, angles over the top of the point and again when you pull it off the structure into deep water."

By doing this, he says, you've messed with the minds of all bass holding along that side of the point. "You weren't moving that lure; the bass were. At least, that's what they probably thought. The bait was doing what prey fish are supposed to do when bass track them—they get pushed into these spots and are eaten."

He throws the knockout punch by repositioning 25 to 30 yards on the opposite side of the point, then angles a second cast toward shore—a mirror image of his previous toss. While winching the bait boatside, he mixes in jerks and pops in the funnel attack spots— these directional changes trigger fish that wouldn't commit on the first foray.

After that, yank up the trolling motor and put the hammer down on your way to the next point. "You've either caught the fish, or they've left—use your time to fish the next point," he says.

## THE DAISY CHAIN EFFECT

Why leave primo structure after just two casts? Unlike most anglers, who think of bass holding on key real-estate, Siemantel is focused on the one or two biggest fish and factors in how his presentations move them on—and off—structure.

"Let's say you cast up near shore along a point and swim

the bait back to the boat," he says. "If a bass is there, it'll leave its holding position and start tracking. If you don't get it to commit, you might pull that fish all the way down that point and out into open water. It could take 20 minutes for that fish to reposition."

But pulling one bass into no-man's land is a conservative estimate. "Fishing like this results in what I call 'Daisy Chaining'. By angling casts over points, you're creating a disturbance that draws in bass," he says. "When bass pick up the trail, the presentation is moving even more water, attracting more fish, and pretty soon you've pulled a wolf pack of bass from their holding points along the

structure. You'll often mark these on your bow-mount sonar just as you're pulling the bait up to the boat."

Siemantel says those big arcs aren't fish suspended off the tip of the point—they're bass that had been holding all along the structure but moved in response to your bait and the activity of other bass.

Where the structure allows, Siemantel exploits this concept. Boat position is key. Rather than hover in deep water off the point's tip, he holds in skinny water next to shore, angles his casts deep and retrieves "uphill" along points.

Instead of pulling bass away from structure, this calls bass from all layers of the water

column and funnels them up the point toward the shallows.

This accomplishes a few key things. First, it essentially creates one prolonged funnel attack, because the lure is being pulled into progressively skinnier water. Siemantel believes this triggers strikes because bass think their prey is backing into a corner—closer to both the bottom and surface.

Second, the uphill retrieve allows for more bottom contact, which creates countless miniature funnel attacks as the bait comes up and over rocks and humps.

The icing on the cake is that after he's pulled his lure out of the water at boatside, Siemantel knows the fish that had been hanging out on the deep-water fringes of the structure likely tracked his bait at least partway back to the boat and are now concentrated along the point, slowly following the contours back to their holding spots.

"You've just pulled fish into structure rather than away from it," he says. "This lets you cast to the point multiple times and mix up your retrieve with pauses and rips until you trigger fish."

# POWER OF PRACTICALITY

As with anything you can't see, it's easy to become overwhelmed by all you *think* you don't know about fishing points.

But fight it. Break down points into the sum of their parts and use that to determine the places where bass will ambush prey. Simply position your boat where your casts will hit as many of those places as possible. Hit them quick, catch the fish, then move on. Now that's a power point presentation.

# OVER THE EDGE

*by Clark Montgomery*

Classic bass fishing focuses on shallow cover. After all, what angler doesn't get a monster adrenaline rush from seeing a largemouth plaster a spluttering buzzbait as it churns over a half-submerged log?

But unfortunately, such shallow-water kicks are becoming more difficult to come by. You've probably noticed a steady decline in the quality and quantity of bass you catch up shallow. There are definite reasons for this.

The shoreline presents an obvious target—so obvious, that on an increasing number of bass waters nationwide, quality bass simply don't hang out there any more.

They've been pummeled and pelted with so many lures for so many years that they've moved off to new haunts where fishing pressure isn't as intense.

Plus, shallow cover doesn't last forever. Wood rots or breaks up from wave action. Vegetation gets sprayed. Seasonal reservoir drawdowns leave shallow cover high and dry.

But there are places where a skilled bass angler can still score big. Ledges and drop-offs are found in virtually every bass lake in the country. Pay attention as some of America's top pros and guides show you how to find and fish these important bass structures.

## LEDGES VERSUS DROP-OFFS

"A ledge and a drop are similar but not identical structures," bass fishing legend Bill Dance explains. "Both are characterized by a rapid depth change—it might be 12 feet on top of a drop or ledge, 30 feet at the bottom."

A true ledge, he says, is a narrow structure that occurs mainly in rocky lakes. Think of a ledge as a shelf associated with a larger structure such as a vertical bluff or a sloping rock bank. A ledge may be only one to four feet wide, but it provides bass with a convenient place to forage and rest.

"A drop is typically a much larger structure," he continues. "In every reservoir, there are drop-offs that extend for miles—the original river and creek channels that were inundated when the lake was formed."

In many natural lakes, drop-offs were created eons ago by natural forces such as glacial upheaval. "As these giant ice formations melted and receded, the earth cracked and shifted, creating dramatic irregularities on the bottom of huge depressions in the landscape. When the depression filled to become a lake, the cracks and shifts remained to form the drop-offs we fish today."

These structures are becoming increasingly critical to bass fishing success, he emphasizes. "In some lakes, highly-pressured bass move offshore and often hold on the first dramatic depth change they encounter, such as a creek channel drop. In others, wood or weed cover

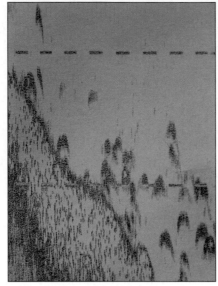

*A graphic portrayal of how bass suspend on a drop. These inactive fish are holding from 15 to 30 feet on the side of a creek channel. Best bets for catching them—vertically jigging a spoon or slow-rolling a spinnerbait.*

may be gone from the shallows, and bass may be forced to move to deep ledges to find concealment and feeding opportunities."

Largemouth, smallmouth and spotted bass all use these structures, with largemouths showing stronger preference than the latter two for shallower structure. "In a lake where all three species exist, I'd expect to catch largemouths on ledges and drops at 12 feet, smallmouths around 18 and spots around 25," he says.

Part of the challenge of fishing drops and ledges, he adds, is that you can never be positive where bass will locate on them at any given time. "Many anglers wrongly believe that bass use only the top or shallowest part of these structures when they are actively feeding.

"I've often found this to be true when power is being generated in a river-run reservoir—baitfish will move shal-

lower as current increases, and bass that are holding on the deeper sections of these structures will follow them up. But you'll make a serious mistake by not checking the bottom of the drop, as well as the open water around these structures."

## MAPS AND FLASHERS

Drops are easy to locate on paper—just pull out your trusty lake map and look for areas where the contour lines run close together, indicating a quick depth change.

Alabama bass angler Jack Chancellor, a master at fishing offshore structure, dedicates hours to scouting drop-offs.

"Before I arrive at the lake, I study lake maps and mark offshore drops. Then, once on the lake, I'll allot several hours during the first day of fishing to simply cruise the water, watching my depthfinder for sudden dips and rises and checking these against the map.

"On older reservoirs, the map may indicate a drop to be sharper or deeper than it actually is because of siltation or other changes that have occurred over time."

Chancellor prefers a flasher-type sonar unit over a liquid-crystal display when cruising for drops. "The rising and falling of the light shows them more dramatically when I'm on the move."

After getting a mental picture of the location of the drops, Jack idles over them, watching for blips on the flasher dial that indicate bass. "If I spot fish, I put out a marker buoy or two and fish the spot to see what's there."

Ledges are much harder to find than drops, says Maryland guide Jay Holt. "You've got to watch your sonar unit closely to find a ledge since these structures are so narrow. Also, locating a ledge on a rocky lake usually means idling right next to the bank, which will often spook the fish below you."

Instead, Holt locates shallow reservoir ledges that are exposed due to the winter drawdown. He records them with a video camera, and pinpoints the locations on his lake map. When the pool fills in the spring, and he's ready to start fishing again, he's got 'em nailed down.

When he has to decipher a ledge during the fishing season, he casts a jigging spoon or some other fast-sinking lure and counts it down to the bottom. He then turns the reel handle once or twice. If the lure starts dropping again, he knows it has come to rest on a narrow ledge.

## CHOOSE YOUR WEAPON

You can fish a ledge or drop with a wide variety of artificial lures. According to Mt. Juliet, Tennessee, bass guide Tony Bean, "When first approaching the structure, try a fast-sinking bait like a Texas- or Carolina-rigged plastic worm, slab spoon or jig. These will allow you to probe both the shallow and deep part of the structure on the same cast."

Bean's "initial approach" in the clear lakes he fishes is to cast a plastic grub body on a ¼-ounce leadhead using a stiff spinning rod strung with 6- or 8-pound mono. "I like a curlytail grub

because it sinks quickly enough to get into the strike zone, yet has a lifelike look when falling.

"Cast to the shallow side, keep the rodtip high and the line semi-tight, then pop it slightly when the line goes slack. This will hop the grub to the next depth level."

Once you know how deep the bass are holding on the structure, you can skip nonproductive water by choosing a lure that keys on this depth zone.

"A crankbait is a great choice for bass holding on the edge of a ledge or drop," adds Florida tournament angler Shaw Grigsby. "I especially like crankbaits on drop-offs that have isolated cover on them in the form of big rocks or stumps."

Grigsby makes long casts using a light-action casting rod and thin-diameter line so the lure dives to its maximum depth.

"It's important to make contact with the stumps or rocks closest to the drop because that's when your

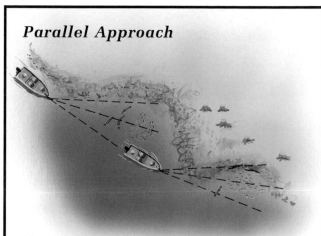

### *Parallel Approach*

*Move slowly along the breakline using a heavy spoon, spinnerbait or crank to target scattered stumps, rocks and grass at the edge.*

### *Top To Bottom Approach*

*Fan-cast to the top of the structure, targeting rocks, weeds or wood cover. Work sinking lures over the breakline for deeper or suspended fish.*

crankbait usually gets nailed. These fish are holding tight to cover and rushing out into open water to grab passing prey."

Grigsby also uses a crankbait to detect patches of weeds along the structure. "If my deep-diver comes back with weeds hanging from the hooks, I'll switch to a slightly shallower-running lure, or rig the same lure on a casting outfit with heavier line. I want the crankbait to run right over the top of the grass."

A heavy spinnerbait is another good lure choice for probing ledges and drops, noted Tennessee bass guide Jack Christian. "At night, fish a 1-ounce spinnerbait with a fat pork frog trailer. Bass often congregate on the shallow, level part of these structures where they forage for crayfish," he says.

"Slow-roll the spinnerbait so it stays very close to bottom. Then when you reach the edge, just let it drop on a tight line—the blade will spin as the lure helicopters down."

Christian fishes heavy spinnerbaits on a 6½-foot medium-heavy baitcasting rod with 14- to 20-pound mono and a slow-retrieve reel.

A worm or lizard fished on a Carolina rig is probably the most popular drop lure of all, Christian adds. "This is a great setup for fishing a big drop-off such as a major creek channel—just cast the rig to the shallow part of the drop, wait for the sinker to clank down, and turn the reel handle slowly.

"The sinker will root and bump along the irregular bottom, causing the lure to dart and settle enticingly." Sooner or later the sinker will tumble over the edge of the drop, and when it does, a fish often responds."

Here's an interesting twist to the standard Carolina rig that Christian uses in clear lakes on sunny days: "I'll replace the worm or lizard with a chrome-finished hardbait like a floating minnow or shad lure. This flashes exactly like a live shad and will draw bass in from a wide area."

Florida bass guide Ray Van Horn puts another unique twist on the popular Carolina rig when probing weedy drops. "I'll rig a huge plastic worm, sometimes 16 inches in length, to a long leader and work it through grassbeds at the edges of drops, usually by drifting with the wind," he says. "Leader length varies with the height of the grass. I want it to suspend just above the grass. I've boated bass up to 14 pounds using this approach."

In clear lakes, bass suspending over a drop-off can sometimes be tempted with topwater lures. "This pattern works best in the fall, when bass routinely use creek channels as migration routes and bunch up on migrating baitfish," says Bill Dance. "A soft jerkbait or noisy propbait will provoke bass, often an entire school of them, into swimming up to grab the lure."

## THREE DEADLY TACTICS

Boat positioning is critical when fishing drops and ledges, our experts agree. "Most of the time you'll want to fish these structures with your boat sitting in deep water," notes Dance. "Cast to the top of the structure and work your lure slowly over the edge into the depths."

Another productive method for fast-breaking structures is to cast parallel to the drop. "This seems to work best when fish are suspended around the drop, and are only moderately active," he says. "I've had the most luck doing it when there are a lot of baitfish in the area. A heavy spinnerbait or suspending crankbait is

your best choice, for once worked into the target zone, they'll stay there."

Jigging a spoon is a third alternative for probing ledges and drops. "I recommend this approach when bass are bunched up around submerged stumps lining the drop. Use a heavy-action baitcasting rod and 14-pound line. Mark the fish on your graph, flip the spoon over the side, then pop the rodtip repeatedly. This is a tremendous way to catch a whole bunch of bass in a very short period of time."

Ledges and drops are the places to catch quality bass these days. So, if your usual shallow spots aren't satisfying your urge to catch fish, break away from the shoreline and head for the edge.

*Tennessee bass guide Jack Christian substitutes a floating crankbait for the usual plastic worm or lizard when probing deep drops with a Carolina rig. The flashy lure attracts bass from long distances in clear water.*

# BIG BASS FROM SECONDARY LAKES

*by Don Wirth*

Most bass fishing today revolves around sprawling waters so immense anglers may run 100 miles before dropping their trolling motors. Tournament anglers race to far-flung fishing holes in 21-foot boats powered by outboards with more horsepower than your old man's Oldsmobile.

It hasn't always been this way. When America's vast reservoir system was created in the last century, it changed our perspective on bass fisheries. Today, a 30,000-acre reservoir is a "primary" fishery, while the 50-acre lake where your grandpa caught bass is considered "secondary."

Pro bass tournaments resembling NASCAR events on water have also contributed to the shift. Not surprisingly, many anglers don't think they're really bass fishing unless they're making payments on a $35,000 rig and running-and-gunning on an 80,000-acre reservoir.

Aside from a few indiscretions, I'm not one of them. You can have your vast reservoirs and long boat rides—my adrenaline starts pumpin' when I'm on a secondary lake.

## LUNKER HAVENS

For our purposes, let's classify a secondary lake as a body of water from 1 to 500 acres. The term is relative— a 500-acre lake is hardly a pond, but if there's a 50,000-acre reservoir close by, it's secondary.

Nationwide, there are thousands of such waters, including small ponds, state-managed lakes, county watershed lakes, "borrow pits" formed during highway construction, state and municipal park lakes, and even golf course water hazards. Add them all up and you've got a lot of great bass water, most of

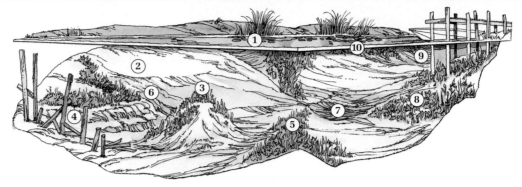

## Natural Pond

At first glance, most natural secondary lakes look like bowls. A closer look reveals many subtleties in cover and structure that hold big bass.

**1.** *Emergent grass along the shoreline feathers out to a long point. Bass use this as a bridge from deep to shallow water in spring.*

**2.** *Sand flat in the northwestern corner of the lake—the first place bass spawn in spring. Cold north winds pass over this area, meaning the water is at least a few degrees warmer.*

**3.** *Submerged hump. Some of the lake's biggest bass may spawn on this offshore structure in spring, then use the areas as a feeding station in summer and fall.*

**4.** *Remains of an old dock. If the bottom is silty, bass will spawn on sunken planks and downed pilings. Good feeding area in summer and fall.*

**5.** *Submerged grass point leads to deep water. Another migration route to shallow water in the spring.*

**6.** *Weedline adjacent to a drop-off. Any abrupt weed edge usually signals a change in depth or bottom composition. Bass stage here before spawning, then feed along the weedline during summer and fall.*

**7.** *Deep hole. Provided there's enough oxygen, this is a great hangout in the summer, when water temperatures in the shallows are high.*

**8.** *Shallow flat where several varieties of vegetation occur. The diversity of plant life provides maximum feeding opportunities.*

**9.** *Boat dock. Provides shade for forage species and largemouths. Bass often spawn in adjacent shallows.*

**10.** *Lily pad bed. When fishing here, look for something different: isolated pads, edges, holes and areas where pads of different sizes grow. Good spring through fall.*

---

which receives minimal fishing pressure.

These lakes aren't the stuff of tournaments, but they offer today's best bets for big largemouths. Need proof?

Paul Duclos was fishing California's 75-acre Spring Lake when he landed what may have been a world-record largemouth. The fish unofficially weighed 24 pounds (the current world record is 22 pounds, 4 ounces). It was deeply hooked, and there were no certified scales handy, so Duclos, an ardent catch-and-release advocate, called his wife and had her bring a bathroom scale to the dock. He weighed and photographed the bass before several witnesses, then released it.

Incidentally, Duclos' scale was later certified accurate to the pound, but in the world record game, a contender must be weighed on a pre-certified scale.

A few years later, Jed Dickerson, another Golden State basser, was chunking an 8-inch swimbait on 70-acre Lake Dixon when he caught a 21-pound, 11.2-ounce largemouth. Only weeks earlier, Mac Weakley, Dickerson's fishing buddy, caught bass weighing 17.5 and 19.7 pounds from the same lake.

Most anglers don't associate New England with giant bass, but the Massachusetts state record largemouth weighed a whopping 15½ pounds. It was caught through the ice of tiny Sampson's Pond by Walter Bolonis in 1975. It was likely the biggest pure northern-strain largemouth ever recorded.

My experiences have also convinced me that secondary lakes rule. Over the past five years, I've devoted most of my bass fishing to secondary lakes across the Southeast, and my lunker catch has skyrocketed. In decades of pounding big

reservoirs, I boated perhaps a dozen largemouths heavier than 5 pounds, with the biggest weighing 7.

In the short time I've been probing secondary lakes, however, I've caught two bass over 9, a dozen 8s and scores of 6s and 7s. I've also lost three in the 12-pound range!

## WATERS OF THE GIANTS

Why do secondary lakes produce such large bass? The reasons are compelling. For one, it's much easier for biologists to manage a small lake than a big one. Today, many secondary lakes, including famous California lunker factories like Dixon, Spring and others, are being managed specifically as trophy fisheries. Strict restrictions minimize harvests and help guarantee that even average fish are real toads. Plus, because you're dealing with waters a fraction of the size of large reservoirs, your odds of hooking them are infinitely better!

Forage availability is another factor. On sprawling reservoirs, bass mainly eat shad. Common small-water forage, however, is generally bluegills, minnows, trout, crayfish, frogs and other beefy prey. This smorgasbord means bass have the opportunity to eat more, and more often.

Finally, light fishing pressure is the single biggest reason to fish secondary waters. Some have no boat launch, and those that do often have horsepower restrictions, both of which eliminate or discourage most boaters. Because they aren't subject to as much pressure, secondary lake bass can grow old and large.

# DO YOUR HOMEWORK

Although secondary lakes are everywhere, not all of them hold trophies. Here's how to sort through the possibilities.

**1. Ask Questions.** Fishermen like to talk. Bait shops and even barbershops are good places to get information. Even if the lake is allegedly "fished out," check it for yourself. Often the water holds big fish, but they've seen too many of the same lures. If you fish smart, you can catch 'em.

Likewise, state fisheries biologists are excellent sources, yet few anglers bother contacting these experts. Big mistake.

A Mississippi biologist once told me he'd netted a 16-pound largemouth from a certain 325-acre lake. Since then, I've fished that lake six times, and although I've yet to hang that monster, I've caught three 6s, two 7s, two 8s and a 9 and I've yet to see another boat there! Some state agencies even offer fish survey information on their websites.

**2. Avoid People And Development.** Case in point, in central Florida small lakes in undeveloped areas that consistently gave up 10 pounders have produced progressively fewer trophies as people move in. Lakes in the least-populated areas generally hold the biggest bass.

**3. Target Weedy Waters.** These can be incredible producers. They are loaded with forage, highly-oxygenated and ignored by most weekend fishermen.

## Man-Made Pond

Man-made secondary lakes typically offer more structure and cover than natural ponds. As a big-bass hunter, you have to pinpoint the more subtle areas that escape the attention of other anglers.

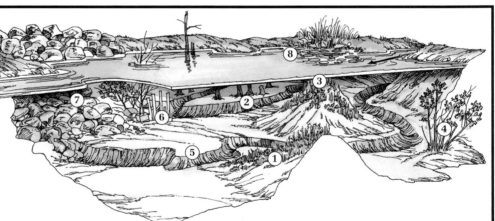

1. *This long, shallow point is one of the most prominent structures on the lake and as such, anglers probably pound it. Bass gather here in summer and fall to intercept passing baitfish, but retreat to more subtle structures when fishing pressure intensifies.*
2. *A large flat with scattered stumps—another spot that probably receives significant pressure. However, note the shallow ditch and deeper outer edge of the structure. Bass here likely escape the eyes of most fishermen. They'll follow the shallow ditch from deep to shallow water in spring. During summer, look for them to suspend at the outer edge.*
3. *A shallow, submerged hump or saddle that rises from 10 to two feet below the surface. Bass will spawn on it and use it as a feeding station in summer and fall.*
4. *Shallow brush. Bass hold around this cover in spring before and after spawning. Great target for a tube bait.*
5. *A creek channel that winds through the reservoir. Bass use it as a migration route into shallow spawning areas in spring. In summer, they'll hold there to ambush baitfish schools.*
6. *A man-made fish attractor of tree limbs and brush. These structures are usually well marked and as a result get hit hard. Fish the outer perimeter, where remnants of wood cover may have been dragged from the main pile by anglers whose anchors tangled in the cover. You'll often catch the biggest bass there.*
7. *An earthen levee lined with rock to prevent erosion. The sun warms the rocks on calm, early-spring days, pulling big bass into shallow water in search of crayfish.*
8. *Lily pads in a shallow cove. Because they provide shade, the water here will be cooler in summer. Fish at midday—the open pad blossoms attract insects and, in turn, bluegills, which big bass feed on.*

**4. Stay Focused.** It can be fun catching dozens of 12-inch bass, but don't get distracted; you're after Mr. Big. Don't hesitate to leave a fast bite in favor of a lake that holds fewer, but bigger bass.

**5. Go Aerial.** It's easier to find untouched bass waters if you have a birds-eye view. A detailed topographical map can help you find out-of-the-way waters, but an aerial photograph is even better. You can order both from the U.S. Geological Survey, (888) 275-8747, or you can download them off the Internet.

## MAXIMIZE YOUR ODDS

To make the most of secondary lakes, start fishing them early in the year. They warm quicker than big lakes, which makes them great places to fish in early spring. Don't wait for 70-degree water, though—you can catch giants when temperatures reach 42 to 44 degrees.

Also watch what other anglers are doing; then do something different. Bass in secondary lakes can be conditioned not to bite certain lures. During spring, for instance, most anglers on lakes I fish pound the banks with spinnerbaits and Texas-rigged lizards and have limited success. I fish right behind them with a floating worm or tube bait and catch big bass.

It often doesn't take much of a change to get big fish to pull the trigger. Cast and retrieve lures from new angles, try extremely slow or fast retrieves, and fish small or large lures—anything that breaks the pattern fish are used to seeing.

On small waters, seek subtle structure. Most have only one or two primary structures like points or flats, which attract most fishing pressure. Unlock the lake's potential by fishing structure everyone else overlooks—shallow ditches connecting deep and shallow water, channel bends, bays and the like.

Key on thick weedbeds, brush piles and logjams with stealth. This is where you'll gain a huge advantage over less-skilled anglers who shy from casting into the thick stuff. Rig a jig or tube weedless, pitch it in the junk—and hang on!

And don't forget to move off the shoreline. Most fishermen are bank-beaters. The biggest bass, however, are often clustered on offshore ledges, channels, ditches and humps, especially in prespawn and summer.

If you fish secondary lakes smartly, you will connect with bruiser bass, and when you do, remember to take care of the resource. Nowhere is it more important to exercise catch-and-release than on waters where numbers of superior fish are limited. Carefully release your trophies, and enjoy these small treasures for years to come.

---

## "FORE" ... Pound Bass, That Is

I still remember the sound of the guy's laugh. Of course, considering his goofy plaid pants and funny shoes, I suppose I should have been the one in stitches. He was on the eighth green; I was in my float tube, casting a spinnerbait along the edge of some matted coontail in an adjacent pond.

"Hey, this guy's fishing," the man chuckled to his buddies. "There aren't any fish in there."

He stopped laughing when a 4-pound largemouth lunged out of the weeds and clobbered my spinnerbait as the blade began to gurgle near the surface. It was no fluke. Golf course lakes, ponds and water hazards are fertile, underfished and can provide stellar bass fishing—if you know where to go.

In the North, the limiting factor in such waters is winterkill. They are often very eutrophic, featuring loads of aquatic vegetation (a situation made worse by fertilizer runoff from the adjacent fairways and greens) and low winter oxygen levels might prevent some ponds from ever growing large bass. In the South, however, your options are more open. In any case, keep an open mind when scouting out golf course bass waters. Ask the course's grounds crew if they've seen fish and consult your local fisheries biologist. If nothing else, they might be able to provide information on what the water was like before the course was built.

Not every water hazard will hold bass, and not every course will grant you access. Some that do might limit the time and dates you're allowed to fish. However, with a little snooping and a few respectful questions, you might find some excellent bass waters that receive no fishing pressure.
—Ryan Gilligan

# ON SOLID GROUND

*by Spence Petros*

I paused for a moment and scanned the lake. A high-powered boat had been flying by every couple minutes, but this time, the wait seemed longer than normal. Finally I heard a roar in the distance and hoped it would come close enough. Yes! A streaking boat buzzed within 75 yards of shore. Perfect.

Within seconds the waves began to slap the riprap bank. My 7-foot spinning rod helped me make a long, tight cast parallel to the rocky bank. I worked the shallow-running minnow plug with a pull-pause, pull-pause retrieve. Suddenly, a smashing strike! Just like the other dozen or so I'd gotten over the last hour. A chunky bass pushing 3 pounds cleared the water; I landed it without getting my feet wet.

When the feeding spree ended, I walked down the bank to a sandy flat where my boat was parked, cranked up the motor and headed out onto the open water to finish the day's fishing. I had parked the boat to fish a wind-pummeled riprap bank with a weed edge that started a few feet out. A tough situation to fish quietly and effectively from a boat.

But not from shore.

If you think shore fishing is only for anglers who don't have a boat, or for those too young, too old or too inexperienced to operate one, think again. I would rather be a knowledgeable shore-bound angler than one in control of "200 horses" who doesn't understand bass and how they react to various weather, water and seasonal conditions.

The major reasons that get me walking the bank are: It's spring and my boat's not ready; I only have limited time to fish; or the biggest reason of all—a particular spot or area is more effectively fished from shore! I guess a little ego enters the picture, too, when you can catch more bass afoot than others flying around in $30,000 boats.

## SHORE STUFF

While shore fishing is an advantage in many instances, you have to use the right tackle. I prefer to use jig-style lures, especially in the spring. A bottom-hopping bait combined with line watching becomes my "underwater eyes." I mentally keep track of the time it takes the lure to fall back down to bottom, which helps me locate slight changes in bottom contour.

With a no-stretch superline, it's easier to feel out particular

## Creek Mouths And Inflows

Creeks and streams flowing into lakes and reservoirs often hold active bass during early-spring warming trends. Casts should cover stained waters (A), and feel for any type of cover along the bottom (B) or any slight depth changes (C). Be sure to note wind direction, which pushes warm water along the shore. Also probe any shoreline cover at the creek mouth (D) that rests in at least 18 inches of water. Check up to the first pool, paying attention to any wood in the water (E) or fertile flat (F) that may support early weed growth.

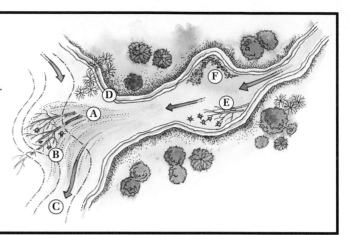

pieces of cover. Plus, it's easier to achieve riveting hooksets, even on long casts. I generally use 10- to 14-pound Flame Green FireLine linked to a 3- to 4-foot leader of mono or fluorocarbon. Upgrade the pound test to cope with bigger-than-average bass and/or heavier cover.

I tend to use 7-foot rods for most of my shore fishing, as they allow longer casts (if needed), and provide better angles when casting parallel to the bank. Also, longer rods let me reach out past shoreline cover to cast, or to better control a fish after the hookup.

# WHERE IT'S WARM

The first warm trends of late winter/early spring signal the start of a shore-fishing bonanza. Many bass move into shallow, sun-drenched waters that heat up quickly. These areas, especially if wind-protected and exposed to a lot of direct sunlight, can easily be 10 degrees warmer than the main-lake waters. Look for these clues that help pinpoint areas of warmer water.

Feeder creeks spilling into lakes or reservoirs are always prime spots to check. Start at

the creek mouth, paying close attention to any changes in water color—darker water usually contains more floating particles, which absorb and store heat. Darker water also attracts forage. Finding structure or cover at the creek mouth is a plus, too. Locating a lip, hole, small hump or scattered cover at the creek mouth may be the key to bigger bass. A good way to uncover these hidden jewels is with a jig, as I mentioned, along with high-visibility line.

Brush, willow or wood-lined banks are a common sight at many creek mouths. If the water is deep enough— 18 to 24 inches is a good rule—you'll generally find bass holding there. This is the type of spot where it's common to contact several bass, then return a few hours later and do it again as migrating fish move in. Under higher water conditions, these areas really heat up.

Cover-lined banks at the creek mouth, in the creek and around the first hole or pool in from the main body of water are all worth checking. I generally use the first widening, or hole, in determining whether or not to head farther upstream. If the first hole produces fish, I continue

upstream to fish another pool. Slower-moving feeder creeks usually hold large-mouths, while swifter creeks may draw early-season small-mouths. Any wood or rock cover is capable of holding bass, but also watch for protected flats on the north shores. These areas foster early weed growth and are always worth checking.

Other areas that warm quickly and draw bass like magnets are backwaters, shallower bays, man-made canals and channels, along with narrows that connect wider bodies of water. In all these instances, the faster a spot warms, the more likely it is to get the first wave of shallow-moving bass. A few more tips: dead-end or T-shaped canals usually warm faster, as do bays and backwaters with darker bottoms that are more sheltered from the main-lake water. Toss various types of cover into the mix and you have the potential for the lake's best spot.

When fishing visible cover in these areas, I've had great success with smaller spinner-baits. A ¼- to ⅜-ounce bait with a single Colorado blade is a favorite, and I either slow-roll it or fish it with frequent drops. Spinnerbait strikes usually come on the

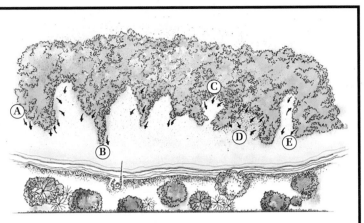
fall, which is another reason to use a no-stretch, visible superline. I generally don't use a trailer this early in the year, and if I start getting short strikes, I clip the skirt so it just comes to the end of the hook's bend. When not casting to visible cover, I cast parallel to the shore.

# 55-Degree Magic

Unless it's spring, I usually don't pay much attention to water temperature when bass fishing. But once the water temperature hits 55 degrees in the spawning areas, both smallmouths and largemouths move in and become very active. This situation is very different from fishing the early-to-warm spots I mentioned above, as most of those areas were not good spawning grounds.

Fifty-five-degree water signals the pre-spawn period, when bass cruise the shallows and begin to search out spawning sites and potential mates. They begin to cross flats, cruise inside weed edges, migrate along channels and move into open bays related to the main body of water.

It's also the time when they'll knock the paint off a fast-moving lure, or quickly suck in a jig or live bait presentation. This aggressive bite lasts until the water temperature reaches the low 60s. Then, you've got to slow down to catch the bigger, non-chasing females.

During prespawn, the shallow "inside edge" of a major main-lake weedbed really starts to turn on. Many bass will spawn along this weedline, often around any type of cover between the weed edge and the shoreline. The most productive zones are the two- to six-foot depths where the edge occurs. If the inside weed edge is visible, it's easy to fish. If it's not easy to see, make sure to use a lure that allows you to feel it out, like a jig or spinnerbait. It's critical you hit that weed edge, since bigger bass often hold tight to the edge where they relate to small weed points, cuts, isolated hard bottoms, or where cover comes into play.

Furthermore, the inside edges of weedbeds are very important throughout the entire year. Not only are they hot during spring, but on many lakes and reservoirs, they can be better than the deeper, outside weed edge. Fishing pressure from boats along the deeper edge and over the weeds can be heavy during the warmer months, but fish along the inside edge often rest unmolested. Inside weedlines can also be very productive on lakes where larger predators such as muskies, pike or big walleyes "rule" the deep edge. They can also get hot under low-light conditions, at night or during fall warming trends—all situations that tend to pull bass in shallower.

Another favorite shore situation that corresponds with 55-degree water temperature is fishing in bays or harbors. Moored boats can be especially productive, as bass mill around the attractive shelter. Be very careful not to hook the boat, or the rope or chain that anchors it. If in doubt, don't cast.

*Soupy shoreline slop is a situation most boaters pass up. Catch the fish they miss while never leaving the bank.*

## Do Northern Bass Need Spawning Sanctuaries?

Recruitment—the number of wild young fish that survive and grow to catchable size—is always a major factor in how many fish are in a lake. That said, does fishing during the bass spawn negatively affect recruitment? After all, black bass, like other Centrarchids, guard their eggs and fry, and the number of fry that survive is largely dependent on how well, and how long, the nest is guarded.

David Philipp, a Senior Scientist with the Illinois Natural History Survey, wanted to know more. Specifically, Philipp set out to discover the relationship between successful nests—those whose fry reached self-sufficient size—and year-class strength.

Over a 10-year period, Philipp and team studied a number of prime bass lakes in southeastern Ontario. Research teams swam the shorelines daily, locating, tagging and monitoring bass nests, then recording which ones were successful and the number of viable fry they produced. The number of successful nests and fry in a lake were then analyzed in relation to the subsequent year class.

Not surprisingly, Philipp found that nesting success directly influenced year-class strength in the waters he studied. It stands to reason, then, that any disruption of the spawning ritual—including the removal of the guarding males—will have a direct negative impact on the size of the fish population.

Philipp notes that, obviously, catch and harvest has the most negative impact. However, he also argues that catch-and-release angling during the spawn negatively impacts a bass fishery. When the protecting male is hooked and removed from the nest, predators like sunfish, small perch and crayfish move in and begin feeding on the unprotected eggs or fry. Even if the male is immediately released, it may still abandon the nest if too many offspring have been lost. Catching males multiple times increases the odds of this happening.

Philipp and his team also tested the effectiveness of protecting prime nesting areas through the establishment of "spawning sanctuaries." These areas were identified through signage asking anglers to voluntarily refrain from fishing them. Interestingly, the signs had the opposite effect. Fishing pressure in the "conservation" zones was often greater than the rest of the lake, with some anglers actively (and illegally) targeting bedding bass, rather than legal pike, walleyes and panfish.

Spawning sanctuaries might find a place in fishing's future, as Phillips showed that bedding bass, at least in northern waters, need protection or anglers may threaten the very fisheries they treasure. But clearly, "volunteer sanctuary" status may not provide that needed protection. —*Jon Storm*

# WORKING THE WEEDS

From the time they are tall enough to provide cover, until cold weather causes them to turn brown, weeds are a blessing to the shoreline angler. Since bass often follow them into shallow water for feeding, safety and spawning opportunities, you may think weeds related to deeper water are a big plus. This is not always the case, especially in this era of "intelligent" fishing pressure. So often, savvy anglers look for prime weeds adjacent to deeper water, and good

spots get hit hard. Here, the shore-bound angler can target fish other anglers ignore.

So too, the shallower areas of thick, matted beds of vegetation such as "slop," reeds or pads can be nearly impossible to fish from a boat. Yet this heavy, shallow cover often harbors the largest bass a lake has to offer. The best shore-fishing opportunity is often the one that looks like it has the least potential to a boater. A wide, weed-choked flat yards from any depth change? Fish it!

It can be difficult to fish these thick weeds from the low angle of the shore, so I use lures made specifically for

the heavy stuff. Top baits include Johnson Silver Minnows with a plastic or pork trailer, the Frogzilla and Weed Demon from Snag Proof, or the Uncle Josh Jumbo Pork Frog on a weedless hook. I tend to use baitcasting rods, rather than spinning, to accommodate heavier line.

When fishing standard weed conditions, such as a good-size bed of cabbage, coontail or milfoil, besides working the inside edge, another excellent condition is to have at least a foot or two of open water over the tops of the weeds. Weedbeds that haven't reached maturity, or those knocked down by fall weather or brisk winds, will have open water over the tops.

Unless the water is stained, the best fishing over the weed tops is usually under periods of lower light penetration, when bass tend to roam more. Low-light periods, cloudy weather, brisk wind or darkness are all conditions that trigger roaming bass. A willow-leaf spinnerbait is a great choice here.

A beach area surrounded by weeds can also be a night-fishing bonanza. After swimmers vacate the area, bass will often roam the edge of the weeds along the sand border. Other times, they cruise the clean sand flats where minnows probably move in at night. If you encounter this situation, think about swimmers using the area and be considerate of hooks.

## ROCKS ARE RIGHT

From acting as heat-absorbing bass magnets in cold weather, to harboring crayfish and baitfish in warmer weather, rocks provide fantastic fishing opportunities. During the cold-water periods of spring and fall, rocks receiving direct sunlight draw bass like moths to a light. I've seen rock-lined banks on one side of a body of water attract bass in the mid-morning after soaking up direct sunlight, then go flat after the sun's rays shift. That's when the opposite shore turns on.

One of the first spots to check during the early season is where a rock-lined culvert connects two areas of water. If one is shallower, so much the better. Under sunny,

warm conditions, schools of baitfish frequently hold at the mouth of the discharge pipe, and a bunch of bass usually aren't very far behind. The bass and minnows are easily spooked by a boat, but a shore-bound angler can have a field day here, often returning several times a day to catch additional fish. Use lures that splash down quietly.

During warmer weather and into fall, rocks that have "something else going on around them" can be consistent producers. Conditions that can make one area of rocky bank better than another are: where deeper water swings in a little tighter to the shore; when adjacent wood, weed cover or structure exists; around points, turns or necked-down areas; when rocks are pummeled by wind; if current influences a particular spot; or where deeper, scattered rocks exist. Parallel cast with shallow-running minnow baits, bigger-lipped floating/diving crankbaits (they usually float out of snags when you stop cranking) and spinnerbaits.

A number of different situations draw bass very close to the rocks. Most often bass will be tight to the bank if the rocks break quickly into deep water, or if the water is cold but sun has been heating the rocks. Also, stained water or fishing pressure can draw bass tight to the bank. In all cases, shore anglers can really get to 'em with tight, parallel casts along the rocks.

A good "secret weapon" in summer and fall along riprap is to fish scattered rocks or rubble that rests slightly deeper than the deep edge of the rocks. Many anglers believe the

base of riprap is a straight edge. Not so. Deeper rocks are often scattered along the edge as a result of erosion, a difference in bottom taper, or some rocks rolling further down into the water than others. Often, shore anglers can find and fish these areas effectively, especially with a Carolina rig.

Instead of using a barrel-shaped sinker, however, I opt for the banana-shaped No-Snagg sinker from Lindy-Little Joe. To further reduce the odds of hanging up, elevate your plastic offering off bottom by using a floating bait rigged with a thin-wire hook, and a small snell float like those used by walleye anglers.

There are a lot of situations when fishing for bass from shore can be more effective than fishing from a boat. Follow the bass through their seasonal cycles and focus on prime targets. You'll better understand the logic of fishing afoot, and in the end, score more bass from shore.

*Spence's two largest Illinois bass were both caught from shore. This 23-inch 7 pounder was pulled from an early-to-warm channel off a large lake.*

# SEASONS

*D*eal with the changing seasons and you will bring more bass into your life.

# Bass Before Bedtime

*by Dan Johnson*

Life should be sweet for the serious bassman during the prespawn period. Winter-weary largemouths move up from deepwater haunts, gravitating to prime structural elements where they hang out for a month or more before spawning.

Easy pickins, right?

Not quite. You may want to bite the bullet sinker while I say this, because it might sting a little: Thanks to media hype and mass misinformation, few of us truly understand the variables affecting where bass go before bedtime, and still fewer know enough to stay put when we find a hotspot.

As a result, we burn a lot of daylight fishing unproductive areas. Then, when we do find a diamond in the rough, we abandon it when the bite changes. It's time to set the record straight. To find the choicest prespawn spots, it's important to understand where the bass are coming from, what they're looking for and where they're easiest to catch.

We've all heard bass go deep during the winter. It's such a common statement, few question its wisdom. Good news is, it's true—at least for the most part. On my home waters in central Minnesota, as well as the lakes and impoundments I've fished from Florida to Arkansas and points west, bass will indeed drop into the abyss come winter. Or at least hang out on the edge. (That's not to say they stay there the whole time, though. Check out the sidebar below for the scoop on that.)

"Deep" is a relative term, of course. In a shallow impoundment, deep might be a 12-foot hole in an old river channel surrounded by six-foot stump flats. In more

---

## On The Move: Study Tracks Seminole Bass

Experienced bass anglers consider season and time of day when trying to pinpoint their quarry. But a recent radio-tracking study by Auburn University fisheries researchers challenges conventional angler wisdom.

The study tracked 3-pound-plus largemouths for a year in Lake Seminole, located on the Florida-Georgia border. Core areas for individual bass ranged from a low of 7 acres in winter to a high of 13 acres in the summer. The fish were most mobile in fall and most sedentary in spring and summer. They moved least during daytime hours, and had higher and similar movement rates during dawn, dusk and night.

The bass occupied water from one to 16 feet deep, but most locations were in water less than three feet deep or eight to 12 feet deep. Their home ranges appeared to include a shallow-water area and a deep-water area. Bass were most likely to be found in deep water in fall and least likely to be found shallow in the winter. However, the fish were located in skinny water 10 to 19 percent of the time—and some bass were

> "The fish were located in skinny water 10 to 19 percent of the time—and some bass were shallow in all seasons."

shallow in all seasons.

The deep-shallow depth distribution was also apparent across all daily time periods, but bass were more likely to go deep during dawn and daytime, and more likely to be shallow at dusk and at night.

More than 90 percent of the radio fixes pinpointed the bass in or near cover. During dawn and daytime, when the bass tended to be deeper, they were most often near wood or hydrilla. At dusk and night, when the fish were more likely to be shallow, emergent vegetation, like cattails and cutgrass, as well as hydrilla, were the prevalent cover.

Seasonal and daily movements undoubtedly are affected by lake and forage conditions. Seminole is shallow, clear, and has abundant cover. And unlike many Southern reservoirs, sunfish, rather than shad, are the preferred forage. The study results may not apply to all lakes, but a few points are worth keeping in mind: the bass were almost always in or near cover; some fish were always shallow; and they didn't stray far throughout a season. *—Dr. Hal Schramm*

## Take Cover

Everything else being equal, you'll find more prespawn bass on structure that has cover than on barren points and breaks. The reason is simple: cover holds more food.

"Bass are programmed to move shallow to feed in preparation for the spawn, which is an energy deficit period," explains Dr. Hal Schramm. "Knowing they are food-oriented can help anglers select the best fishing areas." In reservoirs, look for timber—whether stumps or standing, submerged trees. On both man-made and natural lakes, aquatic vegetation such as peppergrass, hydrilla and cabbage can be bass magnets.

In the North, even "carpet rolls" of last year's dead weeds, rolled by wind-driven floes at ice-out, can attract fish. If weedy and woody cover are relatively scarce in the lake, look for beaver houses and feeder piles, boulders, rubble, ditches—anything that might concentrate baitfish and thus appeal to hungry largemouths. —Dan Johnson

cavernous systems, man-made or natural, a winter haven could be down 50 feet or more.

Regardless of where bass spend winter, as days lengthen and waters warm, the first waves of fish begin washing across the deep ends of promising structure sooner than most anglers think. Depending on your latitude and weather patterns, this exodus can start anywhere from January in the Deep South to late April or beyond in the North.

Bass master Larry Nixon is a longtime student of the prespawn. He says bass show up in staging areas as early as late January in lakes near his Bee Branch, Arkansas, home. "They're just like us, they get spring fever," he says, noting that most of the prespawn action in his area occurs in February and March.

Nixon says savvy anglers can weed out a lot of unproductive water if they know what to look for.

"Prespawn spots vary, but on a reservoir, it's hard to beat a creek channel or river turn, where bass come out of deep water," he says. "Typically, the best structure is also connected to or close to the bank. Like a shoreline point that juts out toward a bend in the main river channel."

The reason is simple. Bass spawn along these banks. Sometimes, though, the best spot will be a sunken island or hump smack dab in the middle of the lake. Just ask Texan Tommy Martin.

A past Classic winner and longtime friend of Nixon, Martin has guided on the hallowed waters of Toledo Bend for 30 years. He even guided with Nixon there once upon a time—but that's another story.

"On Toledo Bend, some of the best prespawn fishing takes place on four- to 10-foot main-lake flats next to 15 to 25 feet of water in the main river channel," he explains. "On a good day in January or February, you can catch 50 to 60 fish."

That brings up a key point. Intuitively, most anglers seek the warmest water possible and start their searches on the shallow, upper sections of a reservoir. That's fine, as long as the water is clear and consistently warm. On Toledo Bend, the water might indeed be a few degrees warmer in the upper lake.

But during the prespawn, it's also a lot dirtier, thanks to sediments washed in from the tributaries. "Always look for the clearest water you can find, because bass respond to artificial lures better in clear water than muddy," says Martin.

Even when the tribs run clear, the upper sections of reservoirs can be fickle places to fish, thanks to fluctuations in water temperature.

"Heavy, cold rains can cause water temperatures to plummet in the upper end of a reservoir," says *North American Fisherman* columnist Hal Schramm, a noted fisheries biologist, professor and devout bassman. "This can really shut down fish that were actively hunting and feeding under stable conditions.

"Whenever I head for a lake, I check the thermal history—in other words, what the water temperature has been the past few weeks," he notes. "That will help me pinpoint the best fishing areas.

"If a steady influx of cold water drops the temperature dramatically in the upper arms, I head for mid-lake structure. If I have to fish the upper lake, I'll slow my presentations and fish closer to, if not right in, any cover located on the structure. Like Martin, I'll look for the cleanest water available. Cold, dirty water is a curse."

A stable thermal history and clear water encourage Schramm to fish classic upper lake hotspots like the backs of coves.

"Natural lakes are less affected by inflows, in terms

# Winning Presentations

Finding prespawn bass is only half the battle. You still have to make 'em bite. Two masters of the game are Larry Nixon and Bill McDonald. Nixon hails from Arkansas and has honed his prespawn presentations on a variety of Southern waters. McDonald, a hard-fishing pro from Indiana, knows the Northern angle well, but also fishes the South extensively.

Both admit that a variety of presentations will take fish, but they agree three of the deadliest are jerkbaits, jigs and cranks. "A jerkbait is my top choice," says Nixon. "Typically, the bass are suspended over a point, about eight to 10 feet down over 20 to 25 feet of water. Keeping my boat over deep water, I throw a Rapala Husky Jerk, on 8- to 10-pound fluorocarbon, up over the point and begin a pull-pause retrieve, with the pauses lasting up to seven seconds. I keep the presentation slow, because the bass are coming in from six or seven feet away from the lure."

McDonald employs a similar approach, casting a suspending jerkbait like Strike King's Suspending Wild Shiner. "I fish jerkbaits 90 percent of the time during the prespawn," he says. "And I fish them a lot slower than most people. Pauses last up to 10 seconds, and I use a gentle rod sweep instead of a pull."

Cold front conditions can tighten a fish's lips and push it close to bottom or deep into cover. In these situations, a jig or bottom-grinding crank is a better call. Nixon throws a $3/8$-ounce jig tipped with a Berkley Power Trailer, while McDonald favors a similar leadhead dressed with a Strike King Plastic Chunk. Browns, blacks and blues are top color options. In cranks, Nixon ties on a Rapala DT6 or DT10, depending on the depth of the fish, while McDonald opts for Rapala Shad Raps, size 5 or 7. "Carp-color browns are the best," he says. Nixon, too, likes brown crankbaits, but says red mixed in is good.

If you're wondering which presentation to fish when, Nixon says, "A lot depends on the conditions. For example, in full sun, a jerkbait can be phenomenal. When it's cloudy, a jig or crankbait fished on bottom is often better." In short, it pays to experiment. *—Dan Johnson*

## Grinding Bottom

*When bass drop tight to cover or structure, both Nixon and McDonald tie on jigs or diving crankbaits. Both are fished slowly along the bottom.*

## Nixon's Husky Jerk

*After making a long cast onto structure, Larry Nixon reels four or five times to get the bait down, points the rodtip low and gives the bait a couple of pops to help it reach maximum depth. "Then I let it hang there before beginning a slow retrieve with smooth, 1-foot pulls, interspersed with two jerks and a five- to seven-second pause. The colder the water, the longer the pause."*

## McDonald's Mantra

*Like Larry Nixon, Bill McDonald fires long casts over bass-holding areas, then pulls the jerkbait down to maximum depth. "A lot of people jerk, jerk, jerk the lure and then let it sit, but I move it extremely slow, pulling it one to three feet with a gentle rod sweep, then pause five to 10 seconds or more. Every third or fourth pause, I twitch the bait just a hair."*

of cold water and suspended sediments," he notes. "As a result, they tend to warm more uniformly and have more consistent clarity, on a lake-wide basis, than impoundments."

In such scenarios, finding promising structure in the warmest water can be key. But even here, it pays to check the thermal history of the areas you plan to fish. Schramm recalls a trip on Lake Erie when the best bite was in anything but the warmest water.

"I was fishing smallmouths on Erie outside Presque Isle Bay," he says. "The water temperature was 60 degrees at the mouth of the bay, but the bass just weren't biting. So I ran out to a rock hump on the main lake. The water there was just 48 degrees, but the bass were actively feeding and I caught a bunch."

Schramm suspects a drop in the water temperature outside of Presque Isle Bay, perhaps due to a spring rain or chilly Lake Erie current, shut down the bass there, while the smallmouths on the main-lake hump were unaffected, and thus still on the bite, even though they were in much colder water.

## MYTH BUSTING

As a trained biologist, Schramm cringes when he hears pro anglers and well-meaning outdoor writers spew misinformation about bass behavior. Over the years, he's heard more than a few prespawn myths.

"You've no doubt heard the one about fishing riprap and shoreline boulders first, because they soak up the sun and warm up the surrounding water," he says. "I wince when I hear that, because unless those rocks are covered with dark algae, they're still cold. Sit your butt on a rock in March and tell me it's warm.

"When you catch bass around riprap or boulders, it's not because the bass are flocking to water two-tenths of a degree warmer than the surrounding area. It's because there's food there, plain and simple."

Same thing goes for concrete boat ramps which, as legend has it, soak up heat and attract bass. "A boat ramp isn't a go-to prespawn location unless something else attracts baitfish to the area, like brush. Or perhaps it's located on an old roadbed leading down into the

*To give suspending jerkbaits like the Strike King Wild Shiner more appeal, Bill McDonald glues a duck feather to the lure's rear treble. "It breathes and moves, giving the bait a more lifelike look even when it's hanging virtually motionless in the water," he says.*

impoundment. Such an area can act like a point and be used by bass coming up from deep water."

Schramm acknowledges that some ramps can be hotspots at spawning time. "You may find bass and, later, bluegills bedding around gravel ramps during the spawn," he says. "But that's due to the hard substrate."

Another big mistake even seasoned veterans make during prespawn is abandoning a productive area in search of greener pastures.

"I'm guilty of it," says Schramm. "If I catch bass on a jerkbait one day on a point, then a front blows through and the fish don't want a jerkbait the next day, I'll often move in search of bass that hit what I'm throwing. That's a major mistake, because science says the bass are still on that point, they just need a different presentation."

It's not easy to hang in there when a bite changes, especially when running and gunning is the mantra of so many anglers. But, in the immortal words of Classic champ and fishing superstar Woo Daves, "More tournaments are lost by anglers leaving fish than are won by anglers finding new ones."

Whether you fish for fun or profit, the moral is the same—don't be quick to give up on an area that holds bass. Especially when you've used these tips to find the best bassin' spots your favorite lakes have to offer.

## Lipless Wonders

While jerkbaits, jigs and cranks are deadly weapons for early season largemouths, Texan Tommy Martin prefers to attack the prespawn Lone Star-style. And make no mistake, his go-to presentation is neither slow nor small.

"In January and February I throw a lot of 1/2- to 3/4-ounce Rat-L-Traps," he says. "Bass often suspend about two feet down over the tops of 4- to 10-foot main-lake weed flats. They seem to be basking in the sun, and even though the water temperature may only be in the high 40s, they'll hit a fast-moving bait."

Martin recommends holding your boat over deeper water and making long casts onto the flats. "Throw as far as you can, then reel as fast as you

can," he advises. "A high-speed reel helps. Mine has a 6.3:1 gear ratio, and some guys even fish 7:1s."

There's no magic to the cadence. No pauses or twitches. Just speed. "Run the bait past 'em extremely fast and they'll hit it," Martin says. He favors lures with red, orange and brown, but it pays to experiment. *—Dan Johnson*

*Texas bassin' ace Tommy Martin throws Rat-L-Traps for high-riding prespawn bass on main-lake flats. He says a blazing retrieve is the key to success.*

## Consider Composition

When it comes to catching bass, it all starts at the bottom. The most successful anglers are those who learn as much about the floor of the area they are fishing as possible. Whether it be a mudflat, chunk-rock bank, gravel shoreline, clay point, mucky ditch, sandy bar or limestone bluff, fishermen need to understand how bass utilize the bottom.

### Bottom Breakdown
Bass generally seem to prefer a hard bottom year-round. If you can keep a good, solid bottom under your boat, your odds of catching fish are going to be better.

In the early spring, dark-bottom bays on the northwestern shores of a lake or reservoir are the first to warm up, attracting forage species, panfish and pre-spawn bass. Early pre-spawners really like the warmer water.

During the post-spawn period in lakes throughout the South, bass relate to soft bottoms like red clay.

Pea-gravel pockets next to chunk-rock banks are areas that bass utilize heavily.

Another prime opportunity is to fish baseball-size rocks, which offer excellent habitat for both bass and forage species.

# BASS BEFORE THE SPAWN

*by Spence Petros*

My partner was nervous and it showed. He could see anglers in two boats feverishly working a stretch of shoreline that produced a catch of big bass for me two days prior. Obviously, the word was out.

"I told you we should have got here earlier," he chastised.

"Don't worry, they won't catch the bigger bass," I assured him. "Their backs are facing deep water, which means they are casting to the shorelines. The sun is up,

the shoreline has limited cover, and the big bass won't be cruising the flats where they can be picked off with sloppy presentations. Just be patient."

We launched the boat, but stayed close to the ramp. I wasn't going to move in until the other boats left the area. In the meantime, I tossed my friend a jig, then explained the aspects of the pattern. He was to cast within a couple feet of where my jig landed and feel for weeds. The prime

area was the inside weedline, not shoreline cover.

The other boats left a short time later, so I eased the electric motor into the water and moved into position. Within minutes, a chunky 3½-pound prespawn bass inhaled my jig. That fish was soon followed by another, then another...and another...and so our morning went.

Prespawn bass can be a challenge in lakes or reservoirs. But then, who doesn't love a challenge?

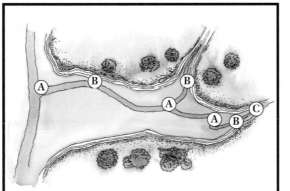

While most anglers probe the shallow, early-to-warm areas and visible cover along the bank, many bass, especially the larger females, hold in deeper water off the bank. A key area is the inside weedline. Bass often tuck up into little slots and cuts (A) created by areas of harder bottoms. If the waters you fish are stained, follow the edge by fishing bottom-bumping baits like jigs. Strips of hard bottom that split the weeds (B) are bass magnets. Also, pay attention to holes (C) or thick clumps (D) in the weeds.

The deep weed edge can also be good early and late; Petros fishes it right through the spawn. Concentrate on inside corners (E) and points (F) with jigs or Carolina rigs.

# TACTICS FOR NATURAL LAKES

Bass anglers head en masse to the shallows during the first warm spells of early spring, and they catch plenty of prespawn bass on spinnerbaits, jerkbaits, worms, jigs and other standard bass lures. But what about those days when big bass are scarce? Or heavy pressure makes fishing tough? These conditions are the norm, not the exception.

Let's break down the success we had that day. Most early spring bass anglers drift the shoreline, casting at visible targets. They catch fish, too, especially when water temperatures hit 55 degrees and hold there.

I prefer to fish the shallow weed edge, especially if temps have yet to reach that magical 55-degree range. When pressured, bass working the adjacent shallows often retreat to the inside weedline, holing up in the slots and openings within the bed. Thick weed clumps are bass magnets, especially if beds are sparse.

The lake we fished was stained, making the inside weed edge difficult to follow. By starting a little later, the sun was higher and by wearing polarized glasses, we could periodically see the weed edge. This helped us stay in contact with the weed edge and probe the cuts, fingers and slots where the bigger fish held, almost immune to fishing pressure.

If a weedline can be visually followed, spinnerbaits, jerkbaits or suspending shallow-running cranks can be very productive. If the weed edge is not visible,

Reservoir bass use the edges of creek channels as they make their pilgrimage to the shallows. Key on channel bends and junctions (A) and saddles. Coves without a lot of cover and structure are easiest to fish. During the early days of spring, look for scattered bass movement on the first available cover near deep water (B). Several days of warm weather is usually needed for bass to move into the shallow back end of the creek arm (C).

the person running the boat should feel it out with a jig (jig-worm or jig-n-pig) or Texas-rigged worm. He or she should also keep their partner informed of where the edge is, so casts consistently hit the best areas.

Weedbeds act as a buffer against water movement. Sheltered inside edges, along with pockets or slots within the vegetation, can become warm cubbyholes for prespawn bass. Holes and slots can often be seen, especially when the sun is at your back, if you're wearing polarized glasses. These openings are best fished with plastics: worm, lizard or craw, using little or no weight.

When working over and into invisible subsurface weedbeds, I frequently use a spinnerbait or jerkbait. Fish a spinnerbait slowly so it brushes across the top of the weeds. Periodically, pump the spinnerbait toward the surface and allow it to flutter back down. This often triggers strikes.

Spinnerbaits with tandem willow-leaf blades shed weeds best. A sensitive rod and smooth reel spooled with a no-stretch

# Where Largemouth Bass Spawn

Reviewing biological literature on the largemouth bass spawn leads one to the conclusion that they nest almost anywhere. Bass do look for sites with firm substrate, some type of structure (vegetation, logs, stumps, rocks) and calm-water conditions, but conditions vary greatly.

**Bottom Type:** Bass appear to prefer gravel and hard sand, but they will build nests on hard clay bottoms. Boat canals are heavily used spawning locations because bass like their typically hard, clean bottoms. Equally, and possibly more important, is a canal's steeply-sloping banks that bring relatively deep water close to shore.

In vegetation-rich Florida lakes, where the lake bottoms often feature thick layers of partially decayed vegetation, largemouths build nests on the thick spatterdock roots (rhizomes) protruding above the soft muck and peat bottom.

**Structure:** As many pond anglers will attest, largemouths can spawn successfully on barren banks. However, the fish seek structure and will build nests adjacent to stumps, logs or clumps of stiff, emergent vegetation such as cattails or bulrushes.

Nesting largemouths seem especially fond of overhead cover. Research in aging Tennessee reservoirs demonstrated that bass readily build nests under horizontal planks suspended a foot or so above the bottom.

**Shelter From Water Movement:** The most consistent feature of bass nesting sites is calm water. In rivers and streams, bass seek coves, sloughs and bays away from the main river. In lakes and reservoirs, nests are generally found on shores sheltered from the prevailing spring winds, in small pockets or in areas of dense vegetation that dampen wave action. Biologists have demonstrated that wave action often destroys bass nests.

Surprisingly, water depth does not seem to be important to bass. Largemouths typically nest in water that's two to four feet deep, but they have been observed nesting in water as shallow as six inches and as deep as 24 feet.

What's more, although the nests observed at 24 feet were in the clear waters of Lake Mead, water clarity does not seem consistently related to nest depth. For example, bass nest in water that's one to three feet deep in clear spring runs in Florida.

## Homing Instinct

Largemouths have preferred conditions for nesting, but do they have preferred spawning areas—a particular cove, a segment of a bank or a certain flat they use year after year? As any dedicated bass angler knows, certain areas are perennial spawning sites, while others are heavily used one year, but used little the next.

Why would an area be used for spawning one year but not the following spring? Conditions may change, and weed growth may be limited, which may allow for an increased amount of water

*Spawning bass (notice fry) prefer to spawn near cover; even more important is finding a spawning area that's protected from current or wind and wave action.*

movement. There may be a better answer, however. Many bass caught in "spawning areas" may actually come from pre-spawn staging areas. In fact, if you catch more than three or four swollen-bellied females from the same spot, it's likely you've found a staging area.
—*Dr. Hal Schramm*

---

superline is a must to allow you to feel the weed tops. Attach a 3- to 4-foot leader of 10- to 17-pound mono before tying on the bait. A double Uni Knot is best for making the connection.

Jerkbaits such as the Smithwick Rogue, Storm ThunderStick, Bomber Long A or Rapala Husky Jerk are also deadly over weed tops, especially under low-light conditions and during warming trends. I want a neutrally buoyant lure that suspends in front of the fish between rod sweeps. At times, pauses as long as 10 seconds are the trick for triggering strikes.

Another area many anglers ignore for prespawn bass is the outside or deep edge of the weeds. Although the vegetation isn't close to being mature, bass still use the deep edge in early spring. It's very common for prespawn bass to retreat to deep water; perhaps the reason why fish "aren't biting" on a particular day.

Another common occurrence during the prespawn is to have smaller "buck" bass working the shallower water, while a school of big, roe-laden females are bunched up on the outside edge of the weeds adjacent to deep water.

Bass holding on the deep weedline are best fished with a jig or a Carolina-rigged worm or lizard. If the fish really turn on and show aggressiveness (i.e., coming off bottom to blast a falling jig), then switching to a deep-diving crankbait can be very productive.

While weed points are the most fished spots along the deep weed edge, inside turns or corners along the sides of these points are usually better for prespawn bass. These slot-like areas offer bass more shelter, a better ambush spot, a shorter route to the shallows, and a place where they are rarely disturbed. Whatever their reasons, a good inside turn near a spawning area can hold a school of big bass!

# RESERVOIRS: ATTACK THE SHALLOWS

Catching prespawn bass on reservoirs can be a lot more difficult than catching them on natural lakes because reservoir bass can be much tougher to locate. There are various types of reservoirs from flatland reservoirs built in flat farm country, to the clearer, deeper highland reservoirs with depths that may plunge quickly to 100 feet or more. One thing is for sure, once water temperatures in the bays, arms and feeder creeks reach 50 degrees or more, and stay there a few days, the bass will start moving shallow.

As a general rule, the shallower upper end of the reservoir (area farthest from dam), warms up the fastest and often provides good early-spring fishing, unless there is an influx of cold or muddy water. If faced with these conditions, try the mid-section of the reservoir or even go up to the dam if there are small, sheltered cuts or coves in the area. The best spots are littered with rocks or wood, and receive long periods of direct sunlight.

Bass move more in reservoirs than they will in natural lakes. As the water temperature nears 50 degrees they usually relate to creek channels that lead into spawning areas. The best coves will be the ones with flats and cover toward the back end.

Fish the edge of the channel with a jig or Carolina rig to try to make contact with prespawn bass. If possible, fish coves with limited cover in the deeper (8 to 15 feet) sections of the channel. This helps concentrate the fish. An area with lots of turns, humps and saddles may look inviting, but it will take you too

*Petros has found that by targeting staging areas rather than spawning areas he not only finds more big bass, he finds success before other anglers even consider fishing.*

much time to check out. Try to establish patterns in areas where bass are concentrated.

Once water temperatures start climbing into the 50s, bass begin to make short forays into the shallows. A great place to intercept these fish is where deeper water brushes up against shoreline cover or structure.

Many anglers head straight for the back ends of the coves hoping for some hot prespawn action. But remember, bass usually follow the creek channels or drop-offs to their spawning sites. It often takes consecutive days of warm weather to pull them all the way into the back of the cove.

The higher water of early spring often draws bass to flooded, cover-lined banks adjacent to deeper water. Skipping a jig under overhanging cover can be a deadly approach. I prefer wide plastic baits such as tubes or craws when skipping. Jig heads or pegged weights get the nod over slip sinkers.

Buckbrush is a favorite spring cover. Key on isolated patches, rather than working solid bands that cover long stretches of shoreline. Not only will you reach a higher percentage of the fish holding in the cover, you will find concentrations of fish a lot faster.

Stumps, docks, fallen trees, rocky points or flats, grassbeds, or just about anything along a sharp-breaking bank, including the drop-off itself, can draw prespawn bass. Be aware that small groups of bass will move up to the cover at various times during the day. By revisiting a hot area over and over again you can pick off fish all day.

# BASS ON TOP

*by Dan Johnson*

*Denny Brauer uses topwaters to find and catch scattered postspawn largemouths.*

Denny Brauer didn't get his face on a Wheaties box by accident. The former Lake of the Ozarks guide climbed the ladder to bass superstardom by fishing hard and smart—and taking seemingly everyday presentations a step or two beyond the competition.

His postspawn topwater approach, for example, involves far more than simply chunking surface baits down the shore. He carefully weighs location, bait selection and presentation in his quest for the most bass possible any given day.

"After the spawn, the fish are scattered and can be tough to find," says Brauer, a multi-time winner on the B.A.S.S. trail, past Classic champ and among the first anglers to break the $1 million dollar mark in career winnings. "Topwaters are a good tool to find and catch them."

He begins his search by locating spawning areas, preferably the actual beds. Gradually tapering, hard bottoms in protected pockets are good places to look. When he finds bedding areas, Brauer doesn't dally; the bass are gone, and this is just a starting point.

"Postspawn bass move off the beds to the nearest cover or structure they can find. In my home lakes of Missouri, they leave protected pockets and move out onto secondary points—especially those with timber. This is particularly true on Truman," he says. "On Table Rock and Lake of the Ozarks, you'll find bass around docks. On other lakes, the inside weedline is the best place in the early postspawn. Later on, the outside edge can be better."

The point is to analyze the lake and assess which location choices bass have when coming off their beds, then fish the most promising areas first.

## MITIGATING FACTORS

Time of day isn't a huge factor. "In the postspawn, topwaters can be good all day," says Brauer. But sun conditions can be key. "If it's clear and sunny, the bass will be tucked into the cover, or deeper on the structure.

"Now's the time to fish noisier baits and slower retrieves. When the sun is low in the sky, or it's cloudy, bass will cruise over the tops of weeds and higher off structure, so you can fish a faster presentation that's not as loud."

Lure style selection is also critical. "Spook-style walking baits call fish from deep water, and are better in clear and calm situations," he explains. "Chuggers are good shallow, in stained water and when you're on numbers of smaller bass. A propbait is a good choice in muddy or choppy water, and at night. 'Crawlers are good night and dirty-water lures, too."

When it comes to color, Brauer warns, "Don't get hung up on shad patterns. Bass have been protecting their beds from perch and bluegills, and these colors work well. Also, your lures should have brighter tones in stained water; more natural shades in clear conditions."

He recommends Mustad Thor Ultra Line in 14- to 17-pound test—no heavier than 20—for chuggers. Walking baits call for a bit lighter, 12- to 17-pound test, and, "Any lure you stop a lot should be on 10- to 12-pound line," he says, adding, "Never use fluorocarbon with a top-water, because it'll sink.

"I use a Palomar knot for topwaters except with chuggers," he adds. "Then I tie an improved clinch because I can keep the knot low on the pull point, for best action. In fact, if all of a sudden your chugger isn't working, check the knot. You may have to slide it down a bit."

Brauer recommends a 7-foot rod, for long casts and taking up line on the hookset. "You want a fast tip with crisp action," he says. "But you don't want it too stiff, either, or you'll take the bait away from the bass on the strike."

## PRESENTATION POINTERS

Any bassman worth his salt knows there's room to get creative with a topwater retrieve. Brauer recommends varying retrieve speed, as well as the number, frequency and duration of pauses.

"Let the fish tell you what they want at the moment," he says. "For example, if you stop your bait and a bass hits while the lure is motionless, you should add more pauses to your presentation. But if a fish hits while you're moving the bait, speed up and stop less."

Brauer also watches where strikes come from. "Post-spawn bass are scattered, so you won't find a school in one spot. But the fish will position the same way on structure or cover throughout a lake. For example, one morning the key spot to fish may be the shady side of the dock, or the rungs of the lad-der—if there is one—or cracks between sections on floating docks. Once you fig-ure out the pattern, focus on high-percentage spots."

## FIGHTING SMART

Drawing strikes is only half the game. Knowing when to set the hook is also critical. "You can't jump when a bass explodes on your lure," he says. "Instead, react to ten-sion on your line. Even when a bass strikes, keep working the bait until you feel the weight of the fish; if a bass misses, it may strike again if you keep the lure moving."

Conversely, waiting too long is just as bad as setting early. "Give a bass too much time and that topwater is going to float back up at you," he laughs.

How you hold the rod dur-ing the retrieve can also play a big role in a successful hookset. "If you hold the rod low to the water in front of you, you'll have a better chance at a good set than with the rod up at 10 o'clock or off to the side."

With the tip low, Brauer holds the rod butt against his forearm for leverage and executes a strong, upward-sweeping set. "Just be careful about that bait coming back at you wide open."

Once a bass is hooked, keep the rod low to keep it from jumping. "If you feel the fish coming up, pull it side-ways to stop the jump," he says. "Sometimes a bit less tension on the line will also make a fish go back down; the key is not getting any slack in the line."

For solid sets and control during the fight, Brauer favors a tight drag, even with 10-pound line. "With a good bass, though, you should back off on the drag or thumb the spool when it gets close, because it's going to run when it sees the boat," he says. "If it runs on a tight drag, it might break the line or tear the hooks out."

Just another pointer in Brauer's total topwater attack. Try it yourself this postspawn and put more bass in your boat.

*Brauer's favorite topwater colors often mimic baitfish that bass have been chasing off their nests.*

# DEEP DOWN BASS

*by Mark Hicks*

Spring through fall, Tennessee fisherman Ricky Shepherd fishes bass in TVA lakes near his home in Mosheim three or more times a week. So, last year, when he heard that Douglas Lake, one of his favorites, would be the site of a MegaBucks tournament, he gladly took a week of vacation from his job as a maintenance manager at an electronics company to fish it.

The May tournament would focus on postspawn bass, and the angler was confident he could dredge up enough largemouths on deep crankbaits to do well on the amateur side of the pro/am event. His hunch proved correct, and he wound up taking fourth place. He also helped legendary bass fishermen Mark Davis and Rick Clunn finish well in the tournament.

"I drew Mark Davis the first day," says Shepherd. "When I found out he planned to fish deep points in my favorite area of the lake, I was pumped."

Shepherd and Davis started fishing depths to 16 feet, but they soon determined that most of the bass had moved out to 20 feet of water. It was too deep for Davis' crankbaits, but he caught bass regularly on a Carolina-rigged lizard.

Shepherd, meanwhile, tossed a modified Mann's 30+ crankbait that plowed bottom like a Massey Ferguson. He, too, caught bass, including some quality fish. After Davis boated his limit, he tried one of Shepherd's special cranks, and on the second cast, caught his largest fish of the day.

Davis accepted the crankbait as a gift and it caught crucial bass for him throughout the rest of the tournament. In fact, it helped him to secure third place in the event.

On day two, Shepherd drew Clunn, who fished shallow early in the day before moving out to deep structure. Though Clunn put together a decent limit on his own lures, he was impressed with Shepherd's success on the Mann's crankbait. Shepherd also gave Clunn one of his lures after their day on the water. It was no coincidence that Clunn eventually won the tournament.

## LOCAL FAVORITE

While the super deep crankbait was an eye-opener to many professional casters, it was an old standby for Shepherd. He and a handful of other Tennessee anglers had been winning local tournaments with the modified lure for years.

"What we do is thin the bill with a file," says Shepherd. "That helps the bait get down faster, run a few feet deeper and stay down longer. I love to feel that bait digging bottom."

The leading edge of the bill on a stock Mann's 30+ is quite thick, but after Shepherd finishes filing the bottom surface, its fine edge slices through the water and forces the lure down close to 30 feet. According to the book *Precision Casting* by Dr.

*Ricky Shepherd's modified super deep-diving cranks are deadly under the right circumstances and on the right waters.*

*Mark Davis' approach to deep structure differs from many pros', but then, who's to argue with his success?*

# Dissecting A Point

Both Mark Davis of Mount Ida, Arkansas, and Alton Jones of Waco, Texas, are skilled and successful professional bass fishermen, yet when it comes to dissecting deep structure, their approaches differ.

The objective is the same—to locate a school of bass that's typically concentrated in a small area.

"The bonus here," explains Davis, "is that you can find a big school that everyone else has overlooked, and instead of catching one or two fish, you'll catch 30, 40 or 50. And they could come from a spot that's half the size of your bass boat."

Our example is a deep point in a reservoir, but the structure could just as well be a ridge, creek channel or hump. Jones prefers to thoroughly fish specific spots on a point, while Davis covers the whole thing. Both anglers catch fish, proving that there's more than one way to skin the proverbial cat.

Study each fisherman's approach to see which best fits your fishing style. Remember, the structure, cover, current or wind could dictate an entirely different approach.

## Davis' Approach

*1. Drops marker buoys on likely spots as he scans the structure with sonar.*
*2. Preference is always to keep boat in deep water and cast shallow.*
*3. Begin at the end of the point, fan-casting the target zone to present the crank from as many different angles as possible (A position on right).*
*4. Move the boat along the side of the point, fan-casting from different locations. Be sure to cast back to water you've already fished to cover it from yet another angle.*
*5. Continue up the point until you reach water too shallow to hold fish.*
*6. Cross the base of the point and begin fan-casting your way down to the end in the same manner.*

## Jones' Approach

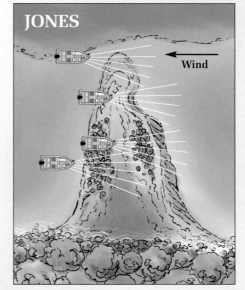

*1. Pinpoint likely hotspots on structure—end of point, cuts, rocks, weeds, etc.*
*2. Prefers to have boat in deep water, but shape of structure and current directions may require the boat be shallow, with Jones casting to the depths.*
*3. Drop a marker buoy, not on the cover, but where you want the boat to be positioned, downcurrent of the cover.*
*4. Keep the bow next to the marker and make long casts upwind/upcurrent so lure swims into fishes' faces.*
*5. When you discover a hotspot, triangulate your position and note the angle of the retrieve. (Jones has an album full of photos of a floating marker buoy accompanied by a note like, "Cast toward the tall tree on the far shore.")*

## Common Denominators

*1. Scan structure with sonar, looking for characteristics or irregularities that might hold bass—a steeper drop-off, proximity to deeper water, rock piles, weeds, stumps, etc.*
*2. Understand the mechanics. Know how deep your lure runs with the line diameter you're using. Thin line allows the lure to dive deeper.*
*3. Boat positioning is critical. Stay close to target zone because a crankbait typically reaches the deepest part of its dive curve 20 to 30 feet from the boat.*
*4. Make long casts. Cast well past the target zone so the crankbait has enough time to reach its maximum running depth.*
*5. Make numerous casts, bringing the lure through the target zone from many different angles. Often, bass will only strike a crank if it approaches from a particular angle.*
*6. When you find the "sweet spot," and know the distance and angle to cast, be ready to duplicate the presentation.*

Steven Holt and Mark Romanack, a stock Mann's 30+ dives to 19 feet on 14-pound mono and 22½ feet on 8-pound line on a cast of at least 100 feet.

It is crucial when customizing this bait that the bill's outside dimensions remain unchanged and that its underside be filed evenly to insure proper balance and action.

When he first started working with the 30+, Shepherd would add weight to make his lures dive even deeper. He no longer does so because his doctored baits dig as deep as he is likely to catch bass on a crankbait.

"I don't like to add weight to a crankbait," he says, "because it hinders the lure's action."

## LONG CASTS REQUIRED

CastAway's 7-foot, 6-inch, Launcher rod (Model LLC76) allows Shepherd to make the 100-foot casts necessary for his crankbaits to achieve maximum diving depth. It takes the lure 70 feet or more for it to achieve that depth, which means his target zone is only 20 or 30 feet from his boat.

He matches this graphite stick with 8- or 10-pound P-Line and a Lew's baitcasting reel. The line's thin diameter, .009 and .011 inches, respectively, and the reel's relatively slow 4.3:1 gear ratio helps the modified crankbaits eke every last inch of depth.

"Where Mark Davis and I were fishing the bottom was only 20 feet deep, so we could get away with fast retrieves," says Shepherd. "But when I really want to get deep, I crank fast to get the lure diving, then slow way down so the bait can maintain its steepest diving angle. It also helps if you plunge the rodtip deep into the water when cranking."

Dropping the rodtip into the water does help increase a bait's running depth. In fact, you will gain a foot of diving depth with each foot of the rodtip you put beneath the surface.

May, June and July present the window of opportunity for super deep cranking from Texas to Tennessee. Farther north, it could begin a few weeks to a month later. This approach appeals to postspawn bass that have migrated from the shallows to deep-water structure connected to the main lake basin or river channel. In the absence of a thermocline, the fish go as deep as they wish. Once the thermocline sets up later in the summer, bass generally move back up within range of crankbaits that run less than 20 feet.

Bear in mind that bass in many lakes rarely venture deeper than 20 feet, so super deep cranking isn't effective everywhere. In Tennessee, Shepherd has caught largemouths on his deep cranks in Douglas, Cherokee, Watt's Bar, Ft. Loudoun and Tellico.

# WHERE THEY SHINE

As productive as the Mann's 30+ was for Davis at Douglas Lake, he believes few bodies of water lend themselves to the big-lipped crankbait. Since the MegaBucks on Douglas, he has experimented with the lure on some of the deep, clear-water impoundments in his home state of Arkansas with limited success. He believes the water has to have some color in order for deep cranking to be successful, but not so much that the fish stay shallow.

"In all my years of fishing, I have never seen a deep cranking pattern as strong as it was on Douglas Lake," says Davis. "But you can bet I'll always have a couple of those baits in my tackle box, just in case I come across that situation again."

Texas bass pro Alton Jones holds a different view. After learning of the success Davis and Clunn had at Douglas, he began pursuing the world of deep crankbait fishing in earnest.

"The Douglas tournament was really educational for me and a lot of other pros," he says. "When I fished that tournament, I didn't have any crankbaits that would catch those deep bass. I do now, and I think they'll pay off for me."

Jones' super deep crankbaits are two lures on which he has performed surgery. One is the Excalibur BSD6F Suspending Fat Free Shad. The other is the discontinued Rebel Deep-R. Jones modifies the lures by shaving the diving bill with a file or Dremel rotary tool, then wet sands it with very fine finishing paper. Even though the bills on these lures are much thinner than that on the Mann's 30+, Jones believes the shaving process gets the baits down to 18 or 19 feet.

"You've got to make sure the lure is tuned to run straight before you start modifying the lip," he says, "then be careful not to take off too much material. So far, I've ruined about one out of four baits I've worked on. I expect my success rate will improve as I get more experience."

One drawback with a shaved lip, warns Jones, is that it becomes more vulnerable to chipping when run over rocks and other hard surfaces. Though the lures are more likely to fail under hard use, Jones feels it is a small price to pay for more bass in his live well.

"If I want one of these baits to break the 20-foot barrier, I add weight," says Jones. "But anytime you add weight, you can adversely alter the lure's action."

Jones drills a 3/16-inch hole through the plastic in the belly of the crankbait halfway between the front hook and the base of the diving bill. Then he fills the opening with silicone to prevent

## *Modifying A Crankbait*

Careful filing on the underside of the bill of the Mann's 30+ helps make it a super deep-diver. Compare the leading edge of the diving bills on the modified lure (left) to that on the standard bait. Alter the bill's thickness, not its length or width.

Modified     Stock

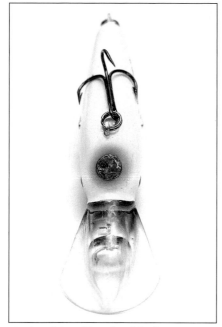

*A tiny bit of lead added to a Suspending Fat Free Shad helps it break the 20-foot mark. Alton Jones explains details.*

water from leaking into the lure's hollow body. Before the silicone sets up, he pushes a depression into it with a pencil eraser. After the silicone hardens, Jones fills the cavity with molten lead, which he later trims with a Dremel tool and smoothes with sandpaper so it's nearly flush with the surface of the lure. Then, he paints the lure, making the modification nearly invisible.

"I figure I add somewhere between ⅛- and 3⁄16-ounce of lead," he says. "It's enough to make the bait sink slowly. If I just crank it back, it will get down about 22 feet. If I'm patient enough to let it sink before I start cranking, I can get it deeper."

When he wants a lure to reach depths of 30 feet, Jones adds a second lead plug directly behind the front treble, using the same procedure. With two weights, the crankbait sinks quickly, as much as a foot per second.

Jones rockets his weighted crankbaits into the distance with a 7-foot medium-action Fenwick Fenglass cranking rod, a SpiderCast SCP600 baitcasting reel, and SpiderLine Super Mono. He opts for 12-pound test if the crankbait has only one weight, 14-pound if the lure carries two.

"I don't need thin line to help the heavier plug get deep," he says. "I just let it sink to bottom, then crank it in. The heavier line has little effect on how deep the plug goes, and it holds up better to abrasive bottoms."

Before fishing any modified crankbait, Jones checks its action in clear, shallow water to be sure the lure runs true and hasn't lost too much of its enticing wobble. To pass muster, the crankbait must run true, even when ripped through the water.

"A crankbait may run fine when pulled slowly, but roll when I burn it in," he says. "Some of them I can fine tune. If I can't, I toss them."

One of Jones' most productive deep crankbait presentations is a quick retrieve with occasional pauses. The pauses ensure the lure maintains its depth. The schools of deep bass Jones targets are unaccustomed to seeing a fast-moving lure. This is why deep crankbaits sometimes have an advantage over Carolina rigs and other slow, bottom-bouncing lures. The crankbaits trigger reaction bites.

Jones has strong opinions regarding where deep crankbaits are most productive. Any long, tapering main-lake point has potential. But the best, he believes, extend farthest into the lake and drop off close to the main creek or river channel.

"Say you're fishing a lake where the main river channel is 50 feet deep," says Jones. "A lot of points that come off the bank have good breaklines out to about 20 feet and then blend into the lake bottom.

"For deep cranking, I'm looking for a point that maintains its integrity until it drops into that 50-foot depth range. Even in a lake that has hundreds of main-lake points, there may be only a handful that qualify."

Super deep cranking is so new to Jones that he hasn't had an opportunity to test his modified lures across the country. However, he has given them a thorough workout in Texas with excellent results. On several trips to Richland-Chambers and Tradinghouse Creek reservoirs, he has cranked up good numbers of bass from structures 30 feet deep, including quality fish weighing more than 10 pounds.

"There's no doubt in my mind," he says, "that I can take these tools to almost any other body of water and do well with them."

# FALL CREEK BASSIN'

*by Mark Hicks*

When Clark Wendlandt's parents took him out on lakes near Austin, Texas, as a child, trolling for anything that would bite was casual family fun. But angling became his passion—and eventually his profession—after an outing on a high school classmate's bass boat. The two caught a passel of largemouths by skipping soft plastics under boat docks, and Wendlandt was hooked on the sport.

He began fishing the Red Man Trail (now called the BFL Tour) way back in 1987 and eventually graduated to the FLW Tour, where he earned many top-10 finishes and some Angler of the Year titles. He has claimed more than $1 million at bass tournaments, using a variety of tactics to catch bass in any season.

Experience has taught him that autumn is the time to key on creeks. Though these waters pose special challenges, he knows how to use their unique features to his advantage. Here are a few of his tips for finding, attracting and catching fall bass.

## FOOD FACTOR

When he fishes reservoirs from September through November, Wendlandt begins searching for bass in the backs of creeks. The creeks may be large or small and found anywhere on the reservoir, from the headwaters to the dam. Shad and other baitfish migrate into the creeks as the water cools in autumn, and the bass follow their food source.

Wendlandt starts as far back in a creek arm as he can get without going up into the original tributary. He studies the creek on the way in, and notes its depth, water color, bottom composition, cover, structure and baitfish, factors that help him decide how to fish it.

"The bass will be where the bait is," he says. "I may not find them until I work back to the mouth of the creek."

## SKIPPING GRASS

If the creek is clear and has weedy flats with three to five feet of water along the outside edge of the grass, Wendlandt opts for poppers such as the Rapala Skitter Pop, Rebel PopR, or his favorite, a Yellow Magic

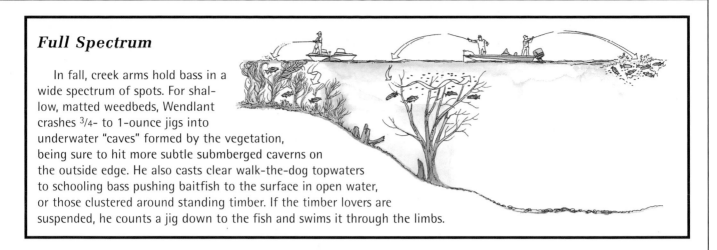

**Full Spectrum**

In fall, creek arms hold bass in a wide spectrum of spots. For shallow, matted weedbeds, Wendlant crashes 3/4- to 1-ounce jigs into underwater "caves" formed by the vegetation, being sure to hit more subtle submberged caverns on the outside edge. He also casts clear walk-the-dog topwaters to schooling bass pushing baitfish to the surface in open water, or those clustered around standing timber. If the timber lovers are suspended, he counts a jig down to the fish and swims it through the limbs.

Popper. He prefers a black back with a pale-gold baitfish pattern and a white belly. He dresses the rear treble with 1½- to 2-inch white hackles to create a livelier teaser.

"I move the bait quickly," he says. "Working fast lets me cover more water, and prevents the bass from getting a good look at the popper. I get more bites, and they take it better."

He keeps his boat moving and makes quartering casts to the edge of the weedline with a 6½-foot medium-action baitcasting rod and 15-pound mono. He never uses fluorocarbon with any topwater plug because fluoro sinks and kills the bait's action.

After casting, Wendlandt points the rod straight at the popper and makes quick, short, downward rod flicks while continually taking up slack with the reel. The rodtip moves only inches up and down. "If you move the rod too far, the popper makes a 'blooping' noise," he says. "That's wrong. Short rod movements skip the popper across the water. That works best."

This pattern produces good numbers of bass up to 3 pounds and an occasional larger fish. It draws strikes all day when he finds enough weedbeds to continue hopping from one to the next.

The popper also comes through for him in clear creeks with rocky banks. He uses the same retrieve and tackle. "I look for rocky shorelines where the bottom gradually slopes from the bank before dropping off into deep water," he says. "I pull bass up from ledges as deep as 10 feet."

## Deep Grass

When aquatic vegetation such as milfoil and hydrilla grows in depths of 10 feet or more, Wendlandt wields a flippin' rod matched with 65-pound-test Power Pro braided line. He ties the line directly to a 3/4- or 1-ounce green-pumpkin or black-and-blue jig. He dresses the hook with Gambler's BB Cricket, a 3-inch craw-style worm.

The heavy jig punches through matted grass on the surface and through submerged grass that forms caves. Bass lounge under the surface mats and in the caves and tunnels formed by submerged weeds. The flippin' rod and no-stretch braided line are necessary to muscle the bass out of the greenery.

Wendlandt prefers weed mats with submerged grass— for example, 8-foot-tall grass in 15 feet of water—and relies

on a flasher depthfinder to keep him on track. Points of grass are key bass locations, and the fish occasionally hold in pockets along the weedline. A ditch within a grassbed should never be overlooked.

When fishing these areas, he moves the boat slowly and pitches the jig to the grass, speeding up along straight stretches and slowing down when he approaches a point or ditch. If the heavy jig lands on a grass mat or on a "roof" of submerged grass, he jiggles the bait until it pops through the vegetation. About half of the strikes occur when the jig first breaks through the grass. If he doesn't get bit when the jig punches through, he lets it sink to the bottom. Then he hops the jig once or twice, pulls it up until it touches the grass, and shakes it for about five seconds before pitching to another spot.

"I drop a marker buoy whenever I get a bite," he says. "Bass really gang up in thick grass. I've loaded the boat with big bass many times by fishing around a buoy. This technique is most productive in the middle of the day."

## Channel Surfing

Creeks without grass typically have stained water,

making bass feel at home in the shallows. This is common in lowland reservoirs with creek channels winding through shallow flats. Wendlandt follows a channel into a creek with his sonar and notes landmarks and waypoints, then fishes it on the way out.

Many anglers stop searching when they come to a section of channel that has silted in, but Wendlandt always ventures upstream and often picks up a well-defined channel again. He looks for channels that are two to five feet deep on the break and drop to six to 15 feet.

"You have to find channel bends that have sharp breaks," he says. "Bass hang on the lips of inside or outside bends. There are usually stumps, sunken logs or some other wood cover on the bends."

He attacks creek bends with shad-color crankbaits like the Bandit 100, which runs three to five feet deep, the Bandit 200, which runs four to eight feet deep, the Norman Middle "N", which runs six to eight feet or the Rapala DT10, which dives to 10. In water shallower than two feet, he opts for a $1/2$-ounce Rat-L-Trap.

A 7-foot Falcon composite cranking rod handles his crankbait chores. He fills a Pflueger Trion baitcasting reel with 12-pound Ande monofilament.

"I keep my boat moving down the middle of the creek and make quartering casts over the break," he says. "I use a steady, medium retrieve. The key is hitting the cover on the edge of the channel. If the crankbait hangs, I stay back and try to snap the bait off. I get a lot of bites the instant it pops free."

When he catches a bass in a creek bend, Wendlandt reworks the bend from different angles until he picks off all of the aggressive fish. Then he finishes with a tube or a jig to catch any finicky leftover fish. "I normally catch two to four bass from one bend and move on," he says. "When you only catch one, it's usually a quality fish."

## SOLITARY SNAGS

Another of Wendlandt's pet patterns is fishing isolated snags in stained water on shallow flats in the backs of creeks. Few anglers bother fishing it because they hate to pick up the trolling motor and move after making only a few casts.

He may run to a snag and make six casts, then crank up the outboard and race to another. If the flat has several isolated snags, he runs his electric motor on high speed from one to the next.

The water on the flat may be as deep as six feet, but it is more often one to three. The tip-off to a productive snag may be only a few inches of a

## Down And Dirty

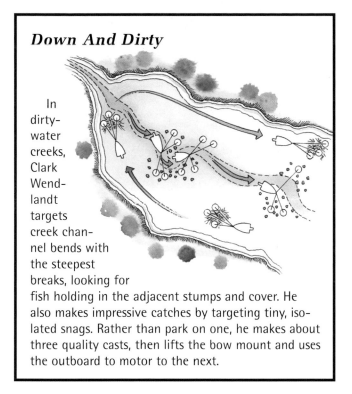

In dirty-water creeks, Clark Wendlandt targets creek channel bends with the steepest breaks, looking for fish holding in the adjacent stumps and cover. He also makes impressive catches by targeting tiny, isolated snags. Rather than park on one, he makes about three quality casts, then lifts the bow mount and uses the outboard to motor to the next.

## Clear Solutions

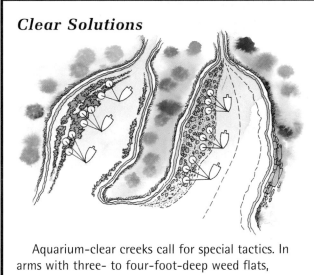

Aquarium-clear creeks call for special tactics. In arms with three- to four-foot-deep weed flats, Wendlandt casts poppers to the deep weed edge, working the bait quickly with short rodtip twitches. This approach also works for rocky banks where the bottom gradually slopes off the bank before dropping into deep water. Look for bass holding down to 10 feet.

limb sticking above the surface. "If the cover is no deeper than, say, two feet, I'll run a ¼-ounce buzzbait over it first," he says. "I've caught a lot of big bass doing that. I use either a white buzzbait with a silver blade or a black buzzbait with a gold blade."

Wendlandt uses a 6½- or 7-foot medium-action casting rod and 17-pound mono—a stiffer rod will typically pull the buzzbait away before the fish can inhale it. He uses a slow to medium-speed retrieve with an occasional pause to goad bass into action.

If buzzing doesn't cut it, he works the snag from different angles with a square-billed, shallow-running crank such as a Bagley Balsa B. This lets him find bass wherever they're holding on the cover.

A 7-foot composite baitcasting rod with 15-pound mono is his rig of choice for cranking isolated snags. He typically ties on shad-color cranks but switches to chartreuse in dirty water.

## SCHOOLING BASS

On clear reservoirs, bass often drive baitfish to the surface in open water, an activity known as schooling. Though this can happen anywhere on a lake, Wendlandt searches for schooling bass in creeks. A whole school may ascend, but it's more common to see one or two bass break the surface between periods of inactivity that may last several minutes.

Casting to schooling bass can be frustrating, because you never know exactly where the fish will come up. One approach Wendlandt takes is to hold off casting until a bass shows itself. Then he chucks a clear Cordell Boy Howdy prop bait to the boil and works it back with a quick dog-walking action.

"You can throw a Boy Howdy a mile with a 7-foot casting rod," he says. "I've always done better with a clear bait, because schooling bass can get finicky. If they're feeding on small baitfish, I downsize to a Lucky Craft

Sammy 65 or a Heddon Zara Puppy in a shad pattern."

When bass school over standing timber or a point, he casts over the cover or structure while waiting for the fish to come up. Because he knows where the bass are holding between surface-feeding forays, he can often bring them up with a topwater.

Another tactic, when bass suspend 10 feet deep over timber or a point that's 20 to 30 feet deep, is to cast a jig-and-grub over the fish, count it down to 10 feet and swim it through them. "I can usually catch them that way when they're not coming to the surface," he says.

Searching for schools, effectively fishing snags, exploring creek channels and using the right approach in weeds can add excitement to fall bass fishing. Try Wendlandt's tactics and your next trip might be your best ever.

# SUSPENDED ANIMATION

*by Don Wirth*

Quick glances at the graph can be enough to ruin your fishing day. Oh, you're on the right spot—the screen reveals a picturebook creek channel drop-off replete with stumps, standing timber and snaggy brush along its edge. Yet ... the fish you're after are neither hunkering tight to the drop nor squatting close to cover, poised to attack passing prey. To your dismay, the hooks on the display indicating bass

appear to be suspended a good 15 feet above the ledge, floating in that awful purgatory beneath the bottom and the surface.

Every serious basser knows suspended fish can be a real downer. They are notorious for being lethargic when not relating tight to a structural edge or cover. Add to this the fact that bass may suspend at extreme depths— 30, 50, even 100 feet—and it's no wonder even the most competent anglers view these

fish as darn near impossible to catch.

Difficult, maybe—but not impossible! Savvy anglers can catch suspending bass— especially once you're armed with the information that follows.

## PROVEN PATTERNS

The pros and guides with whom I've fished over the past 30 years have shared some killer techniques for catching suspended winter bass. The best of these patterns follow. Use 'em right now on your home waters.

## 1. Bluff Banks

Vertical rock bluffs mark the spot where a deep creek or river channel contacts the shoreline in a reservoir. Largemouth, spotted and smallmouth bass will congregate on these massive rock structures, sometimes at extreme depths. Anglers in Georgia's Lake Lanier catch spotted bass as deep as 100 feet on bluffs during February! Fifteen to 30 feet is a good jumping-off zone. Rather than wasting time searching the entire bluff for bass, concentrate on irregular features along the structure, including rock slides, fissures and outcroppings. Be alert for baitfish clouds on your graph —bass are usually close by.

*Inside tip: Bass often suspend over short rock ledges jutting out from the face of a rock bluff. Position your boat tight to the bluff, then lower a blade bait, metal spoon or tailspinner until it makes contact with the ledge. Jig the lure repeatedly with pops of the rod varying from mild to aggressive; if bass don't respond, move to a slightly deeper or shallower ledge until you determine the depth of the most productive outcroppings.*

## 2. "Hollows"

These short, deep V-shaped tributaries are found in clear highland lakes. Southern bass guides often find large numbers of suspending fish schooled here in winter. Bass usually suspend in the middle of the V, but not always. Check close to either bank as well.

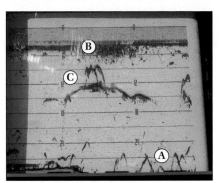

*Typical winter bass scenario: while some bass are holding close to the bottom (A), others are suspending. Tight baitfish school near surface (B) indicates that the suspending bass (C) are probably feeding and susceptible to a properly presented slab spoon, blade bait or tailspinner.*

*Inside tip: Bass suspending in hollows relate closely to large schools of baitfish, which also gravitate to these areas in winter. Look for bait on your sonar— bass will usually suspend at or slightly below their depth level.*

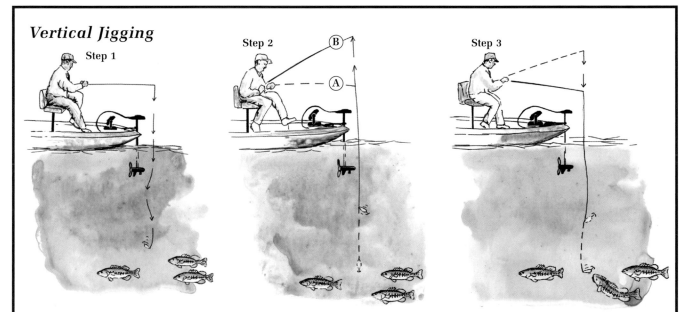

### Vertical Jigging

**Step 1**

**Step 2**

**Step 3**

Step 1. Locate bass on sonar. Drop spoon to fish, keeping it at or slightly above the fish's level. Step 2. Lower rod to position "A," then snap to position "B." The spoon will hop. Step 3. As the spoon drops, lower your rodtip at the same rate the spoon falls to keep a semi-taut line to improve bite detection. If you drop the rodtip too fast, you'll miss strikes. Drop it too slow and the spoon won't flutter enticingly. Vary cadence and intensity of jig strokes until fish tell you what they want.

### 3. Submerged Standing Timber

In some reservoirs, trees were left standing prior to inundation; these bass attractors often line the original creek or river channel and may top out 30 or 40 feet beneath the surface.

***Inside tip:*** *To reduce hang-ups when vertically-fishing deep standing timber, try a heavy metal spoon (⁵⁄₈ to ¾ ounce) with a soft bronze treble hook fished on heavy mono or braided line (or a combination of both). If the spoon hangs on a deep limb, tighten the drag and pull hard to straighten the hook.*

### 4. Spring Holes

These are common in many reservoirs, natural lakes and rivers. Watch your boat's surface temperature gauge—the water is likely to be much warmer near the spring than elsewhere in the lake, attracting baitfish and bass.

***Inside tip:*** *Spring water is typically so clear, bass suspending in it may be exceedingly wary of artificial lures. Try drifting live shad, creek minnows, small suckers or crayfish here instead.*

### 5. Power Plant Canals

Another winter sauna for bass, these man-made

---

## Catching Suspenders Spring Through Fall

Get ready for wearin' out those suspending fish the rest of the year with our hand-picked selection of proven tips from master anglers!

**1. Jerkin' Prespawn Suspenders**—As the water warms to 45-50 degrees, bass move out of their deep winter haunts to stage near spawning areas, often suspending above the first breakline adjacent to the shallows. Your best lure choice here is a jerkbait; pros favor one weighted to be neutrally buoyant or to rise very slowly. Vary the intensity and cadence of the jerks until you find what triggers strikes.

The jerkbait/staging bass pattern works in both clear and stained lakes, but loses its potency in muddy water.

**2. Surface Lures in Post-spawn**—After spawning, bass in clear highland reservoirs and natural lakes often move to adjacent drop-offs, where they suspend prior to scattering on deeper structures. The depth at which these fish will suspend varies greatly—in a rocky Arkansas reservoir, they might be 20 feet down; in a grassy Ohio lake, they may be down only 8 feet. Either way, they're suckers for a topwater lure.

Walk a stickbait like a Heddon Zara Spook over the breakline, and don't be surprised if a big bass swims up to bust it. I've had small-mouths suspending in 30 feet of water hit topwaters after the spawn!

**3. Spinnerbaits Over Deep Brush Piles**—In summer, Kentucky bass pro Dan Morehead targets deep submerged brush piles in flatland and river-run reservoirs. He favors a heavy spin-nerbait with a fat pork or soft-plastic trailer added for buoyancy. He delineates the brush pile with marker buoys, then casts to his target, counts down the lure (1001...1002...etc.) until he feels it make contact with the brush, then slow-rolls it back to the boat.

Morehead favors stout tackle and heavy line here, since a big bass heads straight for the brush pile when hooked.

**4. Crankbaits on "Gravy"**—Florida bass pro Shaw Grigsby knows bass often suspend on main-lake points, ledges and humps in summer and fall. He feels the key to finding big fish on these often large structures is targeting what he calls

*Bass guide Jay Holt uses a floating jerkbait on a Carolina rig for suspending bass during the summer and fall. The lure's flash and rattles call fish in from considerable distances.*

"gravy"—the small pieces of isolated cover that enhance the structure and concentrate fish.

Grigsby will first graph the spot, looking for a rock, stump, brush pile or similar lone piece of cover. Quite often he'll spot several bass suspending above the object. He'll then mark the spot with a buoy and proceed to crank, crank, crank it until he connects with fish.

**5. Carolina Crankbaits in Fall**—In clear lakes and rivers, Maryland bass guide Jay Holt has perfected a unique twist on the popular Carolina rig that's deadly on fall suspenders. Instead of the usual plastic worm or lizard, Holt ties a floating jerkbait to the business end of the Carolina rig's leader, then casts it around deep points, humps and channel drops.

A jerkbait, unlike a worm or lizard, has plenty of flash and will draw suspending fish in from great distances. Holt reels the 1-ounce sinker across the bottom for a few feet, then pauses to let the minnow bait rise slowly—that's when most strikes occur. *—Don Wirth*

structures route the "steam plant's" heated discharge to an adjacent reservoir or river. The water in the canal is likely to be 15 to 25 degrees warmer than un-heated lake water, drawing massive numbers of baitfish in midwinter.

*Inside tip:* *"Too much bait!" is a frequent complaint of anglers fishing power plant canals. Also, the water here is frequently very murky due to heavy plankton growth and turbulence from the power plant's turbines. Try using a highly-visible lure, such as a chartreuse crankbait. Retrieve it rapidly in warm current eddies, where baitfish injured in the power plant's turbines accumulate and the biggest bass often suspend.*

## 6. Bank Transitions

In clear highland reservoirs, very little shoreline cover may be present. To anglers used to fishing weedy, brushy lakes, the banks appear slick and uninviting to bass. However, bass are always attracted to "something different," regardless of how minor this difference may seem.

Experienced highland reservoir anglers know subtle transitions, such as the place where fist-sized rock changes to gravel, can be the key to locating winter bass. Bass will often suspend around these transitions, typically at the depth baitfish are using.

*Inside tip:* *Target transitions on banks being pound-ed by a strong southerly wind with crawfish-patterned crankbaits. Bass that were suspending in deep water often move up tight to these spots to feed on 'dads uproot-ed by wave action.*

## 7. Points

Big bass hold on these key structures, waiting for baitfish to pass by. In winter, bass can suspend near long, tapering points as well as short, fast-dropping ones—be sure to check both by passing over the structures with your sonar.

The depth at which bass are suspending will determine your lure and approach. In natural lakes and flatland reservoirs, they'll probably be no deeper than 15 feet and will hit a horizontal presenta-tion. In highland lakes, 15 to 35 feet is more likely; here, a vertical presentation is best.

*Inside tip:* *On calm, sunny winter days, watch your graph for bass suspending above isolated stumps on the ends of shallow points—these fish have moved up to warm themselves.*

*It's tempting to try for these fish with a crankbait, but these suspenders are lethar-gic, so swim a ½-ounce jig with a fat pork frog past 'em instead.*

*Big spots often suspend in extremely deep water, where vertical jigging is the only reasonable option. Spoon 'em out!*

## 8. Open Water

Sometimes bass suspend in open water, apparently not relating to any structure. In this scenario, baitfish are almost always present, with the bass scattered below the school.

In both highland and lowland reservoirs, this frequently occurs between points, or at the mouth of a major tributary.

Tightly schooled baitfish indicate bass are feeding aggressively and are therefore highly catchable. Depending on their depth, you may need to vertically jig the fish with a spoon or blade.

If the baitfish are loosely scattered, the bass are proba-bly not preying on them. Try drifting live shad, shiners or creek minnows at their level on light line...and expect the bite to be slow.

*Inside tip:* *Winter striper anglers often report catching monster bass from striper schools when using live shad. These bass are hang-ing below the stripers, feed-ing on injured baitfish that drift beneath the larger predators. If you're catching stripers at, say 17 feet, drop a baited line to about 25 feet and see if a lunker bass responds.*

## TIME TO GO

Eight great winter patterns for suspending bass. Chances are at least one of them will work on your home waters right now. Just remember, fish patiently—this is no time for a run-and-gun approach. And once you've caught your winter trophy, send us a picture and tell us about it!

# SMALLMOUTHS

atching
bronzebacks
is easier when you
put these proven
strategies to work.

# SMALLMOUTHS BY THE NUMBERS

*by Spence Petros*

My partner was raring to go. As he pulled his rods from his truck I could see they were already rigged and ready. The first sported a jig, the second a deep-diving crankbait, and the rest various shallow-running minnow plugs and topwater lures. As we motored away from shore he made a remark about me "losing my edge" because my rods weren't rigged. I quickly assured my younger friend that that wasn't the case. With a grin on my face, I let him know that at his age, enthusiasm often controls fishing decisions, but as you get older and wiser you learn to let the water temperature and the fish tell you what to use, especially in the spring.

I'm not an advocate of so-called preferred temperature ranges for the various warm-water species after spring, but early in the season, water temperature can tell you a lot about how active fish should be and what lures to use.

As we pulled onto a favorite spawning flat on the south side of the lake, I dropped a temperature probe into the water. "Fifty-two degrees … let's move!" I shouted, as my partner was just about to make his second cast. He gave me a puzzled look as I fired up the motor and headed to the opposite side of the lake. I was excited because we might find that magic temperature for spring smallmouths, 55 degrees. Fifty-five is more than a speed limit—it's the temp that triggers smallmouths to migrate to their spawning areas where, for a while, they will slam just about any lure that comes in front of them.

I made the quick move to the north shore to find a little warmer water. Water on the north shore of any water body will usually be a little warmer because of the angle of the spring sun, which pounds it with direct, warming rays for longer periods than other banks. Plus, for several days we'd had warm, southerly winds, which also warm the northern banks.

My other ace-in-the-hole for the area to which we were headed was a large creek that poured warmer and slightly stained water onto the flat. Finding stained water in a clear lake is a big plus in spring as large bass seem to seek it out.

While motoring toward the north shore I rigged a couple rods with crankbaits that would cover the five- to 12-foot range. One crank was a crayfish pattern while the other was perch "flavored."

The cranks received a real workout that afternoon as not only did we find water temps

*Petros with two near 5. Water temperature can not only help you locate prespawn bass, it can help you select the most productive presentation. The temperature to seek out is 55 degrees.*

in the perfect 55- to 56-degree range, we found a bunch of big, active smallmouths, too.

## USE WATER TEMPS

It's great to be on a good smallmouth lake when the water temperature in the spawning bays hits the magic 55-degree mark, as the bass will usually be active and roaming until the temperature reaches 60 degrees. Then, they start to bed. Look first to the faster-warming sites, but as the bass in that area begin to bed, shift to spots that are slower to reach the 55-degree range.

But what about those times you get on the water and find water temps less than 55 degrees? Certainly all is not

lost, just learn to use water temperatures to tilt the odds more in your favor.

I'll generally start fishing for smallmouths after we get a few warm, sunny days that get water temperatures into the high 30s or low 40s. Major keys to catching smallmouths during this cold-water period are to fish during the warmest part of the day (noon to 5 p.m.), look for warmer conditions like those already mentioned, and fish cover that's related to deeper water.

While bass usually won't cross barren flats to reach spawning sites until the water gets into the mid-50s, they will move up on shallow cover if there is deeper water nearby. Gravel points, chunk rock banks, shallow-topping rock piles and other rock-based structures located between wintering grounds and spawning sites can hold numbers of bass during warm trends. Even a fallen tree bordering a creek channel is worth a few casts.

A sandgrass (short, crunchy, dill-like weed) flat in natural lakes that's between the spawning grounds and the drop into deeper water can be a hot area during an early-season warming trend. Additional cover mixed with the sandgrass such as limbs, boulders, fish cribs and stumps make this slightly deeper water even more attractive to the bass, and makes them less likely to drop deeper if adverse weather conditions arise.

## JIGGING TACTICS

Jigs are the perfect lure for cold-water smallies, but let the bass and the water temperature tell you which retrieve to use. There are eight jig strokes that I rely on for spring small-mouths. Here they are:

• **Crawl-pause**—This is for the coldest water and inactive bass. I came upon it many years ago when interrupting a retrieve to make a drift correction with the electric motor. When I restarted the retrieve, there was weight on the line. A quick hookset linked me to a 3-pound bass. It was the first of several, all caught on an 1/8-ounce black Fuzz-E-Grub fished "dead" on the bottom. When the bite is tough, try letting the jig rest on the bottom every few seconds during your retrieve. Light jigs generally work best, especially those featuring a marabou tail or light hair dressing, and tipping them with a crappie minnow or sliver of pork improves their effectiveness.

• **Glide**—This is simply swimming the jig inches off the bottom in a slow, gliding manner. A spinning reel that doesn't have a fast retrieve ratio is your best choice since the object is to keep the lure within a foot of bottom. Until a bottom-skimming rhythm is established, stop each retrieve to see how long it takes for the lure to hit bottom. If you are reeling too fast, it will take more than two seconds for the line to bow, which indicates bottom contact. Same jigs previously mentioned, but add tubes and minnow-shaped baits such as Berkley Power Minnows and Lunker City Fin-S Fish to the list of baits to try.

• **Lift-drop**—Just what it implies. Lift the jig up with the rod going from a 3 o'clock position to 1 o'clock, then let it fall straight down on a fairly tight line, and repeat the process all the way back to the boat.

• **Swim-drop**—Sometimes smallmouths want the jigged lure falling on more of a horizontal plane. For this retrieve, hold the rod parallel to the surface and keep it there throughout the retrieve or until you have to set the hook! After the lure hits bottom, crank two to three times at a medium speed, stop, and as the jig is sinking execute a slow crank so the lure swims toward you instead of dropping straight down. Repeat. Watch for a line "tick" as the jig sinks.

• **Snap jigging**—As bass get more aggressive (and crankbaits may not be working due to cover, depth or bass simply not wanting them), try snapping the jig off bottom with an aggressive jig stroke, letting it fall, then snapping it up again. Snap jigging is deadly under the right conditions. Use a heavier jig (usually 1/4-ounce) and make the snaps to the side as opposed to moving the rodtip upward to a 12 or 1 o'clock position.

• **Twitch and drag**—As the water warms and fish move closer to the spawn, slow, teasing retrieves usually work best for big bass. Two favorite lures I fish around bedding sites are a 4-inch lizard thread on a very lightweight (1/16- to 1/8-ounce) stand-up style jig head, or a tube rigged with a light leadhead. Flip the bait gently past the bed, reel it to the fish and gently quiver it on bottom. Watch for the line to move to the side, or for the flash of a bass' side as it turns to take the offering.

• **Flickin'**—Sometimes you see bass in clear water that just won't hit slow-moving plastics, but now and then they will

*Dead vegetation will hold spring smallmouths, especially if the area features scattered rocks. This is a good place to throw small spinnerbaits.*

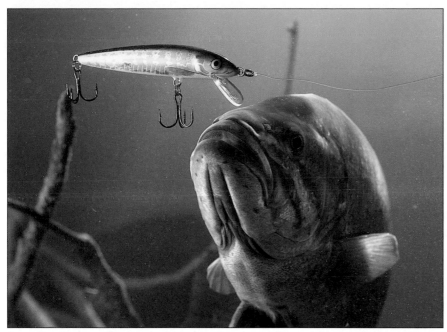

*Inactive bass will respond to small, suspending minnow baits when nothing else seems to work.*

explode into some nearby minnows or panfish. The best way I've found to hook these bass is by using a 1/32-ounce Road Runner. Toss it over the fish and with the rod held high, begin to "flick" it with tiny snaps of the rodtip. This duplicates the flashing sides of small fish. Strikes will be quick, so be ready.

• **Nervous grublet**—Here's a long-time favorite that's the best I've seen for catching neutral-mood bass that aren't on a bed. Cast a 1½-inch curlytail grub on a 1/32- to 1/16-ounce jig head to spring targets such as fallen trees, docks, piers or pilings, shaded spots adjacent to larger rocks, pockets in vegetation—anywhere bass may be holed up. As the lure sinks slowly (and this can be into 10- to 12-foot depths), hold the rod at the 10 o'clock position and softly jiggle the tip to give the lure's tail a nervous, quivering action as the bait settles toward bottom. Make just a couple casts to a specific spot, then move. Don't expect

aggressive hits; watch for the line to tighten.

For most of these jigging techniques, a 5-foot, 6-inch to 5-foot, 8-inch spinning rod and a reel spooled with 6-pound test works best. My favorite is South Bend's model P-244 in the System Series, an IM-6 graphite rod I designed specifically for jigging.

## CRANK 'EM UP

There is nothing more effective for catching numbers of larger spring bass than crankbaits, but again, being aware of water temperatures in the spawning areas puts me a step up on knowing when to use these lures. Once the water temperatures climb into the high 40s on a sunny afternoon, it's time to try cranking. Another good clue for turning to these faster-moving lures is when bass start to hit the more aggressive jigging actions.

When using crankbaits during the early season there

are some very important things to keep in mind. First, take at least twice as long to work a spot as you would during warmer weather. It is very common for a bass to reject a crankbait the first time it passes when the water temperature is in the high 40s to low 50s, but it will often strike if the lure comes by a second or third time. I learned this the hard way when, on several occasions, a boat partner fishing behind me started catching most of the fish.

Minnow-shaped jerkbaits, especially those that suspend, can also be very productive in cold water and will often draw bass up five or more feet off bottom. To get this type of action in colder water, pause the lure at least two to four seconds between pulls. This is also a time when mono works better than any of the low-stretch superlines because it gives the pulled lure a more subdued action.

Another key to catching the most bass when the water is colder than 55 degrees, is to revisit (even three to five times a day) a spot that kicks out a good-size bass or two. Remember, fishing cover adjacent to deeper water is the key early on. Bass will often filter up out of deeper water throughout the day to a key piece of cover or structure. Many times, all cold-water bass caught on a given day will come from just two or three places, though dozens of proven spots may have been fished that day.

When water temperatures are in the mid- to high-50s, crankbaits are usually the best bass catchers unless cover or depth prevents you from using them. Years ago my favorite crankbait, Rebel's

Deep Wee-R, was also the deepest-running small crankbait available (I could get it 10 feet down with a long cast and 6-pound test). Today, there several excellent smallmouth-size crankbaits available such as Luhr Jensen's Hot Lips Express (the deepest small diver I've used), and the various Bomber Model "A"s to name a few. If the bass are shallower than eight feet, consider lipless cranks such as the Frenzy Rattl'r, Cordell Super Spot or Rat-L-Trap. These baits can get hot if bass are up on a rock-studded flat, something that may occur under windier conditions and higher water temps.

As water temperatures near 60 degrees, you'll note that the average size of bass caught on crankbaits usually gets smaller. The bigger

*If you struggle to catch big bass (this one's pushing 20 inches!), fish slower and look for cover with access to deep water.*

females, getting ready to spawn, generally stop chasing lures. About the only hardbait I've had much success with at this time is a small, shallow-running, minnow plug. I toss floating models over suspected bedding areas, and twitch them lightly. Bass will come up and gently take them. Since tight places are usually the targeted areas, I prefer plastic-bodied lures over balsa because they are easier to cast accurately.

## SPINNERBAITS

Small spinnerbaits, models that run about ¼ ounce, can sometimes be the right tools to use. Generally I'll toss them into rushes and reeds in early-to-warm areas, even if this cover is dead. A major key to dead weeds being productive is the presence of large, scattered rocks. Sometimes only a couple rocks may be present, but that's enough to draw bass.

Another place to toss a spinnerbait is around fallen trees. Let it flutter down into openings, parallel to larger limbs, or as it comes off the main tree trunk. Let the water temperature and the bass' mood dictate how it's fished.

If the wood isn't too thick, it can be easily fished with a crankbait such as Luhr Jensen's Brush Baby or Worden's Timber Tiger. This spring don't try to catch smallmouths on the lures you think are best. Let the water temperature and the bass tell you what to use.

---

## Fish-Finding System

The key to catching big spring smallmouths is putting as many odds as possible in your favor. Unless the water temperature is 55 degrees or above, search out spots with the warmest water available. Also pay attention to water color. Areas of stained water in clear lakes have less light penetration due to wind, dirt banks or incoming water and tend to hold bigger, more aggressive fish. When fishing earlier in the year, look for cover near a depth change leading to deeper water and fish it during warming conditions.

Once you locate a prime area, try a controlled drift covering depths from four to 12 feet. Make casts to anything that offers the fish cover. Prime targets include rock piles, points, reefs, piers, pier foundations, the cement-filled tires or cinder blocks to which moored boats are anchored, fallen trees, sandgrass-coated flats, fish cribs, rushes or reeds. The object is to establish whether bass are using the area or not. One of three things is going to happen; you catch some large fish, you catch nothing, or you catch fish, but they are all small.

If you are catching only small bass, you might be fishing too fast for the larger fish (check water temperature), or you may be fishing too shallow. Under most conditions, it's usually faster to find the shallower male bass, then drop to adjacent deeper structure and cover to hunt the larger females, than it is to fish new areas deep and slow. The biggest bass will usually be on the deep edge of the spawning area, or on cover near the drop-off. —Spence Petros

---

# SPRING SMALLMOUTHS

*by Spence Petros*

Forty-degree water; that's the coldest opening day I've ever seen," I shouted as my partner was pulling the trailer out from under my floating boat. To make matters worse, I had all but guaranteed smallmouth action on this early-May bass opener.

Four hours later we had only one 15-inch smallie to show for our efforts. Still, after a quick lunch, we continued with our game plan—jigging piers, sunken cribs and sandgrass-studded, hard-bottom flats. A controlled drift allowed us to fish the desired four- to 10-foot level. If we started catching only the smaller males in that depth range, the plan was to move deeper to adjacent inside turns and points along the drop-off.

Experience on this lake had taught me it was best to first fish active bass on flats that had some cover, then move to adjacent deeper water, if necessary, to locate larger fish. If we worked the deep water first, with slow presentations, we wouldn't cover much territory. And on this type of lake, where 30 to 35 percent of the shoreline had bass-holding potential, we had to fish in a fast and effective manner.

The early-afternoon winds picked up, as they often do, and when one particularly strong gust blew the boat too shallow, I stopped the retrieve to adjust the electric motor. After a few seconds, I moved the jig again and

immediately felt tension. A quick wrist snap connected me to a chunky smallmouth.

After that we landed 18 bass; 17 hit the "dead jig" off the bottom in that numbing-cold water. A two- to three-second pause every 10 feet or so was the key. We never felt a strike or saw the line jump. When we resumed the retrieve, the bass was there.

This unique experience, which occurred years ago, actually offered five lessons concerning cold-

water, prespawn smallmouth bass—lessons that have proven their worth many times through the years. Here's what we learned that day.

## NOT TOO EARLY

Until the water temperatures reach the 50-degree range, or are at least in the high 40s during a sunny, warming trend, the best smallmouth fishing is usually limited to the warmer, after-

## Sand/Rock Smallmouth Lake

This common smallmouth lake is sand/rock based, but will often feature weedbeds, generally in the bay areas. Most of the springtime action will occur along banks bordering deeper water, but the sides of the bays and the bay points can also be productive this time of year.

The key to catching cold-water bass shallower than the edge of the flats is to fish flats with cover (A). Any warm trend after ice-out will usually pull smallies to these areas where they will hold in just about any type of cover. Bass will move across clean flats (B) when the water temperatures rise to the magic 55-degree mark.

Many times one or two stretches of the bank offer consistent action, while you draw a blank at similar sites. Be sure to re-visit productive stretches several times a day as fish will continue to filter up from deeper water.

Springtime smallmouth spots in this type of lake typically lie in the same general areas. Motor around the lake to find shorelines with potential, and focus on the stretches that look the best (C, D and E). Smallies will also hold on deeper turns, points, and rock structures adjacent to spawning flats (F).

noon hours. At such times, I rarely get on the water before 9 a.m., and even then the action generally doesn't pick up until midday.

The exception is when the weather has been consistently warm and a cold front starts to close in. This often triggers a strong, but short-lived, flurry of morning activity before the front arrives.

Sunlight can warm the waters a few degrees during the course of a day, but did you know a smallmouth might physically warm up even more? The dark color on the fish's back absorbs radiant energy from the sun and warms its body.

This explains why the bite usually picks up as the day progresses, or why bass may hit only slow-moving jigs earlier

in the day, but jump all over crankbaits in the afternoon.

## FIRST, ELIMINATE WATER

There are several types of natural lakes that commonly hold numbers of smallmouths. One is relatively fertile with fairly extensive weedbeds, usually in bay areas, but is mostly sand and rock based. These waters may have largemouths in the weeds, while the smallies favor areas sprinkled with sand and boulders; fist-size or chunk-rock; short, dill-like sandgrass; or combinations of all these features.

Lakes like this typically don't have bays with large,

shallow back ends that draw smallmouths. They generally feature weeds, which make them more suited to largemouths.

Smallies, however, often hold along the sides and around the points of the bay, areas that generally have firmer bottoms. They can make fairly short migrations into the shallow water from the drop-off, which usually starts in the 10- to 16-foot range.

When first starting to fish a lake of this type, whether it's 500 or 5,000 acres, I generally motor around the shoreline, looking for submerged rocks. Visible rocks often mean the presence of deeper rocks.

Even gravel shores bordered by muck, marl or sand banks can hold smallies,

## Shield Lakes

Shield lakes commonly feature large, shallow bays and/or long flat arms that smallmouths must cross before reaching the spawning grounds. Before migrating into the shallows, however, they typically bunch up on structure or cover adjacent to the closest, deep water. Spots such as a boulder-studded point (A), rock- and reed-covered reef (B), rocky point (C), and chunk rock bank (D), are all prime pre-spawn areas.

The reef (B) features rock, gravel plus emergent and submerged vegetation. Thus, smallies may spawn near this structure, and may hold there during summer if depths of at least 20 to 25 feet are available in the immediate area.

Once water temperatures in the bays reach the mid-50s, bass will move in and cruise around looking for spawning areas. Cast to any cover available until you discover a pattern. Skinny, limbless trees (E), provide too little cover unless several of them are bunched together, or are inter-mixed with rocks.

Bulrushes or reeds (F) can be good, too, especially if they contain large, scattered rocks. Large logs (G) provide cover and shade, and can be prime sites. Cruising bass often rest up on isolated rock piles (H) and may bed adjacent to their bases. Crevices between large boulders (I) can also hold bass.

Watch for a deeper slot or run (J) that heads into a beaver lodge. This deep cut in the shallow bay can hold a school of big bass, and is usually overlooked by most anglers.

A combination of logs, rocks and reeds (K) is another prime spot, and one that could just hold a trophy. Finally, don't pass up an opportunity to fish any hard- or soft-bottom reef (L), or large scattered rocks (M).

especially if there's sandgrass on the adjacent flats.

Relatively infertile shield lakes are also good spring smallmouth producers. Unlike the more-fertile mesotrophic lakes, the amount of productive shoreline on a shield lake is limited. In a way, that's good, because large numbers of spring smallmouths concentrate in these small areas.

Shield lakes often feature large, shallow bays and/or long arms that warm much faster than the main lake. This means many of the good springtime spots are often hundreds of yards away from deeper water. However, bass won't cross expansive, featureless flats to get to spawning areas

until water temperatures rise above the mid-50s.

This is an important gauge that tells you if the bass have moved shallow. Many times I've checked the water temperature in a shallow bay, found it to be less than 55 degrees, and the bass weren't there. But a day or two later, after the temperature climbed to 55 or higher, aggressive smallies were everywhere.

Because the water is often fairly clear in such bays, I do much more looking than fishing when trying to locate bass. I first investigate bays, or small coves within bays, that are protected from the north wind, and look for fish or signs of fish. Clean spawning beds are a sure sign. It means the fish have been spooked, or moved

deeper because of fishing pressure or weather conditions.

Sight-fishing like this is fun. I start scanning the water after the sun has climbed fairly high in the sky (about 10 a.m.), which makes it easier to see into the water. I try to keep the sun at my back to reduce glare, but you have to be careful that your shadow doesn't fall across the fish. If you see puffs of silt, it means you have spooked the fish.

Wear polarized glasses, a long-billed hat and go as fast as possible while still being able to see the bottom—probably from 2 to 8 mph, depending on depth and water clarity.

If the water is in the 55- to 60-degree range, expect the bass to be on the move, searching for spawning sites.

If the water is warmer than 60 degrees, watch for bass bedding around cover.

# COVER IN FERTILE LAKES

Lakes that are easily accessible generally receive heavy recreational use, so rough, unkempt shorelines (fallen trees, overhanging brush, broken-down docks, etc.) are rare. Consequently, smallmouths and anglers frequently look to man-made cover.

Favorite cover on these well-manicured lakes include fish cribs, rock piles, foundations, pillars, deep edges near a launch ramp, as well as moored boats and the cinder blocks or concrete-filled tires that hold the floating boat markers in place.

Basically, anything that provides cover along a stretch of shoreline can harbor fish. Naturally, deeper cover, or cover that's more difficult to find will tend to hold more and larger smallmouths.

Many of these lakes will be ringed with piers and docks belonging to the homeowners. The bases, or foundations, that anchor these structures to the bottom, if they are located on a firm bottom, are also prime holding spots for smallmouths.

One of my favorite patterns occurs in early spring, before docks are installed. The permanent foundations that support these structures can be smallmouth havens. I motor along the shore, looking for stretches of gravel, sand or rock, and note spots where docks will soon be set up. Usually the telltale sign is a path (stone, wood planks, worn grass or dirt) that leads to water's edge. A cement slab on the shoreline is another indication.

Sandgrass is another type of cover to keep in mind. The

## What To Use When

**From Ice-Out To 43 Degrees**

At this stage, throw small tube jigs, Fuzz-E-Grubs and sparse hair jigs with thin, flexible pork or plastic trailers. All these baits will have enough action, even at slow retrieve speeds.

A slow, bottom-brushing retrieve usually works, but remember to pause the bait for a few seconds—allowing it to lie on the bottom—when the fish won't react to the moving lure. Adding a small minnow or leech is also an option.

**Water Temp: 44 To 49 Degrees**

As the water warms, hop, lift and jump the jig on the retrieve. You can also start fishing neutrally buoyant minnow plugs (jerkbaits), and crankbaits retrieved at moderate speed, especially during an afternoon warm spell. Slow-rolling a 1/4-ounce spinnerbait over or into wood cover or weed clumps can be productive.

**Water Temp: 50 To 58 Degrees**

Bass start responding to more active presentations. Go to a heavier jig (3/16-ounce and up), and add a curlytail or other plastic body that vibrates as it moves through the water.

Lipped crankbaits are also deadly in this temperature range, as are lipless, vibrating cranks and in-line spinners (Mepps, Panther Martin, Blue Fox, etc.). Fish lipless cranks and spinners over flat, shallow (two to six feet) areas, especially if the water is stained.

Jerkbaits can be hot, and in clear lakes they can pull smallies up from a depth of five feet and deeper.

If fish are active, lures that allow you to cover ground quickly—crankbaits, spinnerbaits, jerkbaits—will help you locate scattered fish in a hurry.

In clear-water lakes with lots of fishing pressure, a large, lively minnow on a live bait rig slow trolled or drifted along the deep edges of spawning flats may be the best method for taking big bass. If you locate a concentration of fish, stop and cast.

**Water Temp: 59 Degrees Through Spawn**

As water temperatures in the spawning areas approach the 60-degree range, faster presentations usually produce smaller bass. Large fish, generally females, begin to bed and rarely chase a fast-moving lure. Instead, they'll hang near the beds and aggressively protect them from intruders.

I target these spawning smallies only if there are no panfish around the beds. Panfish often invade largemouth beds if the bass is caught, but this problem often doesn't exist with smallmouths.

Plastic-body jigs in the 1/16- to 1/8-ounce range are tough to beat for bedding bass. And if the jig has to be lifted over wood or snaked through weeds, a thin, wire weedguard will help. Six- or 8-pound-test mono usually works best.

Surface lures like a small shallow-diving minnow plug, downsized topwaters, or even popper flies are other options. Cast them over the beds and retrieve them with a soft twitch.

Live bait behind a split shot will catch virtually every bass you see, unless you come into a bedding area like a moose in rut. Carefully lip-land each bass—no net—and quickly release it.

presence of sandgrass around any structure or cover usually makes it a better option for the fish, and this can help you eliminate a lot of water that has less potential.

Heavy fishing pressure will often chase bass off isolated pieces of wood and rock cover, causing them to shift to adjacent sandgrass-studded flats. Smallmouths will also spawn on these flats, clearing the brittle weeds with their tails until they've formed a bed.

## RETRIEVES AND TACKLE TIPS

In the cold waters of early spring, I like to fish a jig using a swimming, bottom-brushing retrieve. Keep the rodtip low to the water and pointed toward the lure. This keeps the wind from moving the line around, and allows you see a strike more easily.

I favor a 5½-foot spinning rod with a fast tip when fishing jigs, and spool up with 6-pound mono, which is usually strong enough to pull jigs with light-wire hooks free from snags.

Execute the swimming retrieve with the reel, not the rod. Make two or three medium-slow cranks with the reel, pause a second or two until the lure hits bottom (line goes slack), then repeat. In very cold water, or after a cold front, let the jig sit a couple extra seconds between movements.

As the water warms, popping the jig off bottom often triggers strikes when nothing else works. A "double jump," which is a snap followed by another short, quick snap before the lure drops more than a couple of inches, can be very effective.

When fishing is tough—strong winds, neutral fish, or heavy fishing pressure—dress your jig with a minnow and use a slower lift-and-drop, or bottom-dragging retrieve.

When using crankbaits in cold water, it's important to make at least two casts to each spot; three or four to exceptionally good-looking cover. It's very common for smallmouths to ignore the first presentation, but hit the second or third. The first is simply a wake-up call.

Normally I prefer a sensitive, yet fairly stiff rod when casting cranks so I can feel the lure's vibration, or watch the rodtip vibrate. But when tossing smaller crankbaits long distances on light line, a 6½- to 7-foot spinning rod with a softer tip works better. I watch the longer, more flexible tip for sign of a strike.

## TARGETING BIG BASS

When fishing clear lakes, especially those that have a lot of high-potential areas along the shore, I almost always start on the banks that are on the receiving end of a stiff breeze. The more wind the better, as long as it doesn't make casting too difficult.

Wind and wave action roils the bottom, stirring silt and sand, giving the water some color. It cuts light penetration, and gives the smallmouths more confidence.

*Anglers who target spring smallmouths should release fish immediately in case they're protecting spawning beds. Bedding smallies aren't heavily harasssed by panfish, primarily because their preferred habitat is not favored by these species.*

This is where you'll find the biggest fish.

Also, find out what the wind direction and velocity was on the day or two before your arrival. Often areas will still have some color from previous high winds.

Rains can also improve water color on deep, clear lakes. Rarely can you get too much rain or stain on these types of waters.

Watch for soft ground, erosion cuts or feeder creeks that can all contribute to darker water color.

Remember, too, that larger bass sometimes hold a little deeper than smaller fish. While the 1 to 2½ pounders are up on the flats, the 3 to 5 pounders often locate on the drop-off bordering the shelf. Or, maybe on nearby structure that's closer to deep water.

Whether you're going for numbers or targeting trophies, spring smallmouths are predictable, fun to catch and will test the limits of your light tackle. If you haven't already, it's time to put them on your early-season agenda.

# ROCK SOLID SMALLIES

*by Spence Petros*

Somehow, our fishing tactic reminded me of a movie about the Old West. But instead of outlaws on horseback surrounding a circle of covered wagons, we were in a boat going round-and-round a wind-battered rock hump, firing crankbaits at our targets—big fall smallmouths.

I had a feeling it might be an especially successful trip when my partner caught a 5-pound smallmouth on his first cast. And I was right—over the next few days, we boated dozens of large bass.

Though this experience occurred nearly 20 years ago, the pattern we developed then still takes fall smallmouths today. In fact, it's as close to a sure bet as you'll find because smallmouths change their habits as water temps fall. Night-feeding, for example, grinds to a halt and bass begin to concentrate on rock structure, where dwindling forage forces them to feed throughout the day.

So, instead of trying to connect with wary, tight-lipped bass, scattered at a variety of depths and feeding in short bursts, you've got them right where you want them—bunched up on rocky structures and feeding on a limited forage base during the daylight hours.

# SURPRISE BONANZA— SHALLOW LAKES

You usually think of a natural smallmouth lake as being deep and relatively clear, with a sand, gravel and rock bottom. While this is an ideal situation, some of the heaviest smallmouth bass are caught in shallow lakes where smallies are considered a minority species.

In some cases, these fish get virtually no fishing pressure because they are usually scattered and difficult to find during most of the warm-weather season. But come fall, the smallies bunch up on the few decent structures these lakes have to offer.

Since shallow lakes are normally fairly fertile (with at least some weed growth), and generally lack classic, deep-water structure, smallmouth bass aren't overly abundant in these waters. But the fish that are there grow to enormous

sizes. In fact, 5 to 7 pounders are fairly common.

In these shallow lakes, the deeper the rocks, the better. Rock points extending far out into the lake, and rock piles at least 7 or 8 feet deep are prime areas. Rock humps or rocky areas on sand/gravel humps also hold excellent potential, as do rock-studded banks.

A real sleeper spot for big smallmouths in a shallow lake is a fallen tree along a steep bank. I first discovered smallies using this type of cover while working tree-studded banks for muskies and walleyes. Now, it's one of my favorites.

Wind is important. If you fish these shallow areas when the weather is calm and the water clear, you'd swear there wasn't a smallmouth in the lake. However, if a strong wind blasts onto a shallow point or roars over the top of a rock-capped hump near the surface, big, aggressive smallies will knock the paint off your lures.

*Early fall, bright sun and shallow rocks—a perfect combination for smallmouth action. The sun heats the rocks, which warms the water, which draws the fish.*

## TIMING AND TACTICS

The fall bite on shallow lakes normally begins a couple of weeks earlier than it does on classic (i.e.: deep) smallmouth waters, and stays hot right up until turnover. As water temperatures approach the turnover range—58 to 54 degrees— I start thinking about shifting to deeper waters, which will be at least a week or two behind in temperature progression.

After the turnover, I still explore some shallow lakes, but concentrate most of my efforts on deep, clear waters that hold larger numbers of smallmouths. These fish are usually bunched in key areas and generally easy to catch.

Before the lake turns, crankbaits are tough to beat for covering water in a fast and effective manner. Lipped

---

## The Hottest Rocks

During the pre-turnover period, wind-swept humps and points are smallmouth magnets, and are best fished with a crankbait. Pay particular attention to any projections, cuts or concentrations of rocks. Less active bass will hold on these areas, and are more susceptible to a jig or live bait rig.

Shallow, fertile lakes often hold a sleeper population of oversized smallies, and the few good spots that exist may come alive with bass during early fall. If they exist, key areas would be a rocky point, especially if it's pounded by the wind; humps with at least some

larger rocks; deep water near shoreline rocks; and fallen trees along a steep-breaking bank.

But the hottest of all spots for numbers of huge fall smallmouths are rock piles where there is a substantial amount of mid-depth, spring and summer holding areas within 200 to 500 yards.

Smallmouths that related to cover in the 10- to 30-foot range in the warm season will converge on the rocks in the fall. It's the best place to catch bronzebacks that will be at least a pound or two heavier than the average fish in the lake.

---

divers bouncing off rocks trigger a lot of strikes, especially from larger fish.

If the bass have been pressured, or if weather conditions curtail the action, I switch to jigs. A tube or curlytail jig hopped or glided over the top of structure and down its sides works great.

The ultimate presentation for neutral fish, however, is a good-size chub or sucker worked slowly behind a split shot, or a jig-and-minnow combination. I prefer a fairly light jig, such as an ⅛ ouncer, with a grub body, tipped with a 3- to 4-inch minnow. If one of these presentations doesn't trigger strikes, it's time to move on.

If you must fish shallow lakes during the post-turnover period, crankbaits are a good choice during a warm spell, or when the sky is bright and the wind is calm. Sunlight warms the shallow rocks and the surrounding water.

For the most part, live bait rigs and jigs work better when the fish are holding deeper, or if the water is cold and they won't chase a fast-moving lure.

# CLASSIC SMALLMOUTH LAKES

Clear, deep lakes with lots of sand, gravel and rock are ideal waters for smallmouth bass. Unfortunately, these lakes will humble almost any angler who tries to consistently pry "smalljaws" from its depths.

Savvy anglers hit these waters hard during prime times—early or late in the day, when it's windy and/or cloudy, and right after the fall turnover.

During pre-turnover on these clear, deep lakes, I usually take a run-and-gun crankbait approach, especially when it's windy or cloudy. This is a time of transition when bass generally hold on a variety of structures. They'll relate to shallow rock piles, fallen trees and reed beds, deep humps and points, over scattered large rocks in a variety of depths, and may even suspend off of or between structures.

In this situation, it's imperative that your plan of attack cover a lot of water. Bouncing crankbaits over rock-studded

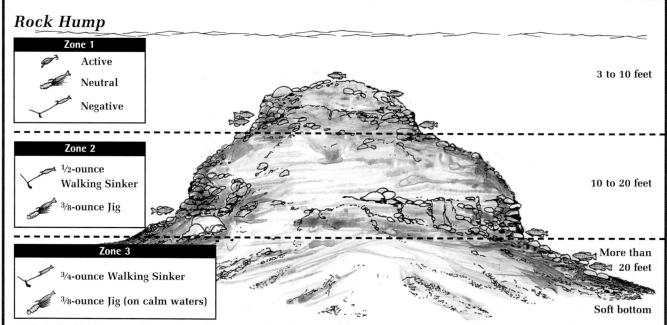

*Rock Hump*

**Zone 1**
- Active
- Neutral
- Negative

**Zone 2**
- ½-ounce Walking Sinker
- ⅜-ounce Jig

**Zone 3**
- ¾-ounce Walking Sinker
- ⅜-ounce Jig (on calm waters)

3 to 10 feet

10 to 20 feet

More than 20 feet

Soft bottom

*Actively feeding bass can be anywhere, but most of the time they'll hold near projections, corners in the contour, heavier concentrations of rocks, lips, and bottom transition areas that change from hard to soft. Use these tips to target fish in specific zones:*
*Zone 1 is best fished with crankbaits for active bass, jigs for more neutral fish and live bait rigs under the toughest conditions.*
*Zone 2 is best worked with a jig-and-minnow combo or live bait rig with a ½-ounce walking sinker and a large minnow.*
*Zone 3 features deep ledges, the base of the structure, and the transition area. Use a ¾-ounce walking sinker on a live bait rig, or a ⅜-ounce jig tipped with a minnow, if it's not too windy. A 10- to 14-pound superline provides great sensitivity and hooksetting power. With a live bait rig, search for bass with a lip-hooked minnow, but once you locate fish, hook the bait behind the dorsal fin. The minnow won't dive into the rocks, plus you can make a quick hookset, which means more smallies are lip-hooked for easy release.*

humps and points is most productive for me, provided there's enough structure in the depth range of my deep-diving crankbait. If the majority of good-looking structure is too deep for casting a crank, jigs and live bait rigs matched with 4- to 5-inch minnows get the nod.

# CRANKBAIT SAVVY

Sometimes the fishing's easy, as it was on that lake so many years ago. Dozens of near-surface rock humps were marked by buoys to warn boaters.

If the humps on the lakes you fish aren't marked, then investing in a GPS unit, or at least a good lake map, is essential. Punch the locations of off-shore structures into your GPS, or mark shoreline sightings right on your map.

Crankbaits should bounce across the top of a hump or point, then make contact down the side for as long as possible. Hold the rodtip high and slow the retrieve when the lure bangs the bottom hard, then drop the rodtip and speed the retrieve when you lose bottom contact.

Generally, I'll cast from deep to shallow water, but may snug up to the structure and cast parallel to its edge if I feel the bass are holding deeper along the breakline. You'll find active bass anywhere along the structure, but when the action slows, rocky fingers, eroded cuts or ledges will be the keys. Switch to a jig when faced with non-active fish.

After the turnover, when surface waters cool and sink, they mix with the bottom layers and the whole lake

## Bottom Bouncing Cranks

Rodtip high, slow retrieve...

...when your crankbait is properly bumping the rocks.

Rodtip low, fast retrieve...

...when your crankbait loses contact with the rocks.

becomes fairly uniform in temperature—usually around 52 to 56 degrees.

Big bass will then abandon shallower water and school on points, humps and sharp ledges that are in or closely related to the main lake basin, or the deepest water in the area.

It's usually no problem catching these bass, as long as you have several good presentations in your bag of tricks. Your biggest enemy is not bright skies, cold fronts, rain, or even snow, but strong winds that make boat control difficult. But even they can be overcome on most occasions.

Smallies can be caught high on structure (4 to 10 feet

or so), under warming conditions, especially if the sun is shining and waves aren't diluting light penetration. At this depth range, try crankbaits first, but always follow up with a jig, jig-and-minnow or a lively minnow worked slowly behind a split shot.

The amount of time you spend fishing the top of a structure depends on its reputation for producing fish, and the amount of potential fish-holding cover it offers.

Generally, the sides and base of a hump or point are the key areas after the turnover. When probing water deeper than 12 feet, I'll generally troll into the wind. Back-trolling with a small outboard or stern-mount electric motor, or forward-trolling with a bow-mount electric motor, allows me to follow tight contours much more effectively than if the boat is being pushed around by the waves.

If the waves become too big, running a boat against them can be virtually impossible.

Rather than getting soaked by the backsplash off the transom, try this trick: Drop a few highly-visible marker buoys slightly shallower than the area you want to fish. Motor upwind and turn your outboard against the waves to slow your drift speed as you float through the zone.

This tactic allows a slow, vertical presentation as you "slip" through the hotspot. Many times I've used the "downwind backtroll" tactic to stay on fish while the other boats either left the lake, or were blown all over the structure.

On deep-water edges like these, the bread-and-butter presentation for big small-mouths is a live bait rig with a ½- to ¾-ounce walking sinker and a 5- to 6-inch minnow. If that's too intimi-

*Here's an important tip—tank every smallmouth you catch (but don't go over your limit) until you plan to move. Releasing a fish back into the school will shut the entire school down.*

dating for you, go to a 3- to 4-inch minnow.

We've all heard that big baits catch bigger fish—well, it's never more true than for big fall smallmouths. Big crank-baits produce big bass when they're holding shallow, and big smallies love big minnows when they're holding deep.

I'll generally slow-troll a lip-hooked minnow around the perimeter of a structure that offers rocks near a drop-off. My feeling is that if you're not getting snagged occasionally, you're not fishing a good area.

The heavy walking sinker allows you to

fish nearly vertically for ulti-mate feel, minimal hang-ups and maximum hooksetting power. I use 14-pound-test FireLine, with a 3-foot mono leader of 10- to 14-pound green mono, and a size 1 or 1/0 hook.

A 7-foot spinning rod with a gradual taper is the ideal stick. You need power to move the weight and hook the fish, so you don't want a fast tip that will collapse before the power is applied to the fish. My two favorite 7 footers are the South Bend System 10, which is my own design, and Quantum's Tour Edition model.

This fall, give smallmouths a go. Most lakes receive little pressure and the fish are bunched on key structures. More importantly—they're eager to bite!

*Anywhere you catch one fall smallmouth, you're likely to catch a bunch. Double, even triple hookups are possible if you find the right spot.*

# LETHAL WEAPONS

*by Don Wirth*

Sometimes the smallest, cheapest weapon in your arsenal is also the deadliest. Remember the Biblical character David? He put big, bad Goliath out of commission with a rock, forever underscoring the adage, "The bigger they come, the harder they fall." That's how it is with grubs.

Compared to flashy crankbaits and topwaters, these dinky little soft plastic lures look impotent. Heck, for the price of one premium hardbait with some bass pro's picture on the box, you can buy dozens of grubs—and still have enough change to pick up a candy bar on your way to the lake.

If you're serious about smallies, you need to know this: Day in and day out, season after season, regardless of where you fish bronzebacks, whether you're after mega-quantities of keeper fish or the trophy of a lifetime … no other lure is more deadly on smallmouths than the simple curlytail grub.

You want numbers? A friend in my bass club recently traveled to Canada for 10 days of backcountry bassin'. He took two spinning rods and a single utility box packed with grubs and leadheads. While he relied solely on curlytails, his partner, an equally skilled angler, fished a mixture of spinners, crankbaits, topwaters and spoons.

My friend averaged 67 smallmouths a day, roughly four times the catch of his partner. He also caught the biggest fish of the trip, a 6 pounder.

You want size? Some of the biggest bronzebacks ever recorded have been caught on grubs. To a man, the smallmouth guides I've met during my 30 years as an outdoor journalist rank the grub as their number one trophy bait.

And, just in time for some serious grub-slingin', here are some grub-fishing tips from some of the nation's leading smallmouth experts.

## BALANCING ACT

Choosing the proper grub and leadhead is a balancing act many anglers simply can't figure out. Enter Tony Bean, legendary Nashville smallmouth guide.

"Smallmouth anglers should focus on three grub sizes: 3-, 4- and 5-inch," he says. "As a rule of thumb, the 4-inch grub is the gold standard, although at times you can catch as many or more smallies on smaller and larger grubs.

"Because 4- to 5-inch baits mimic a wide variety of forage, they'll trigger strikes from bass of all sizes under most conditions. Fish smaller grubs in cold water or when the bite is off; switch to larger sizes when water clarity is reduced, when the bass are really on a tear, or you're fishing areas where trophy bass are likely."

There are numerous styles of grubs you can stick on a jig. A few rules of thumb can help you select the right one every time.

"In general, the clearer and colder the water, the more subtle I want my grub to appear," says Bean. "In a highland reservoir in December, with the water 47 degrees and gin-clear, my first choice would be a slender, ribbon-tail grub. Visibility is high and the fish are likely to be deep and lethargic. I want a low-key presentation.

"But in a lowland reservoir in April, with 62-degree, stained water, I'd choose a bulkier, more visible lure, with a tail that creates some commotion as it swims. The fish will be shallow and in a more aggressive mood; I'll try to turn 'em on with a fatter body with a tail that slaps more water."

Common grub body types include the venerable curly-tail, which works in many situations and is by far the most popular. As its name implies, the bait has a curly, flexible

tail that ripples through the water both on the retrieve and on the drop. Other varieties include:

**Spear-tail**—common among saltwater anglers, they have flat tails that produce less vibration, but their high-speed fluttering action triggers active fish, particularly smallies schooling on baitfish.

**Shad-tail**—the tail is flattened, so the grub body wriggles on the retrieve. Because they fall fast, shad tails are good choices in heavy current.

**Spider**—combines a curly-tail design with a collar comprised of soft plastic legs. A good choice when bass are spitting the jig, because the legs add a lifelike feel that often causes fish to hang on longer than other body styles.

The weight of the leadhead is another key factor. "The three basic head weights will cover most smallmouth scenarios: 1/8-, 1/4- and 3/8-ounce," Bean explains. "When I target

## Heads And Tails

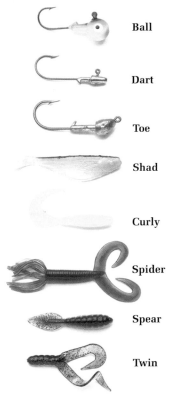

- Ball
- Dart
- Toe
- Shad
- Curly
- Spider
- Spear
- Twin

*Soft plastic grubs may not be the flashiest smallmouth baits around, but they are among the deadliest.*

bass in six to 15 feet of water, which is probably 75 percent of the time I'm fishing for them, I like a ¼-ounce head.

"It gives me a great combination of castability on light line and a realistic rate of descent. In this depth range, a ¼-ounce head works best with 4- and 5-inch grubs; if I'm fishing a 3 incher, I'll usually pair it with an ⅛-ounce head. When smallies are close to the bottom in current, or on reservoir structure deeper than 20 feet, I may use a ⅜-ounce head."

Few anglers bother to consider the shape of the leadhead, yet it can be critical to success, Bean notes. "The three major designs for smallmouth-sized leadheads are ball, toe and dart.

"Round heads are the cheapest and most popular. They're perfect for nearly any presentation that's not bottom- or cover-intensive, but round heads are prone to getting stuck between rocks.

"A toe-shaped head is contoured, sort of like your big toe. It's considerably more snag-resistant, making it preferable for fishing around chunk rock and stumps.

"The dart head's pointed nose and streamlined design allows it to fall faster, an advantage in deep water and current."

Weedguards are another overlooked option. "Some smallmouth anglers argue that they aren't necessary since smallies aren't nearly as cover-oriented as largemouths," Bean says. "Personally, I like a weedguard, but the ones on most leadheads need some tuning."

Bean thins out the fibers with scissors, then separates the strands with his thumb and bends them back and forth to loosen them so they'll compress easier in the jaws of a fish.

"A weedguard will probably cost you a fish every now and then by interfering with the hookset, or by alerting an especially wary fish that the grub it's just picked up isn't real," Bean concedes, "but its advantages outweigh the disadvantages."

## COLOR SELECTION

What color grub should you use? "Grubs, like most bass lures, are available in a zillion colors, but you only need a few to consistently catch big smallmouths," Bean says.

**Smoke**—"A highly realistic baitfish-imitating color, best on sunny days in clear water. My first choice for late spring and fall."

**Chartreuse**—"Totally unrealistic, but extremely visible—bass are highly attracted to it. Fish it wherever visibility is limited—on cloudy or rainy days, around deep structure and in stained water."

**Pumpkin**—"Mimics a crawfish. Ideal for cold, stained water. Works especially well in early spring."

Mixing and matching any of the above colors can help you fine-tune your presentation, as can the addition of reflective or colored flakes to the translucent base color.

"If you're not exactly sure what color the conditions dictate," says Bean, "experiment by combining colors, such as pumpkin with a chartreuse tail.

"Flakes can either increase the visibility of your grubs or make them appear more realistic. On a sunny day, silver flake makes a smoke grub look like a flashing baitfish. When it's overcast, reflective colors lose their impact and you're better off with a flat-colored flake like black or red."

Occasionally, shock patterns like yellow or bubble gum trigger more strikes than Bean's go-to colors. Bass pro Charlie Ingram, a smallmouth fancier when he's not chasing largemouths on the tournament circuit, favors outrageous colors whenever hard rains muddy the waters of a river or river-run reservoir.

# GRUB TACKLE

Most grub experts favor spinning tackle. The all-around favorite is a 6- to 6-foot, 2-inch graphite rod with a medium- to medium-heavy action.

"The biggest mistake most anglers make is fishing grubs on light or ultra-light rods," says Dale Hollow smallmouth guide Bennie McBride. "A grub is a single-hook lure, and it takes a powerful hook-set to sink the barb into the tough jaws of a trophy smallie. It's better to fish grubs on a rod that's a little too stiff than one that's too whippy."

Light line is a must for grubbin'. Most of the guides I talked to use 6- or 8-pound monofilament, and recommend premium, abrasion-resistant line with a little stretch for shock absorption.

"Line that doesn't stretch can break during a big smallmouth's initial run," McBride warns. "I tighten down my reel's drag for a good hookset, then backreel during the fight. Line stretch gives me a good safety margin."

# GRUB RETRIEVES

"Many otherwise-competent smallmouth anglers don't have a clue how to properly fish a grub," says Pickwick Lake guide Steve Hacker. "It works best when you don't overfish it."

There are four basic retrieves to master:

**The Swim**—"A horizontal retrieve for smallies on spawning flats, long points, gravel bars and other structure that slowly tapers into deep water. It's my bread-and-butter spring retrieve.

"Start with the boat in about eight feet of water. This may put you a long way from the bank, but big smallies are seldom shallow. Make a long cast and let the grub sink to bottom with the rodtip steady at 2 o'clock.

"When the jig lands, reel quickly to shoot the grub off bottom, then slow down so the bait swims just off it all the way to the boat. If you feel the lure bottom out, speed up a notch.

"Don't pop the rodtip. Keep it at 2 o'clock; the twisting grub tail is the only action required. Most strikes occur as the grub swims past an isolated stump or rock. When you feel a hit, drop the rodtip to 3 o'clock and set the hook."

## Swim, Dart And Drop

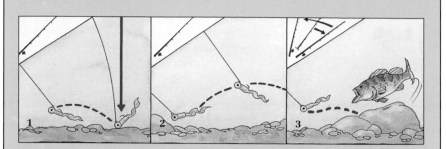

**The Swim**—*With the boat over deep water, cast onto a tapering flat and let the grub sink to bottom with the rodtip at 2 o'clock (1). When it lands, reel quickly so the grub pops off bottom, then slow down so it swims just above it (2). If the jig hits bottom, speed up the retrieve. Keep the rodtip at 2 o'clock until you feel a hit. Then, drop the rodtip and set the hook (3).*

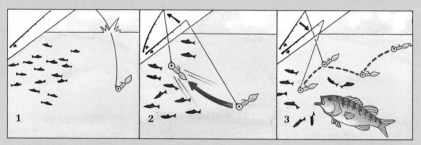

**The Dart**—*Perfect when smallies are schooling in open water or chasing baitfish on flats or points. Cast a spear-tail grub past the fish and let it sink a few feet (1). Pop the rodtip sharply so the grub darts erratically (2). Continue the rhythm, varying the number and intensity of the rod pops (3).*

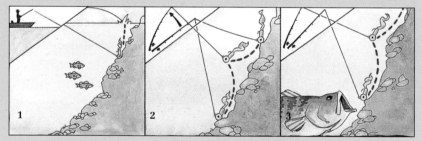

**The Drop**—*Cast to vertical or sloping structure. With the rod between 1 and 2 o'clock, let the lure sink on a tight line (1). Whenever the jig hits the slope, pop the rodtip so it hops over the edge, then return the rod to 2 o'clock (2). If you see the line twitch or jump, set the hook as a bass has taken the bait (3).*

**The Dart—**"A fast-moving retrieve, deadly when smallmouths are actively chasing baitfish on flats or points, or schooling in open water.

"Cast the grub beyond visible baitfish or breaking fish, let the lure sink a foot or two, then pop the rodtip sharply so the grub darts erratically. Let the lure drop a bit, then dart it again, varying the number and intensity of the rod pops. You can substitute a spear-tail grub for a curlytail if you wish. This retrieve will take smallmouths as well as hybrids and stripers."

**The Drop—**"A fall and winter retrieve, ideal when smallies are on vertical or sloping structures such as submerged humps, steep points, chunk-rock channel banks and bluffs.

"Position the boat so you're facing the structure, then cast to it. Engage the reel when the lure hits the water and, with the rod held between 1 and 2 o'clock, let the lure sink on a tight line, pendulum-style.

"When it hits the first stage of the slope, pop the rodtip slightly so it hops over the edge, then return it to 2 o'clock as the bait continues to fall. Repeat until the grub is under the boat. Watch the line; if it twitches, jumps or hops, set the hook—a bass has inhaled the grub."

**Ledge Crawl—**A variation of The Drop, best used when bass are located along a channel drop-off or ledge in 12 to 30 feet of water. With the boat hovering above the deep side of the ledge, cast past it into shallow water and let the lure fall with your rodtip at 10 o'clock.

When it touches bottom, lower the rodtip within two to three inches of the surface, slowly turn the reel handle a few rotations, then pause a few seconds. Continue the cadence until the jig drops off the ledge. Bass may hit during the crawl or on the drop.

## GET GRUBBIN'

Soft plastic grubs may not be the flashiest smallmouth baits around, but they are among the deadliest. And their applications are virtually limitless. Chances are you've already got a bunch of them in your jig box, why not put 'em to use and start catching more smallmouths?

---

## Hard Rock Smallies *by Roland Martin and Bill Dance*

From Volkswagen-size boulders to chunk rock as big as basketballs, from small stones and pea gravel to slab-like ledges, smallies love rocks.

### Rocks And Weeds
Rocks by themselves are great attractors, but the combination of grass and rock together is even better. One of our prime patterns throughout the year involves spots where large boulders have created a hole in the grass.

### Ledges
Smallies also relate to rock ledges. They provide a hard bottom that bass seem to prefer.

For us, a 4-inch grub is the perfect tool to search for smallies on ledges, rocky shelves and drop-offs in seven to 25 feet of water. Drop the grub on a controlled-slack line and watch it closely because, as usual, most strikes come as the bait falls. Once it reaches bottom, I hop the bait way up off bottom, then let it sink back down again.

Another prime location is where there is a change in bottom composition, such as where clay substrate gives way to chunk rock or gravel.

### During The Spawn
The smallmouth/rock relationship is most evident during the spawning season. Smallies will spawn on and around almost everything— from pea-gravel banks to the shadow of a big boulder.

*No matter the season, nor geographic region, giant smallmouths love rocks.*

---

# BIG RIVER SMALLMOUTHS

by Paul Cañada

Experienced river rats know that perhaps the best smallmouth action on big rivers occurs in fall. As the water cools, feeding activity steps up as fish prepare for leaner times. Plus, free-roaming fish are forced to seek shelter from the current and preserve valuable calories for the long winter ahead.

As promising as the fishing can be, changing water conditions and passing cold fronts associated with this transition period make lure presentation critical. Additionally, the characteristics of each river system dictate how smallmouths adjust and react to these seasonal changes. Anglers who understand the interrelation of these factors will not only boat more fish, but will consistently catch the largest smallmouths in their favorite rivers.

Knowing this, I asked four renowned big-river rats from across the country about the excellent fall fishing on their home waters. Each angler—Connecticut's Terry Baksay on the Hudson River, Alabama's Steve Hacker on Pickwick Lake, Oregon's John Eckland on the John Day River, and Pennsylvania's Ken Penrod on the Susquehanna River—tells how he specifically approaches the transition period.

Of course, their methods and tactics will work on other rivers as well. Locate a stretch of water that has similar characteristics to the four rivers mentioned here, and you can use them to your advantage right now.

## WESTERN RIVERS

Oregon's famed John Day River is a classic Western stream, characterized by relatively quiet runs and deep pools. Untouched by hydroelectric projects, the John Day meanders through central Oregon, where it eventually meets the larger Columbia River. Like other Western rivers, the John Day experiences low flows in fall.

Although the skinny water makes navigating the river a challenge, it concentrates smallies into deeper pools and holes. According to outfitter and guide John Eckland, this transition to low water offers anglers some of the most consistent action of the year. "Our biggest smallmouth last year was a 6½-pound, 22½-inch fish,"

> "The key to catching huge smallmouths is understanding how they position themselves and feed in the deep water."

he says, "but we've seen bigger bass, fish in the 7- to 8-pound range."

The key to catching huge smallmouths is understanding how they position themselves and feed in the deep water. Of course, like any river, the John Day's deepest holes occur where moving water meets an unyielding obstacle. The best ones were dredged along rocky bluffs or the hard outside bank of channel bends.

"We target the outside edges of a channel bend," says Eckland, "where there's structure such as rocky points, boulders and bluffs. Some of these holes can drop off into 15 feet of water. Smallmouths concentrate in these pools—cruising the edges and feeding aggressively."

Typically, Eckland and his staff use their oars to keep their craft, a McKenzie riverboat during moderate flows and a self-bailing raft during low flows, moving slightly slower than the current. Where possible, they position outside the faster current and hold the craft while clients work the hole.

However, when fishing bigger, bluff-lined holes, Eckland often beaches the boat and allows his anglers to thoroughly fish the holes from the opposite shore. "Some holes might hold as many as 50 to 60 smallmouths, so we work the entire hole," he says.

The sun, riding lower on the horizon in fall, creates long shadows that blanket the deeper pools early and late in the day. These

## Oregon, John Day River

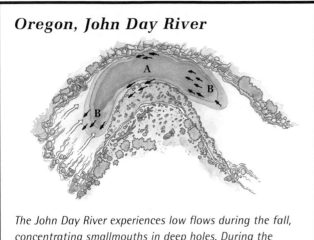

*The John Day River experiences low flows during the fall, concentrating smallmouths in deep holes. During the morning and evening, smallmouths feed near the edges of the pool (A). At midday they occupy the feeding lanes (B), with the biggest fish holding toward the head of the pool.*

shadows encourage bass to move to the edges of the pool, where they root for crawdads and take baitfish. As the shadows recede, the bass become more stationary and take up positions along feeding lanes.

Eckland's experiences have shown that there's definitely a pecking order established during these periods of low flow, with the biggest small-mouths posi-tioned at the front of the hole or eddy. This gives them first shot at food items flushed down-stream. Without exerting much ener-gy, the bigger fish are able to shuffle in and out of the best feeding lanes to secure prey.

Eckland targets small-mouths with fly fishing gear. When shade covers the water, he goes with dark surface poppers; as shadows recede and the canyon light improves, he switches to brightly colored poppers, usually orange or red. Finally, when the sun is directly on the water, Eckland switches to sub-surface presentations.

While the John Day has a reputation as one of the better rivers for fishing pop-pers, anglers using spinning or casting equipment have equal success with topwaters. However, there are days—typically during periods of radical barometric pressure changes—when it's better to fish deep.

This is when Eckland switches to streamer patterns such as a Woolly Bugger, Clouser or Muddler Minnow. Again, for anglers using spin-ning or casting equipment, success can be had with crankbaits and jigs.

## Bass In The Grass

Joe Thomas is widely regarded as one of bass fishing's most experienced smallmouth anglers. His advice may surprise anglers, especially those who rarely target smallmouths in the grass.

"I have spent considerable time fishing smallmouths in big rivers, and during the fall, I concentrate on finding and fishing as many grass patches as I can. On waters like the Detroit, St. Clair and St. Lawrence Rivers, I focus on major current breaks that create enough dead water to harbor substantial patches of grass.

Smallmouths love the grass because it offers oxygen, cover and ambush sites. I love the grass because it offers concentrations of fish.

"The optimum situation is grass that's 2 to 3 feet tall in five to six feet of water. But the key is to find scattered grass mixed in with broken rock. As a rule of thumb, if I'm constantly getting hung in the weeds, they're too thick for smallmouths.

"In the mornings and evenings, the fish tend to roam, and this is when I throw a 4½-inch Husky Jerk around the grass to generate reaction strikes. Really, I only use two color patterns all year. One is a black back with orange sides and gold belly. The other has a black back with silver sides and white belly.

"As the day progresses, small-mouths become stationary and locate on bare spots, or within the grass itself. During the late morning, I'll switch from randomly casting a jerkbait through the grass, to working a jerkbait over isolated clumps of grass. But as the sun reaches its peak, I search for rings of grass with a bare spot in the middle.

"These rings are created by boulders or rocks which impede weed growth. I'll begin by working a jerkbait through these openings, but when the bite slows, I switch to a spider jig like the Arkie Crawlin' Grub. I keep the boat about 15 to 25 feet from the target and pitch the bait to the opening. I let it fall to the bottom, then hop it once or twice.

"Remember, in the morning and evening, cover lots of water. During the afternoon, slow down your presentation and target the openings and bare spots."
—Joe Thomas

## RISING WATERS

Not all rivers suffer low-water conditions during fall. Many rivers like Pennsylvania's Susquehanna River rise during this transition period. The 400-mile Susquehanna is a broad, relatively shallow river with a tremendous smallmouth fishery.

Long-time river outfitter Ken Penrod, a seasoned Susquehanna guide, finds that better fishing occurs between Harrisburg and Montgomery Ferry, where there's no tidal influence.

The fall period on the Susquehanna River actually begins when water levels rise and temperatures start to fall. "On the Susquehanna, the fall period for smallmouths begins when the water temperature dips below 55 degrees," he explains.

"As the water cools and flows increase, smallmouths are forced into very specific areas. The fish don't want to fight that current so they move into eddies adjacent to the shoreline." Many of the best eddies are created by ledges and points extending out from the shoreline.

Similar to most smallmouth rivers in fall, the bigger smallmouths hold in the prime areas found at the head of the eddy. "During the summer," says Penrod, "the bigger fish tolerate the smaller bass because the low flows allow them to leave the eddy to feed.

"However, as the water gets colder, the feeding lanes become more and more important to the bigger fish."

During moderate flows, the smallmouths hold on the edge of the current seam, where fast water meets slow water. However, during high flows, the bass move tighter to shore. Because the whole eddy has the potential to hold bass, Penrod carefully fishes the entire eddy until he identifies exactly how the bass are positioned.

When the bass are aggressive, Penrod works a 4- to 5-inch soft plastic jerkbait along the seam. However, his "go-to" lure is a 4-inch tube, rigged on an ⅛-ounce weedless jig head and delivered by a spinning outfit spooled with 8-pound line.

Penrod hops the tube along the bottom, 4 to 6 inches at a time, on a taut line with his rod in the 10 to 11 o'clock position. The ⅛-ounce lure works as a "check." He tells his clients if the bait isn't reaching bottom, they're fishing the wrong water. In other words, they're fishing too far out in the current.

Finally, as winter approaches, the smallmouths pull even tighter to shore. "In that colder water," he says, "the fish don't want to be in the faster current, burning calories. Instead, they pull tight to shore and feed as food washes past."

## TIDAL INFLUENCE

Like the Susquehanna, the broad Hudson River has a superb population of smallmouth bass. Connecticut's Terry Baksay, a guide and tournament angler who specializes in tidal rivers, finds the better smallmouth fishing occurs near Albany, New York. "The population of smallies in the Hudson has become huge over the last few years," he says. "A 50-fish day is not at all unusual in October."

During fall, Baksay targets midstream structure. "Because the river near Albany experiences water level changes during a moving tide," he explains, "big fish prefer midstream structure over the eddies found along the shore. This portion of the river can experience as much as a 6-foot fluctuation between tides."

Some of the most productive fish-holding structures are the many bridge columns and supports. Large numbers of smallmouths hold in the eddies created by these massive cement and steel structures.

"Normally, the largest number of smallmouths hold in the down-stream eddy," he says. "However, the biggest fish are found on the up-current side."

Anglers must consider tidal influence when approaching these large bridge columns. Like smallmouths on other rivers, the fish hold just outside the fast water. Though, on a strong incoming tide, they will often reposition so as to face downstream and into the tide-driven current.

Baksay makes his first approach with a Rapala Skitter Pop or a Husky Jerk, looking for active fish. After drifting down alongside the structure, he works back up the eddy with a homemade fly-n-rind —a ⅜-ounce hair jig teamed with a 2½-inch Lunker City Piggy Back trailer.

Eventually, the water temperature drops so low, it pushes the smallmouths out of the main river and up into larger feeder creeks where they stay for the winter, according to Baksay.

# RIVERINE RESERVOIRS

The Tennessee River in Alabama was impounded many years ago, but Pickwick Lake, and other riverine areas between the dams, act much like a classic big river system. Pickwick's flow varies greatly, depending on power generation, but guide Steve Hacker, has solved the fall smallmouth puzzle on this large expanse of water.

"As the weather gets colder," he says, "power demand usually peaks on cold mornings as people are getting out of bed and turning up the furnaces. The peak continues into mid-morning as workplaces run their furnaces.

"The fish want to escape the current, so I prefer to fish during times of peak generation because they hold in very specific locations. Beyond doubt, fall is the very best time for sheer numbers of smallmouths."

For most of his fishing, he uses one of his hand-tied white hair jigs, which imitates a shad, the predominate forage in Pickwick. In very light flows, he'll switch to a soft plastic jerkbait.

"I use a ¼-ounce hair jig 80 percent of the time," he says, "but in very shallow water I'll lighten up to an ⅛ ouncer, or during heavier flows, sometimes I'll tie on a ⅜ ouncer. I cast and retrieve the jig along the bottom to locate aggressive fish."

Humps are the primary structure Hacker seeks, and many are symmetrical, resembling an overturned bowl. "During light flows, smallmouths will position both vertically and horizontally throughout the water column.

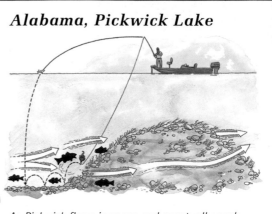

*Alabama, Pickwick Lake*

As Pickwick flows increase and eventually peak, smallmouths hold at the front of the hump near the bottom, in a slack-water area Hacker calls the "push."

"But when current picks up, they group very tightly at the front of the hump, facing into the current. More specifically, they position at the front, near the bottom, in what we call the 'push'—a pocket created by the water deflecting over and around the hump.

"Boat position is critical. I work my boat upstream, and match my trolling-motor speed to the current and hover in a very specific position. This allows me to cast precisely to the spot that's holding fish."

Fall definitely offers fabulous smallmouth fishing throughout the country, and the advice offered by these four guides will help anglers everywhere catch smallmouths in their own backyards. Wherever and however you fish, consider their tips on changing flow conditions and fish positions. Then, use them on your home waters.

The result will be hook-ups with numbers of exceptional smallmouths—an experience no fisherman can afford to miss.

# CRAWDADDY

*by Ryan Gilligan*

The calendar said August, but the truck thermometer flashed 50 degrees as we launched the boat on the Upper Mississippi River that morning. The wispy mist soon turned into a steady, cold downpour pounded into our skin by stiff winds. Even in summer, central Minnesota makes no promises of warmth and sunshine—the massive cold front was proof.

Needless to say, I wasn't brimming with optimism as my fishing partner for the day, Illinois smallmouth guru Curt Samo, lowered the bow mount and began casting to a timber-studded point. Wishing for hot chocolate but settling for cold caffeine, I

reached down to take a swig of Mountain Dew. Before the bottle hit my lips, Samo leaned back into a 3½ pounder. The block-headed brown bass fell for his favorite presentation: a crayfish imitation.

But Samo hadn't chosen the bait simply because it looked roughly like a crayfish. Rather, he picked it by following a complex system he's developed for choosing and using crayfish-style baits. And after spending a cold, dreary day in the boat with him—but catching one bruiser smallmouth after another despite the gloom—I saw just what it can do.

## MATCHING THE HATCH

Color is the first key. If this seems obvious, think again. Samo feels color selection is something most anglers over-simplify. A crayfish is a crayfish? No way.

"On the Winnebago chain of lakes in Wisconsin—lakes Winneconne, Butte des Morts and others—crayfish can be bright orange," he says. "On the other hand, in the South, you'll see a lot more bright red ones."

Samo says bi- or tri-color crayfish often rule a given water. "Before a tournament on Table Rock, I saw a local

*A touch of strategically-placed color can unlock stubborn bass. Curt Samo touches up trailers by painting their pincer tips to match native crayfish.*

lift up his crayfish trap. Even while the trap was underwater, I could already see the crawdads," he says. "It was easy—they had bright red on the underside, but had a lime-green back." In the coming days, Samo made a huge catch throwing red-and-green cranks and tubes with red flake. "Color made the difference," he says.

Although matching these basic color schemes is important, Samo says you often have to don your reading glasses to see the colors you really need to pay attention to.

"I get real anal about colors—more than I used to. Now, whenever I go to a new body of water, I throw out a crayfish trap the night before I fish. Then I can imitate exactly what the fish are keying on."

This insight makes a huge difference when you open your tackle box. Although

crayfish might sport the same overall color regionally, minute variations persist between waters, and Samo believes smallmouths take notice, especially in gin-clear waters or cold-front conditions. Anglers, however, generally don't.

"Crayfish often have tiny spots of bright color on the base and tips of those little legs on their mid-sections, as well as along the tails," he says. "Color most guys don't see."

To account for such details, he chooses baits that match them as close as possible. In the case of cranks, which don't have actual legs or pincers to sport such detailed coloration, he settles for lures that at least incorporate those unique colors somewhere on their bodies. Crank, jig or plastic, however, if his lures don't make the color cut, he takes matters into his own hands.

Such was the case as he and I fished our cold-front bass on the river. As the rain came down harder and the thermometer dipped, the Baby Boo jigs and Yum Chunk trailers we were casting stopped producing. Samo broke out his lure paint.

"The crayfish in this part of the river always seem to have orange pincer tips," he said as he dipped a cotton swab in the dye and dabbed the Chunks. "If the weather is bad and fish are negative, or in clear water where fish can take a really good look at a bait before striking, this can really make it happen."

I must admit the paint job didn't look like much, but the smallies disagreed. After the touch-up, I immediately started hooking smallmouths, including some broad-shouldered brutes.

## UNNATURAL SELECTIONS

Despite his penchant for matching the hatch, Samo says straying from nature is sometimes the only way to go.

Water clarity plays the biggest role. "If the water's muddy or highly stained, you can forget the crayfish traps and lure paint," he says. "Test a lure at boatside—if you can't see it clearly more than a foot away, drop the natural presentations and go for visibility."

Black-and-chartreuse or other highly visible patterns far outproduce the natural greens, browns and rusty reds, despite the fact they might be a spittin' image of the real things.

### *What Are You Looking At?*

Curt Samo catches crayfish-loving bass by matching the coloration of native craws he catches in his traps. But he looks beyond the overall color you see at a glance. Consider this crawdad—olive brown, right? Yes, but that's not the color Samo is most concerned about, especially when fishing clear water.

He's looking at the tiny bits of orange on the tips of the pincers, the underside of the tail, and the tips and bases of the legs. Narrow your focus to see these bits of color—or others found on crawdads where you fish—and match them. The fish will notice. *—Ryan Gilligan*

## CRANK OR JIG

Color is just part of the crayfish equation. When he nails it down, he looks at water temperature to really dial in lure selection. "That dictates bait style—whether I use cranks, jigs or soft plastics."

Fifty-five is the number to know. "When the water's 55 degrees or below, think jigs. If it's that cold, a Baby Boo jig tipped with a small Yum Chunk trailer is the way to go."

Presentation is crucial. Many anglers fish these jigs by holding their rodtip at 10 o'clock and moving it to 12—popping the jig off bottom. Big mistake, says Samo. "You're overworking the jig. Instead, crawl that thing across the bottom like a real crawdad," he says. "Keep in

mind that all the motions you make with your rodtip are magnified underwater, and you need to keep things slow and subtle in water cooler than 55 degrees."

When temps top 55, Samo switches gears to crankbaits, usually a Cotton Cordell Big-O or Bomber Model A. "If I fish a spot and get bit, I'll slowly fish the same spot with a jig, and sometimes boat another fish or two that saw the crank, but didn't respond," he says.

Select crankbaits with a hard-thumping wobble and a lip design that will bang against the rocks without hanging up. "When real crayfish move, they move a lot of water and create tons of vibration," he says. Square-billed cranks crawl right over smallmouth-holding rocks.

## TOUGH TIMES

When things get really tough, Samo prefers tubes. "Crawled along bottom, they can be deadly when bass refuse jigs," he says. "They're a finicky-situation lure."

He also incorporates scent when the bite's off—says he sees a lot of instances when smallmouths hit lures with a closed mouth in an attempt to kill it. Applying crawdad scent can make the difference in your catch rate.

"In cases like those, you not only have to be using a bait that looks exactly like a native crawdad—and be fishing it right—but you need it to smell like food, too," he says. "If it does, they might come back after the initial hit and actually try to eat the bait."

Judging from our success on cold-front smallies on the Upper Mississippi, if you've followed Samo's lure selection system, they probably will!

*System for success! Curt Samo's step-by-step method for choosing crayfish-style baits pays big time.*

# HOT DAM: FOUR TRICKS FOR TAILWATER SMALLMOUTHS

*by Jeff Samsel*

Jerry Crook sees a lot of green faces—fishermen go green with envy as he and his clients battle big brown bass on days when no one else is bringing fish to the boat. Adding to the other anglers' frustration is the fact that they're all using Crook's basic technique—drifting with live bait on a split shot rig—they just haven't mastered its nuances.

When the bite is right on tailwaters, usually during spring or fall, most drifting anglers will catch at least a few smallmouths, and some will even stumble across giants. However, to consistently catch jumbos from vast, complex tailwaters like those on the Tennessee River, anglers must go beyond the basics and do the little things right.

Here are his top four ways to trump trophies. Wrap them into your approach and you'll attract envious stares of your own.

## 1. Go Wild

*Catching and using wild bait is key. "A wild minnow will outfish a bait shop minnow 10-to-1," Crook says. "The hatchery-raised fish has no predator/prey experience. It doesn't react to a big smallmouth, and therefore draws no reaction."*

*In addition, he works hard to keep his baitfish in excellent condition, using a lot of salt and changing water often in his large circular tank. "No self-respecting trophy will eat a shad that has black on its sides or a red nose," he says.*

*Crook's mainstay is live threadfin shad, but when skipjack minnows abound, they're prime. They are extremely hard to care for, however. He catches them as needed with a modified sabiki rig (like those used by saltwater anglers) with only two flies. "If you catch six at a time, numbers one through five will be useless by the time you get number six off the hook," he explains.*

*And if you can catch "crawly bottoms" or "log perch"—darters that hold near dam structures during spring and fall—you've struck baitfish gold.*

## 2. Open The Floodgates

*"When floodgates are open, they can be phenomenal—not when they first open, but after the water has been running for a couple days," Crook says. "By that time, the floodwaters have drawn every big smallmouth in the lake below to the dam."*

*His amazing floodwater catches have included seven or eight smallmouths weighing more than 6 pounds apiece. In fact, he boated his top fish, a 7½ pounder, under flood conditions.*

*When floodgate fishing, Crook recommends that you run as close as safety allows to the concrete wall that separates the floodgate side of the tailwater from the turbine side; then drift straight down the current line that extends downstream from the wall.*

### 3. Toe The Line

Crook drifts with his line at a 45-degree angle and his rig just off bottom—he says both elements are critical. That sounds simple, and it seems easy when Crook is controlling the boat and coaching you along the way. But left alone to deal with powerful, multidirectional currents and fresh, lively baitfish, many anglers wind up chronically snagged or dragging their baits inches beneath the surface—well away from fish.

"A lot of fishermen are too eager to get baits in the water at the beginning of a drift," he says. "If you don't let the boat turn sideways and then gain some downstream momentum before pitching your bait out, the rig will get dragged behind the boat where there's no control, and the drift will be over before it starts."

Crook waits until the boat is angled properly and drifting before making a 12-foot pitch, always aiming toward a seam between current lines. He lets the rig fall until it ticks bottom; then holds the line with his finger for better sensitivity, being careful not to drag bottom. "Hit the bottom three times in a row, and on the fourth hit you'll be hung up."

As important as it is to avoid snags, it's also essential that the bait remain deep enough to attract large fish. Crook points out that fresh baitfish sometimes swim to the surface. "If you've been feeling the baitfish tug and then you notice you're not feeling anything and the line angle has changed, your bait may be right at the top. Reel it in and pitch back out, or wait for the next drift," he advises.

### 4. Find The Spot

Large smallmouths stack up in eddies beside strong currents and along seams, so if Crook sees a current run steady and then split, he drags a bait through that "Y." Specific spots vary by the amount of water running and can change hourly.

He also targets areas where skipjack herring are busting shad on the surface. "The big smallmouths will hang under the skipjack, picking off wounded shad that fall through," he explains.

"You have to start your drift well above them to have your bait near the bottom when you come through. If you pitch in where they are breaking, you'll never get your bait past the skipjack."

Smallmouths typically swim closer to a dam when less water is running and hold farther downstream during high flows. They also tend to be closest to the dam during spring and gradually move down the tailwater as the season progresses. Some of Crook's favorite fall areas are shell mounds several hundred yards downstream from a dam. He also has found that large smallmouths tend to share a common spot. "If you're catching a bunch of small fish, try somewhere else. You're in the wrong place."

Jerry Crook shows off another fine tailwater smallmouth.

# UP, DOWN, ALL AROUND

*by Al Lindner*

We had seen the signs for years. Every so often a smallmouth bass would bust bait on the surface way off structure. From time to time, usually when the fishing was slow, we would race out and fire topwater lures over the deep, open water. Most of the time, it was to no avail.

After a series of frantic, fruitless casts, we would return to whatever sunken island or shoreline drop-off we had been fishing and continue along, frequently with the same slow results. We'd scratch our heads and muse on the reasons behind this bass behavior.

On some waters, a "get on a drop-off and go" approach would work from early spring through fall. But on certain other fisheries, smallies—particularly big fish—became strangely absent after the postspawn dispersal. Oh yes, we could usually catch small fish and even a few quality bass in the morning and toward evening, but the midday bite was tough.

We believed that when the sun was high, big fish lay among the deeper boulders or down the lip of the drop-off, in a negative feeding mood. While this was true on some waters, we found it wasn't on others. Time, plus experience

and observation, as well as technological advances like underwater cameras, multi-transducer sonar and exhaustive electronic tracking studies, would eventually tell us why.

## LEARNING CURVE

Ironically, we got a better handle on the smallmouth's weird ways not through the bass tournaments we fished, but by taping television shows for the Professional Walleye Trail.

On the Great Lakes, as well as many of the lesser, but still relatively large, inland waters

## Double Teaming Summer Smallmouths

This illustrates how summer smallmouths often relate to deep, offshore humps, saddles and other sunken structure—and the Lindners' "one-two punch" system for catching them.

After locating structure and fish with sonar, then verifying the presence of bass with an underwater camera, they begin a two-prong attack. The front fisherman runs a bow-mount electric trolling motor just fast enough to swim the stern angler's jigworm or crankbait (typically a green-back or firetiger, size HJ12 Rapala Husky Jerk).

The boat is positioned anywhere from a cast length from the structure to right on top of it. The lead angler fishes a variety of presentations, including a Carolina rig, mushroom head jig tipped with a 6-inch black Berkley Ribbontail worm, drop-shot rig or Husky Jerk. Huskies are cast and slowly retrieved, while rigs and jigs are slowly dragged along bottom, across the top and down the sides of the breakline, as well as in open water nearby.

Sometimes, the lead angler will swim a jig-and-grub, or prop jig dressed with a small Berkley Jerk Shad. At other times, he'll drag a full-size Jerk Shad under the boat. His partner long-lines a Husky Jerk or a $1/16$-ounce mushroom jig tipped with a white or black Ribbontail, six to eight feet deep, 75 to 100 feet behind the boat.

The pair also has a rod with a hair jig in case bass follow a hooked fish to the boat. The jig is held—not jigged—eight feet under the boat. Both fishermen also have rods with topwater lures close at hand, for when smallies bust bait topside.

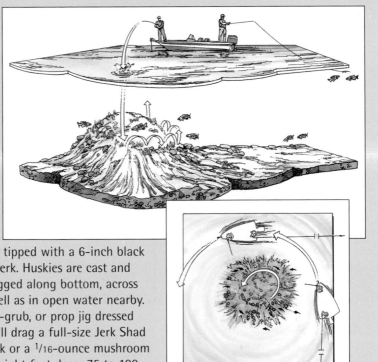

where these events are held, the habitat of walleyes and brown bass overlaps. Michigan's Lake St. Clair, Wisconsin's Sturgeon Bay and the St. Lawrence River in New York are just a few examples.

As it turns out, the walleye anglers proved to be great bass researchers. Except for topwaters, they use just about every presentation bass anglers do, and more. Armed with planer boards, downriggers and flatlines, the 150-boat contingent of competitors common at most tournaments can quickly and effectively seine a water column. If there are any smallies (and we might add spotted bass) roaming open water, they'll find 'em.

On one occasion in the Dakotas, our producer, James Lindner, filmed an angler as

he fished a deep, sunken island with a jig-and-minnow. Problem was, this fellow couldn't get his bait through the suspended small jaws down to the bottom-hugging 'eyes below. After releasing 20 bass (all decent size) he was literally driven off the spot.

A similar scenario played out at an event on Sturgeon Bay. Fishermen pulling Rapalas on planer boards for suspended walleyes were driven off a 50-foot-deep flat by incessant attacks from a school of aggressive bass.

As we added up the evidence and anecdotes from these and other tournaments, a unique "Up, Down, All Around" pattern began to emerge that would forever change our approach to summertime smallmouths.

# FOUNTAIN EFFECT

Biologists say form follows function, and that's certainly true with the smallmouth bass. Its muscular frame, powerful tail, blunt nose and vise-like jaws allow the bronze bass to forage on bottom, rooting crayfish from rocks. Yet it can just as easily swim off structure to attack big, suspended baitfish.

Much of what we have learned about their vertical and horizontal movements, as well as their penchant to periodically suspend off structure—particularly where smelt, shad or alewives are abundant—has to do with what some scientists are now calling the "fountain effect." Bass travel from deep to shallow water, then fan out and suspend near bait, in mini-migrations that occur seasonally, weekly, day to day—even hour by hour!

To fully understand these fish, the fountain effect along with another important factor, the smallmouth's incredible ability to change depths, must be taken into consideration.

It never ceases to amaze me how a smallie can grab a bait in 35 feet of water, rocket to the surface, leap and then dive, put up a sustained battle, and still not blow out its stomach as would a largemouth or walleye. This capacity to quickly equilibrate itself plays a role in the patterns of smallmouth movement.

There is ongoing investigation into this phenomenon. While the smallmouth is not totally immune to the "bends," there's no question it can tolerate quick depth pressure and water temperature changes, beyond the capabilities of many other species. Understanding these two factors allows anglers to look at smallies in a whole new light.

A brown bass is not a walleye on steroids or a largemouth bass that has forsaken cover; under the right conditions, a smallmouth bass that refused offerings dragged in front of its nose in deep water may suddenly rise off bottom in 30 feet of water (20 or less is more common), swim up like a missile and smash a lure on or near the surface.

More amazingly, the fish often brings along three or four buddies, who follow it to the boat during the fight. Even after the hooked fish is netted, its followers may linger below the boat, trailing it for a while before swimming off—either horizontally or vertically.

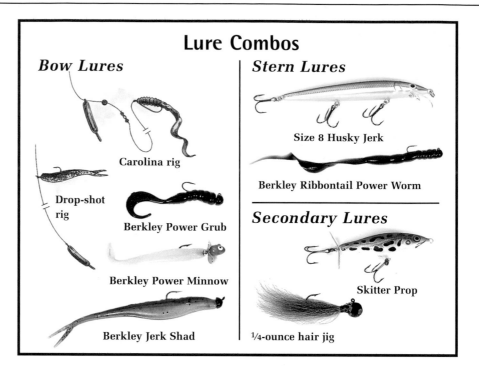

**Lure Combos**

*Bow Lures*

Carolina rig

Drop-shot rig

Berkley Power Grub

Berkley Power Minnow

Berkley Jerk Shad

*Stern Lures*

Size 8 Husky Jerk

Berkley Ribbontail Power Worm

*Secondary Lures*

Skitter Prop

¼-ounce hair jig

This type of behavior baffles anglers, even good ones. Patterns evaporate as bass move up and down in the water column and periodically suspend. In short, the fish are there one moment, gone the next.

## RHYME AND REASON

Forage availability, combined with water temperature and clarity, sets the tune to which smallmouths dance. In some waters they are nomadic—in others, homebodies. For example, in central Minnesota's sprawling Mille Lacs Lake, there appears to be little overlap in the hunting ranges among schools of bass.

Mille Lacs covers 132,000 acres and is just 42 feet at its deepest point. The northern portion of the lake is dominated by mud flats that typically rise from six to 10 feet from the basin floor. The southern section features numbers of gravel and rock bars. The lake provides a very stable environment with plenty of

crayfish, small perch, minnows, mayfly larvae, bloodworms and other forage in the shallows all year long. Thus, the fish become homebodies, and sustained, suspended movements don't occur.

Contrast this with the huge north arm of Rainy Lake in Ontario, Canada. Rainy is a typical Canadian Shield lake dominated by a rocky bottom. Overall, it covers 220,800 acres, with a maximum depth of 161 feet.

After the postspawn dispersal, pods of adult bass may leisurely move to late-summer or early fall haunts, stopping here and there along the way. However, depending upon the weather and available forage, a quantum leap of many miles can happen very quickly. One day a group of fish can be just outside its spawning grounds, the next day it's gone.

And just as suddenly, in another part of the lake, a point or sunken island and the surrounding area will host hundreds of smallies. It appears that once smelt got into Rainy, the big smallmouths said goodbye to crayfish and spottail shiners. Similar scenarios exist in many areas of the Great Lakes, as well as in large, deep reservoirs and natural lakes from East to West.

Once the fish suspend, they apparently switch to an almost exclusive diet of smelt or other pelagic baitfish. They establish new home ranges that may be quite extensive, even overlapping other groups' territory. The size of baitfish schools and where they are located determines these ranges and how long the bass groups utilize them.

As the thermocline forms, it becomes the floor of their vertical movements. When lakes turn over in fall, the fish move steadily deeper. Periodically, they may return to shallow water, but they will eventually move to deep-water flats where they spend the winter.

## FEEDING PATTERNS

The most common behavior we've observed is when a wolfpack of bass swims up or out from a deep hump or point to attack forage suspended nearby, then returns to the structure to rest and digest their huge meals. This behavior appears to be temporary and opportunistic.

We know smallies, like walleyes, can and do school up, suspend and roam over open water for extended periods of time. What we still do not know is how far they will wander, how tightly they group and how long they will stay there before resting on some sort of structure. In our experience it's usually a smash-and-grab, hit-and-run situation.

Even while suspended, the bass relate in some way to structure. While they may hold six to 10 feet deep in 30 to 50 feet or more of water, the bottom is often a saddle between two shallower humps, a ridge of rock or a hump surrounded by deep water. Bass will also suspend in deep water adjacent to a steep bluff wall or an extended deep lip off some shallow point.

Smallies hunting smelt, shad or alewives like to hover above a deep flat between two landmasses (an island

> "Once the fish suspend, they apparently switch to an almost exclusive diet of smelt or other pelagic baitfish."

and the shoreline, or two islands). Neck-down areas where baitfish are funneled by wind or current are perennial hotspots.

## TOOLS AND TACTICS

When smallies root crayfish on bottom or scrounge the shallows for perch and shiners, location and presentation are pretty straightforward. Get on a drop-off and cast toward or parallel to a shoreline bank of some sort. Keep your eyes open; look in enough areas long enough, and eventually you'll find 'em.

A potent arsenal of angler-friendly and familiar lures can help, including tubes, craws, spider grubs, lipless cranks, spinners and topwaters. But it's a different matter once smallmouths zero in on pelagic, offshore forage and play the "upsey-downsy-daisy" game.

A pod of bass may start the day at 30 feet or deeper, then move up, suspend and end up six feet beneath the surface, only to return to deep water in late evening. These movements are tough to pattern.

To boost our efficiency, we usually don't fish unless we see smallies in an area first. It's sight fishing, all right, but with electronic gear. Armed with an Aqua Vu camera (with depth and temperature display), we establish the thermocline. Then we motor over deep structural areas with a dual-transducer, Vexilar Edge 2 graph (with 10-degree narrow and 40-degree wide cones), augmented by a Vexilar FL-18 flasher with a 20-degree cone. We mount the transducers so the cones overlap approximately 20 feet below the boat.

If a lot of targets appear on the graph or flasher, we drop the camera to determine if the fish are indeed bass.

When this pattern emerges, smallies' foraging demeanor takes a peculiar twist. They tend to quit feeding on bottom, preferring overhead or eye-level prey. They also quit chasing fast-moving, tight-wobbling and erratic lures—baits that work very well a month earlier. Lying under or near immense clouds of suspended bait, the hovering groups of bass watch for easy meals. Any weak, injured or dying baitfish that flutter out become potential targets.

Once bass focus on suspended bait, they're more attracted to slow-moving, slow-falling, gliding, suspending and slow,

*When summer smallies suspend, long-line a slim-profile crankbait or jigworm 100 feet behind the boat over open water adjacent to structure.*

start/stop types of presentations. As a bonus, there are also just enough occasional dramatic topwater episodes, when bass drive baitfish to the surface, to keep everyone on their toes.

Our favorite approach involves two anglers. The first is a lead man, who uses a bow-mount trolling motor to guide the boat within a cast-length of the edge of a submerged island, point, saddle, or other sunken treasure. From this vantage point, he fires casts toward the structure with a variety of standard bass presentations—including topwaters, Carolina rigs and jigworms.

Our favorite topwaters are Rapala's Skitter Pop and Skitter Prop. A typical Carolina rig consists of a ½- to ¾-ounce No-Snagg sinker, 6-foot, 10-pound mono leader, and 4- to 7-inch, black or white Berkley Ribbontail worm on a Mustad jerkworm hook. When we use a jigworm, we keep it light, say, a ³⁄₃₂- to ¹⁄₁₆-ounce head with a 3-inch grub.

When the rig or jig hits bottom near the top edge of the structure, the lead angler uses the motion of the boat to drag and swing it along bottom down the drop-off.

This phase of the retrieve ends when the rig reaches the depth of the thermocline, and he'll slowly reel the rig back to the boat, checking for suspended fish on the way. Sometimes, he'll zigzag the boat over the top of deep structure, other times he'll work open water as well.

Drop-shotting is another option. Here, we use a ½- to ¾-ounce No-Snagg, five to six feet beneath a 4-inch Berkley Jerk Shad or 4- to 7-inch Ribbontail. Don't cast the drop-shot, though. Drop it and use the trolling motor to slowly swim it at the depth of the fish.

The rear angler serves as tailgunner. He long-lines either a ¹⁄₁₆-ounce mushroom head jig tipped with a 6- to 7-inch, black or white Ribbontail worm, or an HJ12 Rapala Husky Jerk. The jig or Jerk should run 75 to 100 feet behind the boat, six to eight feet down. This often catches the biggest bass.

When one person hooks up, his partner reels in and drops a ¼-ounce hair jig eight feet down, directly off the side of the boat. You'd be surprised how many quality-size bass will nail the jig after following the hooked fish to the boat.

Another variation is when bass blow up on top. Then, both anglers fire topwaters toward the surfacing fish.

## FINAL THOUGHTS

Anytime from late summer to early fall, you'll frequently face fish that have recently fed. In some cases, they may be totally bloated. Presentation—or rather, exacting presentation—takes on a whole new perspective.

Keep in mind, these observations are general in scope. There are times shallow fish will take slow-falling baits, and deep fish will take rigs on bottom. And when smallmouths get into one of their ravenous moods, anything can happen.

That aside, the patterns and tactics I have revealed are deadly. By gradually applying them to our bass fishing endeavors during the two tourneys we fish in Canada each year, we have, since 1992, logged three wins, two seconds and four thirds. On one circuit, my brother Ron has posted six top 10s. Interestingly, each year, half of the bass he weighs are caught suspended six feet down over 15 to 30 feet of water.

You can do it, too, when you acknowledge that big smallmouths run open water on certain lakes. Learn to find and stay on the fish—anticipating their movements and moods—and figure out how to successfully angle for them, and your summer smallmouth success will blossom. With trial, error and patience, you'll tap bronze beauties other anglers only dream about.

# INDEX

## A

Autumn fishing
  creek fishing, 112-115
  small bait tips, 56
  smallmouth bass and rocky
    structures, 132-136

## B

Bait
  progressive retrieve, 23
  small bait tips, 51-56
Baksay, Terry, 145-146
Bank transitions
  suspended winter fish, 119
Barracuda, 10
Bass
  anatomy of, 10-11
  feeding behavior of, 10-11
  mouth size, feeding mecha-
    nism and location of, 9, 11
Bean, Tony, 81, 138-139
Bichanich, Matt, 15
Biting, as feeding behavior, 10
Blow-up
  feeding mechanism and, 13
Bluffs
  fishing tips for, 49
  shallow-running crankbait, 68
  suspended winter fish, 117
Boat docks
  as cover for smallmouth bass, 130
  fishing tips for, 60-63
  small bait tips, 56
Bolonis, Walter, 84
Boomerang rig, 37
Brauer, Denny, 104-105
Bridges
  fishing tips for, 45-46
Bruce, Mickey, 34-37
Brush piles
  full-circle technique for, 69-71
  shallow-running crankbait, 67
Buzzbait
  making own clacker, 20
  tips for choosing, 20

## C

Cañada, Paul, 143-146
Carolina crankbait
  in fall for suspended fish, 118
Chancellor, Jack, 80
Christian, Jack, 82
Chuggers
  customizing, 21
  hooksetting technique, 22
  tips for using, 21-22
Clunn, Rick, 65, 107

Cold fronts
  prespawn fishing and, 97
Cold water fishing
  deadsticking and, 24-26
  jerkbait technique, 42-43
  spinnerbait in deep water, 39
Color
  crawfish, plastic, 147-148
  deep water fishing, 109
  grubs, 139
  jerkbait, 19-20, 44
  spinnerbait, 41
Crankbaits
  defining small bait, 52
  for drop-offs and ledges, 81-82
  in fall for suspended fish, 118
  gravy cover and suspended fish, 118
  lipless, 53, 66
  plastic crawfish for small-
    mouth bass, 148
  rock humps for smallmouth
    bass, 134-136
  shallow lakes for smallmouth
    bass, 133, 134
  shallow-running, 64-68
  short-lipped, 65-66
  small bait tips, 51-56
  spring smallmouth bass, 125-126
  super deep fishing, 107-111
Crawfish, plastic, 147-149
Crawl-pause jigging, 124
Creek fishing
  channel surfing, 113-114
  clear water tips, 115
  dirty-water tip, 115
  fall fishing, 112-115
  schooling bass, 115
  shore fishing creek mouths
    and inflows, 88
  solitary snags, 114-115
  weeds and, 112-113
Crook, Jerry, 150-151

## D

Daisy chaining, 77-78
Dance, Bill, 13, 25, 38-41, 45-49,
  53, 57, 79-82, 82, 141
Dart retrieval method, 140, 141
Davis, Mark, 27-28, 107-111
Deadsticking, 24-28
  bedding fish, 27-28
  coldwater treatment, 24-26
  rubber-skirted jig and, 25
  windy spring days, 26-27
Dean, John, 18
Deep fishing, 107-111
  fishing point, 108
  long cast required, 109
  spinnerbait in, 38-41
Dickerson, Jed, 84
Docks. *See* Boat docks
Drop-off fishing, 79-82
  characteristics of, 80

  finding with maps and
    flashers, 80
Drop retrieval method, 140, 141
Duck blinds, 48
Duckworth, Jim, 26-27
Duclos, Paul, 84

## E

Eckland, John, 143-144

## F

Fall
  creek fishing, 112-115
  small bait tips, 56
  smallmouth bass and rocky
    structures, 132-136
Feeding behavior, 9-13
  of bass, 10-11
  blow-up, 13
  mechanics of, 9-10
  ram-feeding, 10
  ram-suction feeding, 10
  suction feeding, 10
  types of, 10
Finesse tactics, 57
Fisher, Mark, 54, 56
Fishing tips and strategies
  for boat docks, 60-63
  bridges, riprap banks, bluffs, 45-49
  deadsticking, 24-28
  fall creek fishing, 112-115
  feeding behavior and, 9-13
  floating worm, 29-33
  full-circle technique for brush
    pile, 69-71
  how bass attack, 9-13
  jerkbait technique and water
    temperature, 42-44
  jig hopping, 34-37
  ledges and drop-offs, 79-82
  mat fishing, 72-75
  for points, 77-78
  secondary lakes, 83-86
  shallow-running crankbait, 64-68
  shore fishing, 87-91
  small bait tips, 51-56
  spinnerbait in deep water, 38-41
  suspended winter fish, 116-119
  topwaters techniques, 15-23
  water temperature and small-
    mouth bass, 122-126
Flickin' jigging, 124-125
Floating worms, 29-33
  arrow straight technique, 31-32
  backup lure technique, 32
  extreme worming technique,
    32-33
  open hook rigging method, 33
  outrageous vs. natural color
    for, 30-31
  skip casting, 31, 32
  swimming worm rigging, 33
  swivel rig, 33

topwater fishing, 30
wacky worm, 33
Floodgate fishing, 150
Florida bass, 9, 11-12
Fountain effect, 153-156
Frogs, plastics, 15-17
Full-circle technique for brush
   pile, 69-71
Funnel attack, 77

**G**

Gilligan, Ryan, 15-18, 42-44, 77-
   78, 147-149
Glide jigging, 124
Golf course water hazards, 86
Gowing, Jim, 65
Grass
   fall creek fishing, 112-113
   grass shrimp, 9, 11, 12
   smallmouth bass, 144
   spinnerbait in deep water, 39
Grass shrimp, 9, 11, 12
Gregg, David, 16
Grigsby, Shaw, 81, 118
Grinding bottom presentation, 97
Grubs, plastic, 137-141
   choosing proper grub and
     leadhead, 138-139
   color of, 139
   retrieval methods, 140-141
   shad-tail, 138
   spear-tail, 138
   spider, 138
   tackle for, 140
   why smallmouth bass eat, 138
Gulp! BatWing, 16

**H**

Hacker, Steve, 140, 146
Hannon, Doug, 73
Harp, Rickie, 32-33
Hicks, Mark, 107-111, 112-115
Hite, Davey, 75
Hollows
   suspended winter fish, 117
Holt, Jay, 81
Holt, Steven, 109
Hooksetting technique, 22
Howell, Randy, 16, 30-31, 31-32
Huskey, S., 9-13

**J**

Jerkbait
   adding a prop, 20
   color, 19-20, 44
   deadsticking, 24-28
   defining small bait, 52
   prespawn fishing, 97
   for prespawn suspended fish, 118
   size, 20
   small bait tips, 51-56
   water clarity and, 44

water temp 38 to 42, 42-43
water temp 43 to 48, 43
water temp 49 to 55, 44
water temp 55 to 65, 44
weeds and prespawn fishing, 102
wind and, 44
Jigging
   crawl-pause, 124
   flickin', 124-125
   glide, 124
   lift-drop, 124
   nervous grublet, 125
   snap, 124
   swim-drop, 124
   tactics for cold water small-
     mouth bass, 124-125
   twitch and drag, 124
   vertical jigging for suspended
     winter fish, 117
Jigging a spoon
   for drop-offs and ledges, 82
Jig hopping, 34-37
   boomerang rig, 37
   tackle for, 35-36
   technique for, 34-35, 36
   where and why, 34
Jig-jerking, 34
Jigs
   for jig hopping, 35-36
   plastic crawfish for small-
     mouth bass, 148
   rubber-skirted jig and cold
     water, 25
   water temperature and small-
     mouth bass, 130, 131
Johnson, Dan, 51-56, 95-99, 104-105
Jones, Alton, 108, 110-111

**K**

Kile, Mark, 69-71
King, Stacy, 54-55
Klinger, Tim, 69-71

**L**

Lake maps
finding drop-offs with, 80
Lakes
   classic smallmouth bass lakes,
     134-135
   cover in fertile lakes and
     smallmouth bass, 130-131
   sand/rock lakes for small-
     mouth bass, 128
   secondary, 83-86
   shallow and smallmouth bass,
     133-134
   shield lakes for smallmouth
     bass, 129-130
   tactics for natural, 101-103
Leadhead
   grubs and choosing, 138-139
Ledge crawl retrieval method, 141
Ledge fishing, 79-82

characteristics of, 80
jig hopping and, 36
locating, 81
smallmouth bass, 141
Lift-drop jigging, 124
Liles, Scott, 45-49
Lindner, Al, 152-156
Lindner, Ron, 60-63
Line
   grubs, 140
   jig hopping, 35-36
   progressive retrieve, 23
   shallow-running crankbait, 66
   shore fishing, 88
   small crankbait and jerkbait, 52
   spinnerbait in deep water, 41
   for topwater fishing, 23
Lipless crankbait, 53, 66

**M**

Man-made ponds, 85
Martin, Roland, 13, 25, 49, 53, 57, 141
Martin, Tommy, 96, 98, 99
Mats
   benefits of fishing, 73
   fall creek fishing, 113
   feeding mechanism and, 12
   finding sweet spot, 73-74
   over the top, 75
   punch the mats, 75
   steps for fishing, 74
   as top spot for topwater
     plastics, 17
   types of, and bait choice, 74
   working the edges, 74-75
McBride, Bennie, 140
McDonald, Bill, 97
Menendez, Mark, 34-37, 42-44
Michigan bass, 9, 11
Montgomery, Clark, 79-82
Mudlines
   shallow-running crankbait, 68

**N**

Natural lake tactics
   for prespawn fishing, 101-103
Nervous grublet jigging, 125
Nixon, Larry, 74, 96, 97

**O**

Open hook rigging method, 33
Open water
   suspended winter fish, 119

**P**

Padgett, Bob, 55, 56
Parallel approach
   for drop-offs and ledges, 81, 82
Pauley, Scott, 47-48
Paullo, Jordan, 75
Penrod, Ken, 145

Petros, Spence, 87-91, 100-103, 122-136
Philipp, David, 90
Plastics
    crawfish, 147-149
    grubs, 137-141
    soft plastic topwater, 15-18
Points
    daisy chain effect, 77-78
    deep fishing, 108
    funnel attack, 77-78
    suspended winter fish, 119
Ponds
    man-made, 85
    natural, 84
Poppers, 112-113
Postspawn fishing
    small bait tips, 56
    sun conditions, 104-105
    topwaters and, 104-105
Power plant canals
    suspended winter fish, 118-119
*Precision Casting* (Hold &
    Romanack), 107
Prespawn fishing, 95-103
    bass location in winter, 95
    full-circle technique for brush
        pile, 71
    grinding bottom presentation, 97
    McDonald's mantra presenta-
        tion, 97
    natural lake tactics, 101-103
    Nixon's husky jerk presentation, 97
    reservoirs, 103
    shore fishing and, 89
    water temperature and, 96, 98
    weeds and, 101-103
Prop baits
    tips for using, 22-23
    windy conditions, 22-23
Protrusible premaxilla, 11

**R**

Ram-feeding, 10, 11, 13
Ram-suction feeding, 10
Reaction Lures Ribbit, 18
Reels
    shallow-running crankbait, 66
    small bait fishing, 52
    for topwater fishing, 23
Reservoirs
    fall creek fishing, 112
    prespawn fishing, 103
    schooling bass, 115
Rigging methods
    boomerang rig, 37
    floating worms, 33
Riprap structure
    fishing tips for, 47-48
    shallow-running crankbait, 68
    shore fishing, 91
River fishing
    rising waters and smallmouth
        bass, 145

river bars and shallow-
    running crankbait, 67
riverine reservoirs, 146
small bait tips, 54-55
tailwater tips for smallmouth
    bass, 150-151
tidal influence and small-
    mouth bass, 145-146
western rivers for smallmouth
    bass, 143-144
Rocks
    crankbait over rock humps for
        smallmouth bass, 134-136
    rock humps in riverine
        reservoirs, 146
    shore fishing, 91
    smallmouth bass and, 132-136, 141
Rods
    grubs, 140
    jig hopping, 35
    progressive retrieve, 23
    shallow-running crankbait, 66
    shore fishing, 88
    small crankbait and jerkbait, 52
    spinnerbait in deep water, 40-41
    for topwater fishing, 23
Romanack, Mar, 109
Round blade spinnerbait
    in deep water, 39-40
    retrieving, 40
Rowland, Zell, 19-23
Runoff
    shallow-running crankbait, 67

**S**

Samo, Curt, 147-149
Samsel, Jeff, 150-151
Scalish, Frank, 15, 17, 18
Schooling bass
    fall fishing, 115
    shallow-running crankbait, 68
Schramm, Hal, 12, 28, 95, 96, 98-
    99, 138
Schultz, Bernie, 75
Schultz, Bill, 55
Seasons
    bass location in winter, 95-96
    fall creek fishing, 112-115
    fall smallmouth bass and
        rocky structures, 132-136
    prespawn fishing, 95-103
    spring smallmouth bass, 122-131
    super deep fishing, 107-111
    suspended winter fish, 116-119
    topwater fishing postspawn,
        104-105
Secondary lakes, 83-86
    cover and structure of natural, 84
    defining, 83
    finding best, 85-86
    man-made, 85
    reasons for large bass in, 84-85
Section feeding, 13
Seminole bass

seasonal and daily movements
    of, 95
Seward, Tom, 65
Shallow fishing
    with crankbait, 64-68
    reasons for decreasing numbers
        of bass in, 79
Sheepshead, 10
Shepherd, Ricky, 107-111
Shield lakes
    smallmouth bass, 129-130
Shore fishing, 87-91
    creek mouths and inflows, 88
    rocks, 91
    tackle for, 87-88
    weeds, 89-91
    winter/early spring, 88-89
Short-lipped crankbait, 65-66
Siemantel, Bill, 26, 37, 77-78
Situations, 60-91
    fishing docks, 60-63
    full-circle technique for brush
        pile, 69-71
    ledges and drop-offs, 79-82
    mat fishing, 72-75
    points, 77-78
    secondary lakes, 83-86
    shallow-running crankbait, 64-68
    shore fishing, 87-91
Skip casting
    floating worms, 31, 32
Small bait tips, 51-56
    after summertime cold front,
        54-55
    autumn and stained water, 56
    best situations for, 51-52
    boat docks, 56
    defining small, 52
    matching tackle for, 52
    river fishing, 54-55
    weed flats, 53-54
Smallmouth bass
    classic lakes for, 134-135
    cover in fertile lakes and, 130-131
    crankbait for spring, 125-126
    crankbait rock humps for
        smallmouth bass, 134-136
    crawfish, imitation, 147-149
    double teaming summer
        smallmouth bass, 153-156
    fountain effect, 153-156
    grass and, 144
    jigging tactics for cold water, 124-125
    ledges, 141
    retrieves and tackle tips, 130, 131
    river fishing for, 143-146
    rocky structures, 132-136, 141
    sand/rock lakes, 128
    in shallow lakes, 133-134
    shield lakes, 129-130
    spinnerbait for spring, 126
    tailwater tips, 150-151
    tips for finding fish in spring, 126
    using grubs, 137-141

water temperature and, 122-126, 127-128
windy conditions, 131, 133
Snap jigging, 124
Spawning
catch-and-release impact during, 90
deadsticking and, 27-28
homing instinct, 102
lake bottom and, 102
shelter from water movement, 102
structure, 102
Spawning sanctuaries, 90
Spinnerbait
color, 41
for deep brush piles, 118
in deep water, 38-41
for drop-offs and ledges, 82
spring smallmouth bass, 126
weeds and prespawn fishing, 101-103
Spring fishing
floating worms, 30
shore fishing, 88-89
smallmouth bass, 122-131
water temperature and smallmouth bass, 122-126
Spring holes
suspended winter fish, 118
Stained water
small bait tips, 56
Stone, Marty, 75
Storm, Jon, 19-23, 34-37, 69-71
Strikes
reasons why bass strike, 13
Stroking, 34
Structures
boat docks and small bait, 56
bridges, riprap banks, bluffs, 45-49
duck blinds, 48
fishing large structures, 45-49
ledges and drop-offs, 79-82
points, 77-78
suspended winter fish and, 117-119
Stumps
fishing tips, 49
Suction feeding, 10
Summertime
river fishing with small bait, 54-55
small bait after summertime cold front, 54-55
Sun conditions
topwater fishing postspawn, 104-105
Suspended fish
spring through fall tips, 118
winter tips for, 116-119
Suspended winter fish, 116-119
Swim-drop jigging, 124
Swimming worm rigging method, 33
Swim retrieval method, 140-141
Swivel rig method
floating worms, 33

**T**

Tailwater tips, 150-151
Thomas, Joe, 53-54, 55
Thurmond, Dan, 73, 75
Timber. *See* Wood
Top to bottom approach for drop-offs and ledges, 81
Topwater fishing
buzzbait, 20
chuggers, 21-22
feathers, 22
floating worm, 30
jerkbaits, 19-20
line for, 23
painting, 21
for postspawn suspended fish, 118
postspawn tips, 104-105
prespawn fish and, 19
progressive retrieve, 23
prop baits, 22-23
reels, 23
rod choice for, 23
soft plastics, 15-18
tops spots for, 17-18
walking stickbait, 20-21
Treat, Lou, 24-26
Twitch and drag jigging, 124

**U**

Uncle Josh Sizmic Toad, 15

**V**

VanDam, Kevin, 41, 114
Van Horn, Ray, 82
Vegetation
grass shrimp, 9, 11, 12
holding food for bass, 12
Vertical jigging
suspended winter fish, 117

**W**

Wacky worm rigging method, 33
Walking stickbait
add treble hook, 21
line wait, 21
tips for using, 20-21
walk-the-dog motion, 20-21
Walleye, 152-153
Warm water fishing
jerkbait technique and, 44
spinnerbait in deep water, 38-39
Water temperature. *See also* Cold water fishing; Warm water fishing
jerkbait technique and, 42-44
reservoirs and prespawn fishing, 103
shore fishing and, 88-89
smallmouth bass, 122-126, 127-128, 130, 131
Weakley, Mac, 84
Weather

small bait after summertime cold front, 54-55
Weedguard, 139
Weeds
deep weedlines, 114
fall creek fishing, 112-113
grass shrimp, 9, 11, 12
holding food for bass, 12
mat fishing tips, 72-75
mats and feeding mechanism, 12
mats as top spot for topwater plastics, 17
prespawn fishing and, 101-103
shore fishing, 89-91
smallmouth bass and grass, 144
spinnerbait for deep brush piles, 118
submerged weedbeds and shallow-running crankbait, 67
weed flats and small bait, 53-54
Wendlandt, Clark, 112-115
Wilkes, Dustin, 55, 56
Willow-lead spinnerbait
in deep water, 39-40
retrieving, 40
Windy conditions
jerkbait and, 44
prop baits, 22-23
smallmouth bass, 131, 133
Winter
bass location during, 95-96
tips for suspended winter fish, 116-119
Wirth, Don, 24-33, 64-68, 72-75, 83-86, 116-119, 137-141
Wood
brush piles and shallow-running crankbait, 67
downed timber and shallow-running crankbait, 67
fishing with topwater plastics, 17-18
full-circle technique for brush pile, 69-71
shallow-running crankbait in timbers, 66
solitary snags, 114-115
spinnerbait in deep water, 39
stump flats and shallow-running crankbait, 67
stumps fishing tips, 49
submerged standing timber and suspended winter fish, 118
Worms
floating, 29-33

**Y**

Yelas, Jay, 32
Yum Buzz Frog, 17

**Z**

Zoom Horny Toad and Horny Toad Hook, 16